Genealogy Online
Eighth Edition

About the Author

Elizabeth Powell Crowe has been writing for over 30 years. Her previous editions of *Genealogy Online* have sold a combined total of nearly 200,000 copies. Crowe has been a contributing editor for *Computer Currents* magazine and the author of numerous articles in both popular and technical publications. Her work has appeared in *Civil War Times*, *PC World*, C|Net, *Digital Genealogist*, and other publications and websites. She has been a guest on WashingtonPost.com's chat with Jacquelin D. Salmon (http://discuss.washingtonpost.com/wp-srv/zforum/01/salmon0731.htm), DearMYRTLE's Family History Internet podcast, and other national news programs. Ms. Crowe often makes speeches and conducts workshops on online genealogy; she has been a presenter at the Institute of Genealogy and Historical Research at Samford University and at GENTECH; and she has edited genealogy publications. She lives in Navarre, Florida, with her husband, Mark.

Genealogy Online
Eighth Edition

DISCARD

Elizabeth Powell Crowe

New York Chicago San Francisco
Lisbon London Madrid Mexico City
Milan New Delhi San Juan
Seoul Singapore Sydney Toronto

The McGraw·Hill Companies

Library of Congress Cataloging-in-Publication Data

Crowe, Elizabeth Powell.
  Genealogy online / Elizabeth Powell Crowe. –8th ed.
      p. cm.
  Includes index.
  ISBN 978-0-07-149931-6 (alk. paper)
  1. Genealogy—Data processing. 2. Internet—Handbooks, manuals, etc.
I. Title.
CS21.C67 2007
025.06'9291—dc22

                              2007049247

Genealogy Online, Eighth Edition

1234567890   DOC DOC   0198

ISBN   978-0-07-149931-6
MHID   0-07-149931-8

Sponsoring Editor	**Indexer**
Roger Stewart	Kevin Broccoli
Editorial Supervisor	**Production Supervisor**
Patty Mon	George Anderson
Project Manager	**Composition**
Vastavikta Sharma,	International Typesetting
International Typesetting and Composition	and Composition
Acquisitions Coordinator	**Illustration**
Carly Stapleton	International Typesetting
Copy Editor	and Composition
Lisa McCoy	**Art Director, Cover**
Proofreader	Jeff Weeks
Manish	

This book is dedicated to my mother, Frances Spencer Powell
1926–2007
"Her children will rise up and call her blessed."— Proverbs 31:28

Contents at a Glance

Contents

Part II
General Genealogy

Part III
The Nitty Gritty: Places to Find Names, Dates, and Places

Part IV

The Genealogy World

Part V
Appendixes

Acknowledgments

As with any book, this one was made possible by the efforts of many people besides the author. First, I'd like to thank each and every person mentioned in this book, as I obviously couldn't have done it without all of you.

Special thanks go to Jeanne Henry, Bill Ammons, Pat Richley, Jeri Weber, and Linda Mullikin of the FHC in Navarre, as well as Myra Vanderpool Gormley, Dick Eastman, Randy Hooser, Liz Kelley Kerstens, Roger Stewart, Carly Stapleton, and all the staff at McGraw-Hill. Immense gratitude is due to all my family and friends, who were more than patient with me while I was writing this book.

Most of all I want to thank my mother, Frances Spencer Powell. Mama died January 8, 2007.

Introduction

"I've gotten more genealogy done in one year on Prodigy than I did in 20 years on my own!" my mother exclaimed some 15 years ago. This quote, from a genealogy veteran, shows how technology has changed even this popular hobby. The mind-boggling mass of data needed to trace one's family tree has finally found a knife to whittle it down to size: the computer.

The early editions of this book assumed you knew how to do genealogy but not how to use the Internet. Since that time, commercial online services and the Internet have added, expanded, revised, and changed what they offer, as well as how and when they offer it. From having to use a dial-up connection over a modem in 1992 to cable and satellite connections to today's iPhone, we've come a long way. In fact, it has become almost impossible to escape the Internet. We've all had a chance to surf on the Net without a life jacket. Therefore, the current iteration assumes you know most Internet technologies and programs, and that you want to know how to use them to do your genealogy.

The potential for finding clues, data, and other researchers looking for your same family names has increased exponentially since the last edition of this book was published. Since 2002, push technology, streaming video, blogs, podcasts, and indexed document scans have radically changed what can be found on the Internet and how we search for it. If you feel you need formal instruction, online courses, from basic self-paced text to college-level instruction, can now make that happen.

In short, online genealogy has never been better and it's a good time to try your hand at it!

Bill Ammons' Story

How does online genealogy work? Let's look at a case study.

Bill Ammons is a friend of mine who used a few hints on online genealogy from me to break down a brick wall in his genealogy research. Here is what he wrote to me about his quest:

> I started my genealogy research 16 months ago with the name of the only grandparent I knew from my childhood. The journey has taken me from knowing a very small family to discovering an enormously large family. I have learned a lot about history, our society, family secrets, and what not to say in e-mails, even jokingly to family. I have hit roadblocks and gotten through some, while others are still being researched.

> Some roadblocks will never be resolved, as the documents were destroyed because of Civil War or mysterious fires at the courthouses or newspaper offices. However, on your journey, you, too, will become a collector of websites, books on dead people, and American history.

> Roadblocks are very interesting challenges, in that one must begin to be creative in their research to find clues to get them through the roadblocks. If the information on the Internet leads to roadblocks, then try going to the county historical society office and then to the county courthouse to look for wills, land documents, bible records, newspaper articles, and even personal letters. I have found old bible records at the historical societies that have provided clues to names I was uncertain of and even provided insights into cemetery records.

> I started my journey with a simple posting to the Horry County, South Carolina Historic Society home page (http://www.hchsonline.org/), shown in Figure 1.

> From a simple posting on the message board of the four family surnames (Ammons, Denton, Martin, and Tompkins), I received a response the next day that solved the Martin branch of my tree to 1810. My cousin is, in fact, one of the contributors of documents to the Horry Historic Society site. Sometimes, one can find a new family member and genealogy at the same time.

> The next day brought another surprise when I received an e-mail from a gentleman in Atlanta and he provided the Denton branch of my family tree. His mother was my grandmother's sister. I never met my grandmother's

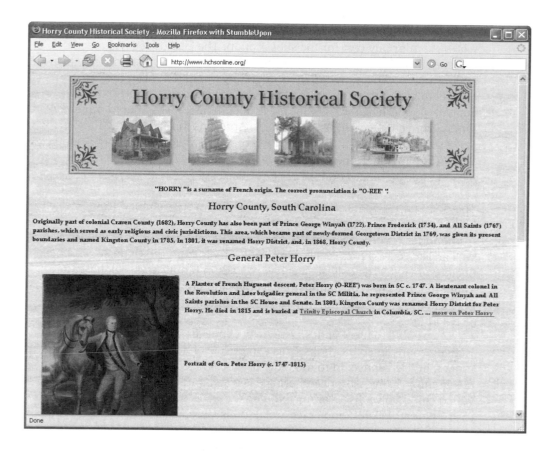

Horry County Historical Society

"HORRY "is a surname of French origin. The correct pronunciation is "O-REE" ".

Horry County, South Carolina

Originally part of colonial Craven County (1682), Horry County has also been part of Prince George Winyah (1722), Prince Frederick (1734), and All Saints (1767) parishes, which served as early religious and civic jurisdictions. This area, which became part of newly-formed Georgetown District in 1769, was given its present boundaries and named Kingston County in 1785. In 1801, it was renamed Horry District, and, in 1868, Horry County.

General Peter Horry

A Planter of French Huguenot descent, Peter Horry (O-REE') was born in SC c. 1747. A lieutenant colonel in the Revolution and later brigadier general in the SC Militia, he represented Prince George Winyah and All Saints parishes in the SC House and Senate. In 1801, Kingston County was renamed Horry District for Peter Horry. He died in 1815 and is buried at Trinity Episcopal Church in Columbia, SC. ... more on Peter Horry

Portrait of Gen. Peter Horry (c. 1747-1815)

FIGURE F-1. *Local organizations can be a big help in online genealogy research.*

sisters, but this posting yielded another new family member and also information about the Denton family as a bonus. This family member pointed me to documents and newspaper articles that were available online that provided personal insight as to the possibilities that my grandmother and grandfather were Native Americans.

Then I had to really get into the digging mindset to start finding information and documents on the other surnames. The Ammons surname has taken me from the coast of South Carolina to the Appalachian Mountains and back to Sampson County, North Carolina. I never had any idea that the Ammons family came from North Carolina, because I grew up with the understanding that the Ammons were "Black Irish" that migrated to South Carolina. The real surprise has been in the documentation I have obtained that does not support this idea.

Census reports from Ancestry.com (www.ancestry.com) have been well worth the monthly cost for the subscription. The census reports are searchable and easily accessed, even with a dial-up connection. They provide a road map of where the family is migrating or settled. Also, the census reports tell something about the family's living conditions, employment, education, and neighbors. From these documents, I was able to trace my family from 1780 to 1920s. I found the Ammons family around 1780 in Sampson County, North Carolina, then they migrated to Marlboro County, South Carolina, after the American Revolution, and the children migrated to Macon and Cherokee counties of North Carolina.

The documents from the American Revolution were obtained from Wallace State College in Hanceville, Alabama. This community college has a tremendous records area on the American Revolution and the Civil War, as well as access to the 2.5 million microfilm reels from the Genealogical Society of Utah. The college also has courses in family and regional history. I know that the Ammons family received a land grant in Marlboro County because they served in the American Revolution.

I also was able to use Cyndi's List (www.cyndislist.com) to help search the Native American connections. This can be a useful page when researching roots that are connected to the federally recognized tribes. The issue of researching Native American heritage is a separate and interesting journey, which can involve discovering your genetic markers, such as Asian shovel teeth, anatomic knot, and "race"-related diseases.

Another helpful resource was the Melungeons page (http://homepages .rootsweb.com/~mtnties/melungeon.html). Some people are really confused about this group of folks that lived in North Carolina. The more I read about the forgotten Portuguese, the more interesting this hidden part of America's history became in tracking the family history.

To date, the journey has brought me to the Waccamaw Indian people of South Carolina (I am a tribal member) and the Croatans of Sampson, County North Carolina (http://docsouth.unc.edu/nc/butler/menu.html), on the University of North Carolina at Chapel Hill Library site (see Figure 2).

The book, written by George Butler in 1916 and now available online, was a jewel of a find in this surname search. The book discusses the Croatans' possible connection with the lost colonists of Roanoke. This discovery led to researching the census records. The census places family in the correct place at the correct time to strengthen the argument of where they originated. Currently, I plan to continue my research focused on the county, state, and federal records of the time. A big plus was the photos in the book, with people that resemble family members who I know today.

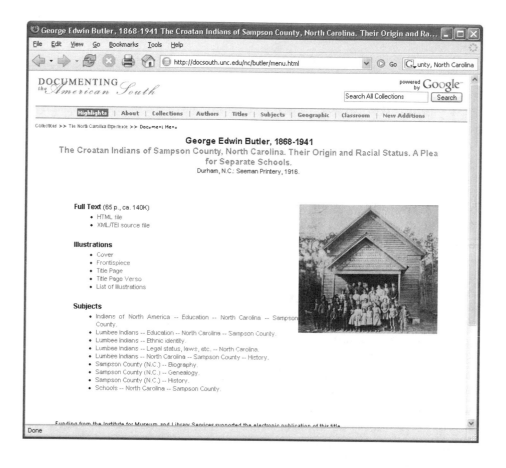

FIGURE F-2. *A full-text online book at the NCCH Library site helped Ammons with his genealogy.*

In my research for records, I have been to the archives in Raleigh, North Carolina. (A word to the wise: Don't take any ink pens and/or briefcases; you will not be allowed into the records area.) Believe me, it is a tremendous treat to see the historical records that remain. The information you can discover is well worth the frustration.

As you can see, Bill Ammon's journey took him to many different online and offline resources:

♦ Sites such as Cyndi's List to find online information about Native Americans (see Chapter 6)

♦ Local college resources for genealogy materials and knowledge (see Chapter 3)

- Online queries (see Chapter 8)

- Vital records from government archives (see Chapter 9)

- Online libraries (see Chapter 10)

- Ethnic resources online (see Chapter 13)

- Ancestry.com (see Chapter 17)

Bill took what he knew from his own immediate family, plus the family legends and gossip, to begin searching for the original records he needed. He went to some resources in person, such as the North Carolina archives and Wallace State College Library, but only after *online research* told him that's where he needed to go. This is an excellent example of genealogy online.

Where Computers Come In

Databases, online services, online card catalogs, and bulletin boards are changing the *brick wall syndrome*, that frustrating phase of any lineage search where the information needed seems unavailable. Genealogists who have faced the challenges and triumphed are online, helping others.

State governments and the federal government have recently started to put data, such as death records, veterans' records, and so on in computer-readable databases, which can then be accessible via the Internet. The Bureau of Land Management, the Library of Congress, and the National Archives and Records Administration are just a few examples of government sites that can help the family historian.

The United States alone has numerous genealogical societies that trace people's descent. Some of these are national, but many more are local or regional, such as the Tennessee Valley Genealogical Society or the New England Historical Society. Others are specific to certain names. Many patriotic organizations, such as the Daughters of the Confederacy, limit membership to descendants of a particular historical group. Many of these groups offer courses in genealogy, which can help you with online and offline research.

There's no denying that the computer has changed nearly everything in our lives, and the avocation and vocation of genealogical research is no exception. Further, the Internet has added to the ways a genealogist can research, as with Bill Ammons' example, to find those elusive primary sources that are essential to any family history. This book explores many different networks, services, and websites that can help you in your pursuit of your ancestry.

Stories about how online communities have helped people in their genealogical research abound. Here are some examples.

DearMYRTLE Finds a Patriot

DearMYRTLE, a daily genealogy columnist on the Internet, was helping a friend move files, data, and programs from an old computer to a new one. In the course of the conversation, DearMYRTLE's friend wondered aloud what online genealogy could do for him, but expressed doubt anything useful could turn up online.

Then the conversation turned to the new United States quarters celebrating the states in the order they joined the Union, specifically, the one with the Delaware patriot Cesar Rodney on the reverse.

"Who was he?" asked DearMYRTLE's friend.

"All right," DearMYRTLE replied, "let's run a test. Your wife here will look up Cesar Rodney in the *Encyclopedia Britannica.* You look him up on your old computer using Microsoft Encarta 97. I'll look him up on the Internet with your new computer."

Faster than the other two could use either a book or a CD-ROM, DearMYRTLE found a transcription of a letter from George Washington to Rodney, as shown in Figure 3.

Nancy's Story

Nancy is a friend of mine from high school who knows more about computers and the Internet than I do, but not quite so much about genealogy. When her stepmother died recently, Nancy got a large box of her father's memorabilia and photos. She called to ask me about genealogy, and I showed her some good genealogy sites on the Internet on her laptop computer.

I didn't think much more about it until she called me a few weeks later in considerable excitement. She had not only found the USGenWeb (www.usgenweb.org) site for her father's home county in Texas, but also that the moderator of the site had known both her father and her grandfather. She was scanning in the old photos and e-mailing them to the fellow, and he was identifying people in them left and right. One was of Nancy's grandfather as a child. Another showed her father as a teenager. Every day, the USGenWeb moderator was helping her fill in more holes in her family history.

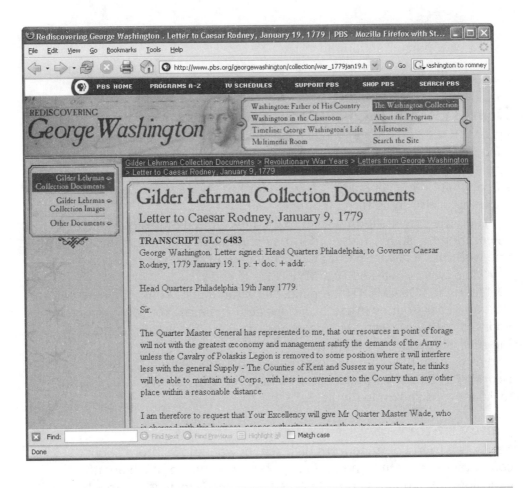

FIGURE F-3. *Online research leads to unexpected treasures, such as this letter from George Washington to Cesar Rodney.*

What's a Hoosier? Genealogy Has the Answer

Randy Hooser of Huntsville, Alabama, has been working on his genealogy for years. One result has been his work with a University of Indiana professor to publish a white paper to prove that his family is the origin of the nickname "Hoosier." A fascinating story, the migration of Randy's family involves religious and political movements of this nation's history, which was published and is posted at http://www.geocities.com/heartland/flats/7822/ . In it, Randy postulates that his pioneer ancestors, being usually the farthest west of civilization, were the origin of the nickname "Hoosier." Randy has also used the Web to maintain an active mailing list, organize a family reunion at Pleasant Hill in Kentucky (where an ancestor had been a neighbor to the Shaker religious community), and helped others with their genealogy.

A Quick Look at This Book

Part I: The Basics   We'll look at doing genealogy in general in the first part of the book.

Chapter 1: Beginning a Genealogy Project   If you already have some knowledge of family history research, you may want to skip this chapter. If you are skipping this chapter, please take this one phrase from it: BACK UP YOUR WORK REGULARLY.

Chapter 2: Software You'll Need   Here the book will explain some of the software that can make online genealogy easier, both the searching and the sharing.

Chapter 3: Genealogy Education   This section examines the online and offline ways you can improve your level of genealogy expertise, up to and including formal accreditation.

Chapter 4: Online Communities   This is a quick look at online etiquette. This chapter is a holdover from the earliest editions of the book, but I think we all need to be reminded that on the Internet, common courtesy still applies.

Chapter 5: Ethics, Privacy, and Law in Genealogy   This is a sticky subject in genealogy and getting more so all the time. When you find crime, illegitimacy, and surprise ancestors, you are faced with some interesting choices.

Part II: General Genealogy

Chapter 6: Revving Up Search Engines   Oh, those wonderful search engines! How to best use them to find the secondary and primary sources you need.

Chapter 7: Chat   People still chat on the Internet, as real-time communication gets easier and easier.

Chapter 8: Genealogy Mailing Lists and Forums   Worldwide, continual discussions on any topic you can imagine is one more resource. And, of course, queries are our best friends!

Part III: The Nitty Gritty: Places to Find Names, Dates, and Places

Chapter 9: Vital Records and Historical Documents   This chapter explores how and where to get those important government documents and certificates.

I hope you'll find in this book the tools you need to get started—or continue—pursuing your genealogy with online resources, to share data with other genealogists online, and to participate in the online society in its many facets. Happy hunting!

Part I

The Basics

Chapter 1

Beginning a Genealogy Project

To paraphrase the Chinese, a journey of a thousand names begins with yourself. If you are just starting your genealogy, with or without the Internet, the process is simple, if endlessly fascinating. This chapter will help you understand that process.

Organize from the Beginning

Friends often call and ask, "Okay, I want to start my genealogy. What do I do?" The process of genealogy has these basic steps: Look at what you already know, record it, decide what name to pursue next, research and query to track that information, analyze what you have to see what's needed next, and then do it all again.

Experienced genealogists are more than willing to help the beginner. Pat Richley, also known as DearMYRTLE, has a lot of great advice on her site, www.dearmyrtle.com. Here are what she feels are the important points for the beginner:

- Just take it one step at a time.

- Devise your own filing system.

- Don't let the experts overwhelm you.

- Use the Family History Library's Research Outline for the state/county where your ancestors came from. They get you quickly oriented to what's available and what has survived that might help you out.

- Don't invent your own genealogy program. You can get Personal Ancestral File (PAF) for free from www.familysearch.org, or you can choose one of the commercially available ones.

- Only use a GEDCOM-compatible software program, because it is the generic way of storing genealogy data. This way, you can import and export to other researchers with common ancestors in the future.

That's the "what" to do, and soon we'll look at that more closely. "How" to do it includes these basic principles: document and back up. From the start, keep track of what you found, where you found it, and when. Even if it's as mundane as "My birth certificate, in the fireproof box, in my closet, 2007," record your data and sources. Sometimes genealogists forget to do that and find themselves retracing their steps like a hiker lost in the woods. Backing up your work regularly is as important as recording your sources is. Both of these topics will be covered in more detail in this chapter.

Your System

Software choices are covered in Chapter 2, where you will see how modern genealogy programs help you to do this. However, remember the good old index card (see Figure 1-1)? These can be useful to record data you find in a library, a friend's book, or even an interview with older relatives until you can get back to your computer.

The handwritten index card also serves as a backup, which brings us to the second most important thing: Back up your data. For most of this book, I assume you are using a computer program to record and analyze your data, but even if you are sticking to good old paper, typewriter, and pencils, as my fourth cousin Jeanne Hand Henry, CG, does, back that up with photocopies. Back up your computerized data in some way: CD-ROMs, flash drives, or online storage sites (see the following box) are all options,

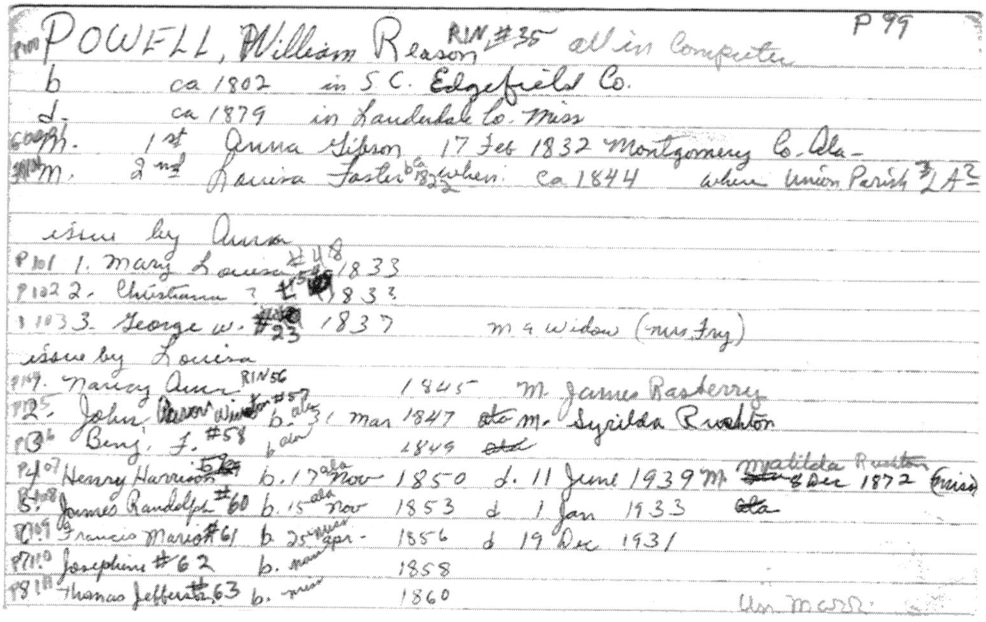
POWELL, William Reason RIN #35 all in Computer P 99
b ca 1802 in S.C. Edgefield Co.
d. ca 1879 in Lauderdale Co. Miss
m. 1st Anna Gibson 17 Feb 1832 Montgomery Co. Ala-
m. 2nd Louisa Foster ca 1844 Union Parish
issue by Anna
1. Mary Louisa #48 1833
2. Christiana 1833
3. George W. #23 1837 m a widow (mrs Fry)
issue by Louisa
4. Nancy Ann RIN 56 1845 m. James Rasberry
5. John Reason Winston #57 b. 31 mar 1847 m. Syrilda Rushton
6. Benj. F. #58 1849
7. Henry Harrison #59 b. 17 Nov 1850 d. 11 June 1939 m. Matilda Rushton 8 Dec 1872
8. James Randolph #60 b. 15 Nov 1853 d. 1 Jan 1933
9. Francis Marion #61 b. 25 apr. 1856 d. 19 Dec 1931
10. Josephine #62 b. 1858
11. Thomas Jefferson #63 b. 1860 Un marr.

FIGURE 1-1. *A sample index card with page numbers indicated for the data collected. The name of the book is written on the back.*

but you must back up. Grace happens, but so does other stuff, like hurricanes, wildfires, and hard drive crashes.

Most people feel that finding a good genealogy program that enables them to record sources (as noted in Chapter 2) is the way to go. Paper sources can be scanned into digital form and/or stored in good old-fashioned filing cabinets. Remember to keep a record of all your research findings, even those pieces of information that seem unrelated to your family lines. Some day that data may indeed prove pertinent to your family; or you may be able to pass it on to someone else.

Even if you decide to do the bulk of your research on a computer, you might still need some paper forms to keep your research organized. The following box lists some Web sites where you can find forms to use as you research censuses and other records so that you can document your findings and sources. There's more about documentation later in this chapter.

A Baker's Dozen of Free Forms

You can find free, downloadable forms to record and track your research. Here are just a few places:

♦ Ancestry.com has PDF files of useful forms, such as a research calendar and source summary. Check out http://www.ancestry.com/save/charts/ancchart.htm.

♦ Another generous genealogist, Judith Haller, has developed templates for spreadsheets and word-processing programs, and offers them free for personal use at http://www.io .com/ ~ jhaller/forms/forms.html.

♦ From the Family Search home page (http://www .familysearch.org), click the Search tab. Click Research Helps. Click Sorted by Document Type. Click Form. You'll find a list of forms, from charts to timelines to census worksheets. These files are in PDF format. You must have Adobe Acrobat to read and print them.

♦ Genealogy.com has a chart to keep track of your correspondence at http://www.genealogy.com/00000007 .html?Welcome = 991338571.

- Mary (Hagstrom) Bailey and Duane A. Bailey are two generous genealogists who have posted forms they developed for their own use at http://www.cs.williams.edu/ ~ bailey/genealogy/. They are free for nonprofit use.

- Ontario GENWEB has a collection of forms useful for recording Canadian research: census, vital statistics, and so on, at http://www.rootsweb.com/ ~ canon/needhelp-genforms.html.

- Free-Genealogy-Forms (http://www.free-genealogy-forms .com/) has forms to help you record data from North America and the United Kingdom.

- Several members have posted their most useful forms at http://www.rootsweb.org/ ~ ilfrankl/resources/forms.htm. For example, you'll find PDF files of family group sheets and a census summary chart.

- The Genealogical Society of Washtenaw County, Michigan, Inc. has a page at http://www.hvcn.org/info/gswc/links/ toolforms.htm with links to forms and articles discussing how to use them.

- Search for Ancestors (http://www.searchforancestors.com/ genealogyfreebies.html) has a set of links to other sites with free genealogy forms.

- The Mid-Continent Public Library has a whole section on genealogy and four PDF files to help you record research at http://www.mcpl.lib.mo.us/ge/forms.

- Microsoft Office Online (http://office.microsoft.com/en-us/ templates) has five different templates: four sample letters requesting information and one book template for sharing your finds.

- *Family Tree Magazine* has a page of forms in text and PDF formats for note-taking, checklists, and more (http://www .familytreemagazine.com/forms/download.html).

Good Practices

To begin your genealogy, begin with yourself. Collect the information that you know for certain about yourself, your spouse, and your children. The data you want are birth, marriage, graduation, and other major life milestones. The documentation would ideally be the original certificates; such documents are considered primary sources. Photographs, with the people in them identified and the date on back, can also be valuable. Such documents are considered primary sources because they reflect data recorded close to the time and place of an event.

> ## Note
>
> *A primary source is an original piece of information that documents an event: a death certificate, a birth certificate, a marriage license, etc. A secondary source is a source that may cite an original source but is not the source itself: a newspaper obituary or birth notice, a printed genealogy, a web site genealogy, etc.*

Pick a Line

The next step is picking a surname to pursue. As soon as you have a system for storing and comparing your research findings, you're ready to begin gathering data on that surname. A good place to begin is interviewing family members—parents, aunts, uncles, cousins, and in-laws. Ask them for stories, names, dates, and places of the people

Adventures in Genealogy

Family legend can be a good starting place, but don't accept what you hear at face value. I will give you an example from my own experience.

When my husband and I were dating, his family's stories fascinated me. One is that his mother is descended from Patrick Henry's sister, who settled in Kentucky soon after the Revolution. Her Logsdon line was also said to be descended from a Revolutionary War hero. T. W. Crowe, Mark's paternal grandfather, said his grandmother was full-blooded Cherokee.

The maternal line was researched and proven by Mark's mother as part of a Daughters of the American Revolution project. Documentation galore helped provide the proof. But the paternal line was more problematic. While T. W. Crowe had some physical characteristics of Native Americans, as does my husband, no documentation of marriage or birth is available to prove the connection. Had I been able to prove it, our children might have been eligible for scholarships and special education in Native American history. After we married and had children, I asked T. W. for the details that would qualify our children for this, but he would not discuss it with me. Indeed, the more I pressed for information, the more reticent T. W. became, and he died in 1994 without my finding the evidence. Finally, a relative told me that T. W., in effect, had been testing me: The Native American grandmother was something not talked about in his generation or the one before him. By telling me what was considered a "family scandal", T. W. was trying to find out if I would be scared off from dating his grandson. The poor man had no idea he had chosen to test me with something that would get my genealogy groove on!

Which brings up this point: While all family history is fascinating to those of us who have been bitten by that genealogy bug, to others, some family history is, at best, a source of mixed emotions and, at worst, a source of shame and fear. You must be prepared for some disagreeable surprises and even unpleasant reactions. You will find out more about this in Chapter 5.

and events in the family. When possible, get documents to back up what you're told. Family bibles, newspapers, diaries, wills, and letters can help here.

A good question to ask at this point is whether any genealogy of the family has been published. Understand that such a work is still a secondary source, not a primary source. If published sources have good documentation included, you might find them a great help.

Visit a Family History Center (FHC) and the FamilySearch site (www .familysearch.org), which has indexes to The Church of Jesus Christ of

Latter-day Saints' (LDS) genealogy information (see Chapter 14). This includes the following:

- ◆ **International Genealogical Index (IGI)**   The event-based International Genealogical Index is the largest single database in the world. Use it with care, though, because sometimes mistakes are included.

- ◆ **Ancestral File (AF)**   A patron-submitted pedigree format genealogy.

- ◆ **Old Parochial Register (OPR)**   These are indexed and microfilmed vital records for Scotland before 1855. They are far from complete, as registering with a local parish was not required, and cost money, but they are still a valuable resource.

All the previous databases are made up of research done by LDS members, but they might include data on people who aren't members.

Record all you find in your system of choice. This is tedious, but necessary. Get someone to proof your entries (typing 1939 when you meant to type 1993 can easily happen).

References to Have at Hand

As you post queries, send and receive messages, read documents online, and look at library card catalogs, you will need some reference books at your fingertips to help you understand what you have found and what you are searching for. Besides a good atlas and perhaps a few state or province gazetteers (a geographic dictionary or index), having these books at hand will save you a lot of time in your pursuit of family history:

- ◆ *The Handybook for Genealogists: United States of America* **(9th Edition) by George B. Everton, Editor (Everton Publishers, 1999)**   DearMYRTLE says she uses this reference book about 20 times a week. This book has information such as when counties were formed; what court had jurisdiction where and when; listings of genealogical archives, libraries, societies, and publications; dates for each available census index; and more.

◆ *The Source: A Guidebook of American Genealogy* by Sandra H. Luebking (Editor) and Loretto D. Szucs (Ancestry Publishing, 2006) or *The Researcher's Guide to American Genealogy* by Val D. Greenwood (Genealogical Publishing Company, 2000)   These are comprehensive, how-to genealogy books. Greenwood's is a little more accessible to the amateur, whereas Luebking's is aimed at the professional, certified genealogist, but still has invaluable information on family history research.

◆ *Cite Your Sources: A Manual for Documenting Family Histories and Genealogical Records* by Richard S. Lackey (University Press of Mississippi, 1986) or *Evidence! Citation & Analysis for the Family Historian* by Elizabeth Shown Mills (Genealogical Publishing Company, 1997)   These books help you document what you found, where you found it, and why you believe it. The two books approach the subject differently: The first is more amateur-friendly, whereas the second is more professional in approach.

Analyze and Repeat

When you find facts that seem to fit your genealogy, you must analyze them, as noted in the section "How to Judge," later in this chapter. When you are satisfied that you have a good fit, record the information and start the process again.

Success Story: A Beginner Tries the Shotgun Approach

My mother shared some old obits with me that intrigued me enough to send me on a search for my family's roots. I started at the ROOTSWEB site with a metasearch, and then I sent e-mails to anyone who had posted the name I was pursuing in the state of origin cited in the obit. This constituted over 50 messages—a real shotgun approach. I received countless replies indicating there was no family connection. Then, one day, I got a response from a man who turned out to be my mother's cousin. He had been researching his family line for the last two years. He sent me census and marriage records, even a will from 1843 that gave new direction to my search.

In pursuing information on my father, whom my mother divorced when I was two months old (I never saw him again), I was able to identify his parents' names from an SS 5 application and, subsequently, track down state census listings containing not only their birth dates, but also the birth dates of their parents—all of which has aided me invaluably in the search for my family's roots.

Having been researching only a short while, I have found the online genealogy community to be very helpful and more than willing to share information with newbies like myself. The amount of information online has blown me away.

— Sue Crumpton

Know Your Terms

As soon as you find information, you are going to come across terms and acronyms that will make you scratch your head. Sure, it's easy to figure out what a deed is, but what's a cadastre? What do DSP and LDS mean? Is a yeoman a sailor or a farmer?

A cadastre is a survey, a map, or some other public record showing ownership and value of land for tax purposes. DSP is an abbreviation for a phrase that means "died without children". LDS is shorthand for the Church of Jesus Christ of Latter-day Saints, or the Mormons. And finally, a yeoman can designate a farmer, an attendant/guard, or a clerk in the Navy, depending on the time and place. Most of this is second nature to people who have done genealogy for more than a couple of years, but beginners often find themselves completely baffled.

And then there are the calendars—Julian, Gregorian, and French Revolutionary—which means that some records have double dates.

No, wait, don't run screaming into the street! Just try to get a handle on the jargon. I have included a glossary at the end of this book with many expressions. As the book progresses, many words are defined in context. But here are a few terms you need to know:

- **(c.) About (or circa, in Latin)** Often used in front of uncertain dates.

- **ahnentafel** An "ancestor table" that organizes information along a strict numbering scheme. An alternative to the pedigree chart.

- **BCG** Board for Certification of Genealogists.

- **CG** Certified Genealogist by BCG.

◆ **CGI**   Certified Genealogical Instructor by BCG.

◆ **CGL**   Certified Genealogical Lecturer by BCG.

◆ **CGRS**   Certified Genealogical Record Specialist by BCG.

◆ **GEDCOM**   The standard for computerized genealogical information. It's a combination of tags for data and pointers to related data.

◆ **family group sheet**   A one-page collection of facts about one family unit—husband, wife, and children—with birth and death dates and places.

◆ **French Revolutionary calendar**   The French Revolutionary calendar (or the Republican calendar) was introduced in France on November 24, 1793, and abolished on January 1, 1806. It was used again briefly during the Paris Commune in 1871.

◆ **Gregorian calendar**   The Gregorian calendar was introduced by Pope Gregory XIII in 1582 and was adopted by England and the colonies in 1752, by which time it was 11 days behind the solar year, causing an adjustment in September 1752.

◆ **Julian calendar**   The Julian calendar was replaced by the Gregorian calendar, which had also fallen behind the solar year.

◆ **NGS**   The National Genealogical Society, U.S.

◆ **pedigree chart**   The traditional way to display a genealogy—the familiar "family tree", where one person's ancestors are outlined. Other formats are the fan chart, the decendency chart (starts with the ancestor and comes down to the present), and the timeline.

◆ **Soundex**   A filing system, usually for recording surnames, using one letter followed by three numbers. The Soundex system keeps together names of the same and/or similar sounds, but of variant spellings.

◆ **SSDI**   The Social Security Death Index. Details from the SSDI often can be used to further genealogical research by enabling you to locate a death certificate, find an obituary, discover cemetery records, and track down probate records. Several sites offer online searching of this resource for free.

Sources and Proof

Most serious genealogists who discuss online sources want to know if they can "trust" what they find on the Internet. Many professional genealogists I know simply don't accept what's found on the Internet as proof of genealogy, period. Their attitude is this: A source isn't a primary source unless you've held the original document in your hand. And a primary source isn't proof unless it's supported by at least one other original document you've held in your hand. To them, seeing a picture of a scanned original on the Internet isn't "proof".

For example, as you can see in Figure 1-2, *The Mayflower* passenger list has been scanned in at Caleb Johnson's site, Mayflower Passenger List (http://members.aol.com/calebj/passenger.html). Would you consider this a primary source? A secondary source? Or simply a good

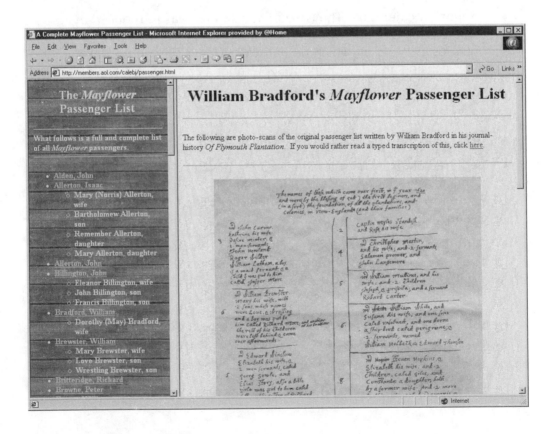

FIGURE 1-2. *Is a picture of an original source as good as holding it in your hand?*

clue? It's a decision you must make for yourself as you start climbing that family tree.

Some genealogists get annoyed with those who publish their genealogy data on the Internet without citing each source in detail. Once, when I was teaching a class on how to publish genealogy on the Internet at a conference, a respected genealogist took me to task over dinner. "Web pages without supporting documentation are lies!" she insisted. "You're telling people to publish lies, because if it's not proven by genealogical standards, it might not be true!"

I have to admit I don't see it that way. In my opinion, you must evaluate what you find on the Internet, just as you evaluate what you find in a library, courthouse, or archive. Many a genealogy book has been published with errors, and the same is true of online genealogies.

On the Web, no real editors exist. You can find all kinds of information and sources on the Internet—from casual references in messages to documented genealogy to original records transcribed into HTML. The range is astounding. But the same can be true of vanity-published genealogies found in libraries.

You *can* find some primary materials online. People and institutions are scanning and transcribing original documents onto the Internet, such as the Library of Virginia and the National Park Service. Volunteers are indexing census records and marriage records at www.FamilySearchIndexing.com. You can also find online a growing treasure trove of indexes of public vital records, scanned images of Government Land Office land patents (www.glorecords.blm.gov), and more (see Figure 1-3).

Don't be put off by those who sneer at the Internet, saying nothing of genuine value can be found there. This might have been true only a few years ago, but not today. Now you can find scanned images of census records going online at both the U.S. Census Bureau site (www.census.gov) and volunteer projects, such as the USGenWeb Digital Census Project (http://www.rootsweb.com/census/). Looking at these records on a web page is as good as looking at them in microfilm or microfiche, in my opinion, and often much cheaper, even if you have to pay a subscription to a site such as Ancestry.com to find them.

I say this as a hobbyist, mind you, not someone trying to impress anyone with my family history, and no important issue hangs on whether I have managed to handle the documents myself. If I wanted to register with the College of Arms, then the original documents would be necessary. If I just want to know what my husband's great-grandfather did for a living, reading a census taker's handwriting on the Internet will do.

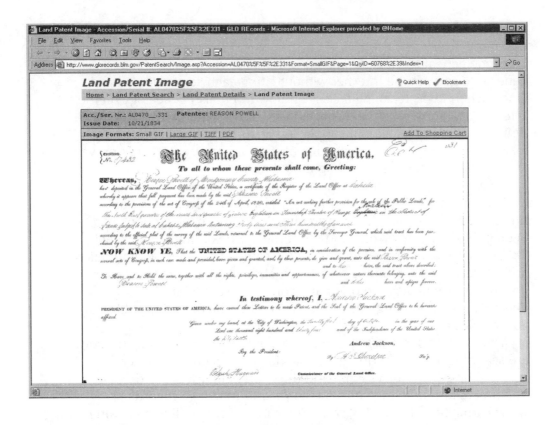

FIGURE 1-3. *You can view original land grants, and order certified copies, online.*

That said, secondary sources are much easier to find than primary sources. The main value of these secondary sources on the Internet is finding other genealogists who are researching the same lines. In addition, you might uncover leads to finding primary and secondary sources offline and, in rare cases, get a glance at an actual data source, perhaps even a primary source. Simply knowing that a source such as a diary, a will, or a tax document *exists* can be a breakthrough.

You will find many people are putting their family trees online. Although many of these websites don't have the disk space available to include complete documentation, most people who publish online are willing to provide pertinent details to anyone who has data to exchange with them. Therefore, I still believe in publishing and exchanging data over the Internet as long as you remember to use good judgment.

How to Judge

The criteria for the evaluation of resources on the Web must be the same criteria you would use for any other source of information. Be aware that just because something is on a computer, this doesn't make it infallible. Garbage in, garbage out. With this in mind, ask yourself the following questions when evaluating an online genealogy site.

Who Created It?   You can find all kinds of resources on the Internet—from libraries, research institutions, and organizations such as the NGS, to government and university resources. Sources such as these give you more confidence in their data than, say, resources from a hobbyist. Publications and software companies also publish genealogical information, but you must read the site carefully to determine whether they've actually researched this information or simply accepted whatever their customers threw at them. Finally, you can find tons of "family traditions" online. And although traditions usually have a grain of truth to them, they're also usually not unvarnished.

How Long Ago Was It Created?   The more often an HTML page is updated, the better you can feel about the data it holds. Of course, a page listing the census for a certain county in 1850 needn't be updated every week, but a pedigree put online should be updated as the author finds more data.

Where Does the Information Come From?   If the page in question doesn't give any sources, you'll want to contact the page author to acquire the necessary information. If sources do exist, of course, you must decide if you can trust them—many a genealogical error has been printed in books, magazines, and online.

In What Form Is the Information?   A simple GEDCOM published as a webpage can be useful for the beginner, but ideally, you want an index to any genealogical resource, regardless of form. If a site has no search function, no table of contents, or not even a document map (a graphic leading you to different parts of the site), it is much less useful than it could be.

How Well Does the Author Use and Define Genealogical Terms?   Does the author clearly know the difference between a yeoman farmer and a yeoman sailor? Does the author seem to be knowledgeable about genealogy? Another problem with online pages is whether the author understands the problems of dates—both badly recorded dates and the 1752 calendar change. Certain sites can help you with calendar problems.

Does the Information Make Sense Compared to What You Already Know?   If you have documentary evidence that contradicts what you see on a webpage, treat it as you would a mistake in a printed genealogy or magazine: Tell the author about your data and see whether the two versions can be reconciled. This sort of exchange, after all, is what online genealogy is all about! For example, many online genealogies have a mistake about one of my ancestors because they didn't stop to analyze the data and made erroneous assumptions.

In Figure 1-4, you can see a transcription of the 1850 Census of Lake County, Indiana. The column labeled HN is for household numbered in order of visitation; the column labeled FN is for families numbered in order of visitation. You can see Abraham Spencer (age 58) and his wife Diadama (age 56, her name is misspelled on the census form) have children Stephen through Elisabeth, and underneath are Amanda, age 27, and then three children under the age of 5.

Some genealogies I have found on the Web assume that Amanda and the following children are also offspring of Abraham and Diadama, but if you look at the ages and how the families are listed—with Amanda and the younger children under the youngest of Abraham and Diadama's children—you see this doesn't make sense. On the other hand, if you were to look at the mortality schedule for the county for that year, you would see that Orsemus Spencer (Amanda's husband and Abraham's son) died in February before the census taker arrived in October. Amanda and her children moved in with her in-laws after her husband's death. The three youngest ones are part of the household, but they aren't Abraham Spencer's children; they are his grandchildren.

Note

A mortality schedule contains data collected during a census about those who died before June in the year of the census. For each person, the following information is listed: name, age, sex, marital status if married or widowed, state or country of birth, month of death, occupation, cause of death, and the length of the final illness. In 1918 and 1919, many of these records were returned to the states; others were given to the Daughters of the American Revolution. Many volunteer-run genealogy websites have posted transcribed mortality schedules for specific counties.

```
1850 Census of Lake County, IN p.156B - Netscape 6                          _ □ ×
File  Edit  View  Search  Go  Bookmarks  Tasks  Help

  ←  →  ⟳  ⊗     http://www.rootsweb.com/~inlake/census/1850/156b.htm    ▼   Go   Search   ⟲   N

CENSUS YR:  1850   STATE or TERRITORY:  IN  COUNTY:  Lake  DIVISION:  Hobert  Township  R
REFERENCE:   5 Oct 1850;  B. McCarty Ass't Marshal;  MF#312
=================================================================================
 LN  HN   FN   LAST NAME       FIRST NAME      AGE SEX  RACE  OCCUP.        VAL.    BIR
=================================================================================
  1  34   34   ENSIGN          Edward          31   M          Cooper       180    Ohi
  2  34   34   ENSIGN          Emmarilla       30   F                              New
  3  34   34   ENSIGN          Clarissa D.     4    F                              Ohi
  4  34   34   ENSIGN          Sarah           2    F                              Ohi
  5  34   34   ENSIGN          Linus           3/12 M                              Ind
  6  35   35   CRAGE           George          24   M          Sawyer              Can
  7  35   35   CRAGE           Cornelia        19   F                              Can
  8  36   36   ALBY            Jesse B.        34   M          Carpenter    200    Ver
  9  36   36   ALBY            Sarah A.        24   F                              Ohi
 10  36   36   ALBY            Americus S.     7    M                              Ohi
 11  36   36   ALBY            Alonzo C.       2    M                              Ind
 12  37   37   SPENCER         Arza            21   M          Farmer              Ohi
 13  37   37   SPENCER         Eliza           16   F                              Ohi
 14  38   38   SPENCER         Abraham         58   M          Farmer              New
 15  38   38   SPENCER         Deidama         56   F                              New
 16  38   38   SPENCER         Stephen         23   M          Farmer              Ohi
 17  38   38   SPENCER         Eleazer         18   M          Farmer              Ohi
 18  38   38   SPENCER         Phineus D.      16   M          Farmer              Ohi
 19  38   38   SPENCER         Elisabeth E.    12   F                              Ohi
 20  39   39   SPENCER         Amanda          27   F                              Ohi
 21  39   39   SPENCER         Stephen M.      5    M                              Ill
 22  39   39   SPENCER         Deidama         3    F                              Ind
 23  39   39   SPENCER         Nelson          1    M                              Ind
 24  40   40   HALE            Jacob           50   M          Farmer              New
```

FIGURE 1-4.   *Census records sometimes need careful study and interpretation.*

    With this in mind, becoming familiar with the National Genealogical
Society's Standards for Sharing Information with Others, as shown in
Appendix A, would help. Judge what you find on the Internet by these
standards. Hold yourself to them as you exchange information, and
help keep the data on the Internet as accurate as possible. After you
have these standards firmly in mind, a good system to help you track
what you know, how you know it, and what you don't know, as well as
the surnames you need, is simply a matter of searching for the facts
regarding each individual as you go along.

Look Far and Wide

Some steps you might consider to gather the information:

◆ Find published genealogies with your surnames. You can do that
with search sites and catalogs such as Cyndi's List (Chapter 6),
Family Search.com (Chapter 14), ROOTSWEB (Chapter 17),
Ancestry.com (Chapter 17), and genealogy databases (Chapter 11).

◆ Interview older family members now, with tape or video running,
before they and their information are beyond your reach.

◆ Communicate with other people searching the same family lines
as you. You can do that with search engines (Chapter 6), through
chat programs (Chapter 7), mailing lists (Chapter 8), ROOTSWEB
and Ancestry.com, and other sites (Chapter 18).

◆ Find original documents or historical information. Sometimes,
historical information (such as the fact that mortality schedules
are included with some censuses) will help you decide where to
look next, whether online or offline. You can do that with the
World Wide Web; certain vital records (Chapter 9); Ellis Island
Online (Chapter 15); The Library of Congress, the National
Archives and Records Administration, and online library catalogs
(Chapter 10); international genealogy sites (Chapter 12); ethnic
genealogy sites (Chapter 13); and many other sites, such as state
archives (Chapter 9).

◆ Learn more about genealogy techniques and practices. Chapters 3
and 4 will give you pointers.

Standards of Genealogical Research

Genealogy is a hobby for most of us, and we do it for fun. The average
genealogist is not doing this for fame and fortune, but because of an
insatiable curiosity about the people who came before us. Given that,
this little section may seem a bit too serious, even "taking all the fun
out of it." Still, I believe that if you approach this hobby with the right
attitude and care, it will be more rewarding than if you just dive in
without a thought to the best practices and ethics of this rewarding
pastime. Despite the fact that there are no official "rules" to this when
you are a hobbyist, following guidelines and standards can, in the end,
make your experience easier and more enjoyable.

Sources That Can Help a Genealogical Researcher

- **Vital records** Birth, death, marriage records and the Social Security Death Index. Many states did not require these before the 20th century.

- **Court records** Wills, adoptions, land and property bills of sale, tax rolls, deeds, naturalization, and even lawsuits.

- **Church records** Baptisms, marriages, burials, etc.

- **Newspapers and magazines** Not only obituaries, marriage, and birth notices, but also social news; perhaps parents, siblings, or cousins are mentioned.

- **Military records** Enlistment, commission, muster rolls, and veterans' documentation

- Fraternal organizations

- **Ships' passenger lists** Not only for immigrants to your country, but travel within. Also, some rivers, such as the Tennessee, were the site of many a pioneer marriage.

- Family History Centers have resources such as the International Genealogical Index, Ancestral File, and Old Parochial Register. More about these in Chapter 14!

- State archives and libraries (many online!)

- Census records, not only federal, but also local and state

- Published genealogies

- Aunts, uncles, cousins, grandparents, and folks who knew them before you were born.

As mentioned previously, in the appendixes to this book you will find the latest standards and guidelines from the National Genealogical Society (www.ngsgenealogy.org), and I suggest you study them. Though you can (and should) take many excellent courses in genealogy, if you review and understand these documents first, you will be better prepared to proceed on your family history quest in the best manner.

To summarize them briefly, these NGS standards and guidelines emphasize the following:

♦ Taking care not to assume too much from any piece of information and to know the differences between primary and secondary sources

♦ Keeping careful records

♦ Giving credit to all sources and other researchers when appropriate

♦ Treating original records and their repositories with respect

♦ Treating other researchers, the objects of your research, and especially living relatives with respect

♦ Availing yourself of all the training, periodicals, literature, and organizations you can afford in time and money

♦ And finally, taking the time and effort to mentor other researchers as you learn more yourself

Joining the NGS is a good first step!

Another good outline to the best way to practice genealogy is the Board for Certification of Genealogists Code of Ethics and Conduct on their website at www.bcgcertification.org/aboutbcg/code.html. This is also a guide to choosing a professional, should you decide to get some help on your genealogy along the way!

How to Write a Query

Genealogy is a popular hobby, and lots of people have been pursuing it for a long time. When you realize that, it makes sense to first see whether someone else has found what you need and is willing to share it. Your best tool for this is the query.

A query, in genealogy terms, is a request for data or at least for a clue where to find data on a specific person. Queries may be sent to one person in a letter or in an e-mail to the whole world (in effect). You can also send queries to an online site, a magazine, a mailing list, or another forum that reaches many people at once.

Note

Do not ever send a letter or query that says, "Send me everything you have on the Jones family" or words to that effect. This is not a game of Go Fish. It is rude and unfair to ask for someone to just hand over years of research. When you ask for information, have some data to exchange and a specific genealogy goal to fill. Also, always offer to pay copying and/or postage costs.

Writing a good query is not hard, but you do have to stick to certain conventions for it to be effective. Make the query short and to the point. Don't try to solve all your genealogical puzzles in one query; zero in on one task at a time. You must always list at least one name, at least one date or time period, and at least one location to go with the name. Do not bother sending a query that does not have all three of these elements, because no one will be able to help you without a name, date, and place. If you are not certain about one of the elements, follow it with a question mark in parentheses, and be clear about what you know for sure as opposed to what you are trying to prove. Here are some points to keep in mind:

- Use all capital letters to spell every surname, including the maiden name and previous married names of female ancestors. Include all known relatives' names—children, siblings, and so on. Use complete names, including any middle names, if known. Finally, proofread all the names.

- Give complete dates whenever possible. Follow the format DD Month YYYY, as in 20 May 1865. If the date is uncertain, use "before" or "about" as appropriate, such as "Born circa 1792" or "Died before October 1850." Proofread all the dates for typos; this is where transpositions can really get you!

- Give town, county, and state (or province) for North American locations; town, parish (if known), and county for United Kingdom locations, and so on. In other words, start with the specific and go to the general, including all divisions possible. If you are posting your query to a message board, it is helpful to include the name, the date, and if possible, migration route using > to show the family's progress.

♦ Finally, include how you wish to be contacted. For a letter query or one sent to a print magazine, you will want to include your full mailing address. For online queries, you want to include at least an e-mail address.

Here's a sample query for online publication:

```
Query: Crippen, 1794, CT>MA>VT>Canada
I need proof of the parents of Diadama CRIPPEN born 11 Sept
1794 in (?), NY. I believe her father was Darius CRIPPEN, son
of Samuel CRIPPEN, and her mother was Abigail STEVENS CRIPPEN,
daughter of Roger STEVENS, both from CT. They lived in
Egremont, Berkshire County, MA and Pittsfield, Rutland County,
VT before moving to Bastard Township, Ontario, Canada. I will
exchange information and copying costs. [Here you would put
your regular mail address, e-mail address, or other contact
information.]
```

As you can see, this query is aimed at one specific goal: the parents of Diadama. The spelling matches the death notice that gave the date of birth—a secondary source—but because it is close to the actual event, it's acceptable to post this with the caveat "I believe." It has one date, several names, several places, and because this one is going online, a migration trail in the subject line (CT > MA > VT > Canada). If the author knew Diadama's siblings for certain, they would be in there, too.

When you have posted queries, especially on discussion boards and other online venues, check back frequently for answers. If the site has a way to alert you by e-mail when your posting gets an answer, be sure to use it. Also, read the queries from whatever source you have chosen to use, and search query sites for your surnames. As you can see from the previous information, queries themselves can be excellent clues to family history data!

Documentation

Document everything you find.

When you enter data into your system, enter where and when you found it. Like backups of your work, this will save you countless hours in the long run.

A true story: At the beginning of her genealogy research in the late 1960s, my mother came across a volume of biographies for a town in Kansas. This sort of book was common in the 1800s. Everyone who was "someone" in a small town would contribute toward a book of history of the town. Contributors were included in the book, sometimes with a picture, and the biography would be a timeline of their lives up to the publication of the book, emphasizing when the family moved to town and their importance to the local economy. One of these biographies was of a man named Spencer and included a picture of him. He looked much like her own grandfather, but the date was clearly too early to be him. Still, she photocopied it, just in case. However, she didn't photocopy the title page or make a note of where she had seen the book, which library, which town, and so forth.

Fast-forward 15 years to the early 1980s. At this point, my mother is in possession of much more data, and in organizing things, came across the photocopy. Sure enough, that biography she had found years before is of her grandfather's grandfather; she had come across enough primary sources (birth certificates, church records, and so on) to prove it. And now, she knew this secondary source had valuable information about that man's early life, who his parents were, and who his in-laws were. However, all she had was the page, with no idea of how to find the book again to document it as a source! It took days to reconstruct her research and make a guess as to which library had it. She did finally find it again and documented the source, but it was quite tedious. Just taking an extra two minutes, years before, would have saved a lot of time!

Backup

Back up your data.

I'm going to repeat that in this book as often as I say "Document your sources." Documentation and backup are essential. On these two principles hang all your effort and investment in genealogy. Hurricanes happen. Fire and earthquakes do, too. Software and hard drives fail for mysterious reasons. To have years of work gone with the wind is not a good feeling.

Pick at Least One System

If you are sticking to a paper system, make photocopies and keep them offsite—perhaps at your cousin's house or a rental storage unit.

If you are using a computer, as most of us are these days, then back up on whatever you have: floppies, CDs, thumb drives, whatever. Or print it all out on paper as a backup to the digital files. Then be sure to keep a copy offsite, and update your backup often.

An alternative is online backup—that is, using someone else's computer to hold your data files. Again, you may have family at a distance that can do that for you, but you may also consider one of several free online storage services.

Free Online Storage Services

Online storage services are a convenient way to store offsite backup copies of critical information. Some services that are free until you reach some level of use are Xdrive, box.net, mozy, DropBoks, iBackup, eSnips, MediaMax, OmniDrive, openomy, and more. If you need more than the basic free space, they all offer additional storage, costing from $5 to $30 a month, depending on how much room you need. Several of these services will let you make some files available to other people while keeping other files secret and secure. Although all of them will work with both Macintosh and PC computers, some of them are picky about the Web browser you use. Experiment with several of these services and find the one with the right fit for you. Then use it often!

My favorite is Xdrive, a service of AOL (see Figure 1-5). I use this not only for personal files, but also to "take work home" by uploading a file at the office, downloading it at home to write, and uploading it again. The default setting on Xdrive offers 5 gigabytes (GB) of free storage space, with preconfigured folders for your documents, photos, and music.

Macintosh and Linux/UNIX users can only access Xdrive by using a Web browser. For Windows-based systems, there are three ways to access your Xdrive account: Xdrive Web, Xdrive Desktop, and Xdrive Mobile. Xdrive Web is the interface through your browser. No matter where you are, you can log in and upload and download files. Xdrive Desktop is software that allows dragging and dropping entire folders from your computer to your Xdrive account, as if it is another drive or

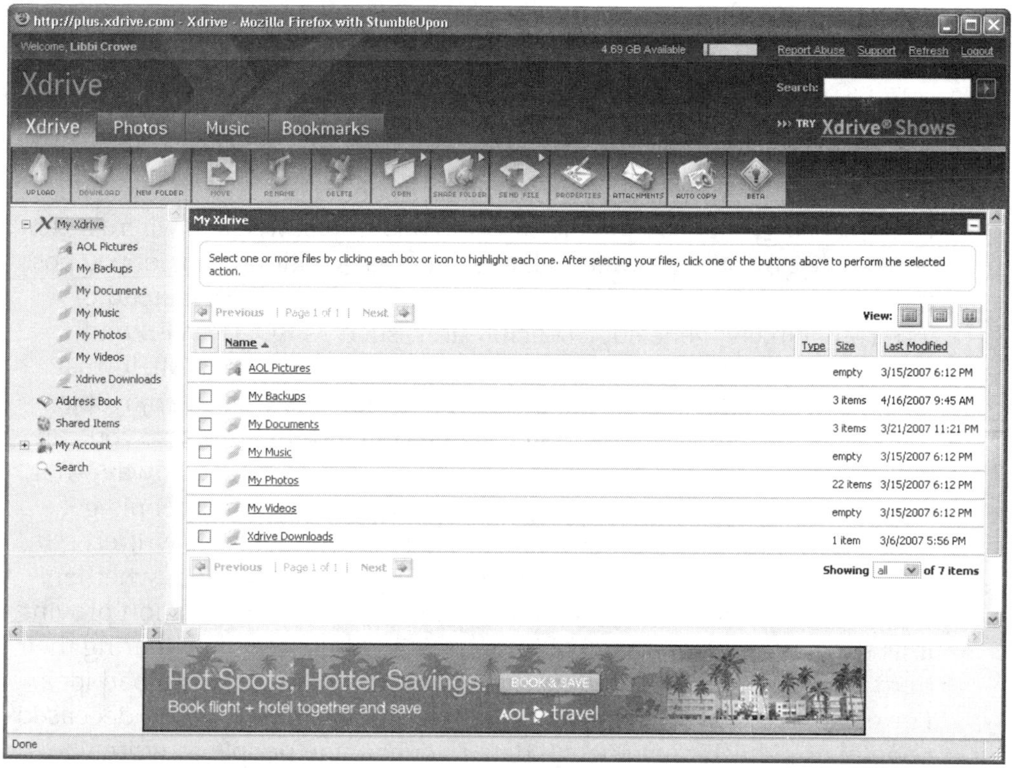

FIGURE 1-5.   *Xdrive Desktop from AOL acts like a hard drive and backs up your
important data offsite.*

device on your computer. Xdrive Desktop can even back up files and
folders automatically on schedule for you! Xdrive Mobile gives you
wireless access to your cell phone, personal digital assistant (PDA), or
other Web-enabled device.

Publishing Your Findings

Sooner or later, you're going to want to share what you've found,
perhaps by publishing it on the Internet. To do this, you need some
space on a server of some sort. Fortunately, your choices here are wide
open. You can publish your genealogy on the Internet in many places.

Most Internet service providers (ISPs) allot some disk space on their servers for their users. Check with your ISP to see how much you have. Dozens of sites are out there, offering up to 10 megabytes (MB) of space for free, including AOL's Hometown, Yahoo!, Xoom, Angelfire, and more. Most of these are free, as long as you allow them to display an ad on the visitor's screen. Some software programs, as noted in Chapter 2, will put your genealogy database on the software publishers' website, where it can be searched by others. Some websites, such as WorldConnect, let you post the GEDCOM of your data for searching in database form instead of in HTML. Finally, genealogy-specific sites, such as ROOTSWEB and MyFamily.com, offer free space for noncommercial use in HTML format.

In short, publishing on the Internet is doable, as well as enjoyable. By publishing at least some of your genealogy on the Internet, you can help others looking for the same lines. But don't get carried away—not everyone may be thrilled to be part of your project. Some people get upset at finding their names published online without their written permission. Some genealogists consider anything published, whether it's online or in hard copy, to be false unless the documentation proving it as true is included in the publication. Still others feel that sharing their hard work without getting data and/or payment in return is a bad idea. For these and other reasons, you want to publish data only on deceased people, or publish only enough data to encourage people to write you with their own data.

So, be careful about what you post on the Web and how you post it. The National Genealogical Society recently adopted a set of standards for publishing genealogy on the Internet. With their permission, I included these standards in Appendix A.

Almost every good genealogy program now includes a way to publish on the Web. Ultimate Family Tree, Family Origins, Family Tree Maker, The Master Genealogist, Generations Family Tree, and Ancestral Quest are only a few of the programs that can turn your genealogical database into HTML. Most of them simply create a standard tree-branching chart with links to the individuals' data. Others may create a set of family group sheets. Many of them let you have "still living" replace the vital statistics for certain people. In many of these programs, the process is as simple as creating a printed report, and you simply choose HTML as the format.

Some of the programs, however, don't give you a choice of where you post your data. Family Tree Maker (FTM), for example, publishes your data on its site. Once there, your data becomes part of the FTM database, which is periodically burned to CD-ROMs and sold in stores. Simply by posting your data on the site, you give them permission to do this. Quite a bit of discussion and debate is ongoing about this privatization of publicly available data. Some say this will be the end of amateur genealogy, whereas others feel this is a way to preserve data that might be lost to disaster or neglect. Still others say it takes money to store and maintain this data. It's up to you whether you want to post to a site that reuses your data for its own profit.

Success Story: Finding Cousins Across the Ocean

After ten years of getting my genealogy onto computer, I finally got the nerve to "browse the Web," and to this day I don't know how I got there, where I was, or how to get back there—but I landed on a website for French genealogists. I can neither read nor speak French. I bravely wrote a query in English: "I don't read or speak French, but I am looking for living cousins descended from my ancestors ORDENER." I included a short "tree" with some dates and my e-mail address.

Well, within a couple of hours I heard from an ORDENER cousin living in Paris, France. She did not know she had kin in America and had spent years hunting in genealogy and cemetery records for her great-great-grandfather's siblings! She had no idea they had come to America in the 1700s and settled in Texas before it was a state of the union.

So, while I traded her hundreds of names of our American family, she gave me her research back to about 1570 France when the name was ORTNER! About four months later, another French cousin found me from that query on the Web. He did not know his cousin in Paris, so I was able to "introduce" him via e-mail. One of them has already come to Florida to meet us!

What keeps me going? Well, when I reach a brick wall in one family, I turn to another surname. Looking for living cousins is a little more successful than looking for ancestors, but you have to find the ancestors to know how to go "down the line" to the living distant cousins! Genealogy is somewhat like a giant crossword puzzle—each time you solve a name, you have at least two more to hunt! You never run out of avenues of adventure—ever!

— Patijé Weber Mills Styers, Sarasota, Florida

Caveats

In discussing how to begin your genealogy project, we must consider the pitfalls. This chapter has touched briefly on your part in ethics and etiquette, and Chapters 4 and 5 will expand on that. We must also consider the ethics of others, however, and be careful.

In the 21st century, genealogy is an industry. Entire companies are centered on family history research and resources. Not surprisingly, you will find people willing to take your money and give you little or nothing in return in genealogy, just as in any industry. Many of them started long before online genealogy became popular, and they simply followed when genealogists went online. "Halberts of Ohio" is one notorious example. Dick Eastman covered this in a March 2001 article that is still worth looking up at www.ancestry.com/library/view/columns/eastman/3538.asp.

Books with titles such as *The World Book of [YOUR SURNAME]* and *Three Centuries of [YOUR SURNAME]*, sold via junk mail flyers as well as online, often turn out to be nothing you couldn't find in a telephone book. You have to read such pitches carefully, and before you send any money, ask on the e-mail lists, chat rooms, and blog sites whether anyone has had experience with the company.

And, of course, don't believe anyone who tells you the College of Arms has a coat of arms or a crest for your surname. These are assigned to specific individuals, not general surnames. (Although a crest may be assigned to an entire clan in Ireland—the crest is the part above the shield.) Today, as always, coats of arms come only from letters patent from the senior heralds, the Kings of Arms. A right to arms can only be established by registering in the official records of the College of Arms a pedigree showing direct male line descent from an ancestor who was granted a letter patent or by making application through the College of Arms for a grant of arms for yourself. Grants are made to corporations as well as to individuals. For more details, go the college's site: www.college-of-arms.gov.uk.

Always check a company's name and sales pitch against the following sites, which list common genealogy scams.

♦ **Cyndi's List Myths, Hoaxes, and Scams (http://www.cyndislist .com/myths.htm)** Cyndi Howells keeps on top of myths, lies, and scams in genealogy on this page, and has a good set of links to consumer protection sites, should you fall prey to one of them.

◆ **Kimberly Powell's Genealogy Hoaxes page (http://genealogy .about.com/cs/genealogyscams)**   This site lists some current and historical cases of people losing good money for bad genealogy.

If you feel you have been scammed, report it to the Federal Trade Commission (FTC) at https://rn.ftc.gov/pls/dod/wsolcq$ .startup?Z_ORG_CODE = PU01.

Wrapping Up

A genealogy project involves specific steps. Here are the most important points:

◆ Record your data faithfully. Back it up faithfully. These two things will save you a world of grief some day.

◆ To begin your genealogy project, start with yourself and your immediate family, documenting what you know. Look for records for the next generation back by writing for vital records, searching for online records, posting queries, and researching in libraries and courthouses. Gather the information with documentation on where, when, and how you found it. Organize what you have, and look for what's needed next. Repeat the cycle.

◆ Beware of scams!

Chapter 2

Software You'll Need

Online genealogy is only different from the old-fashioned kind in the type of tools you use. Instead of using a photocopier, you make copies using your printer. Instead of sending queries in an envelope, you send them by e-mail. Instead of reading an article in a magazine, you read it in a browser. And instead of going to the library in person, you can search the card catalog and even the text of whole books from home!

Please understand—I don't mean to imply that you won't ever do things the old-fashioned way again. Of course you will! But you'll use these online techniques much more often, sometimes even before you try to do research the traditional way. These are new tools for age-old genealogical tasks.

You'll need to learn the ins and outs of the Internet, software, and techniques for online information exchange to get the most out of the experience. This chapter covers such considerations and the software you might want to use. Of course, it's assumed you will need a computer with some connection to the Internet. High-speed connections are best, as so many primary sources are now available as images online and they take up a lot of bandwidth. Some folks use dial-up at home just for checking e-mail, and they surf the Web at a local library using their high-speed connection. The disadvantages to that are obvious: You can only work on your genealogy when the library is open in such a setup, and you certainly can't work in your pajamas at the library, which is part of the fun of online genealogy!

Still, there will be days when you do go to the library, and then a laptop and a wireless card are useful. For example, at the Family History Library in Salt Lake City (and many other libraries), you can now use your own laptop computer or handheld personal digital assistant (PDA) with Wi-Fi wireless networking to check your e-mail, visit genealogy sites, or otherwise surf the Web. You can do all this without connecting any network cables; the wireless networking card in your device will connect via low-power radio waves to the building's network.

Often, you will find all a library's computers are taken on a busy day, but you can pull out your own laptop and use that instead when it has Wi-Fi network capabilities. You do not need to wait for someone else to give up their seat at a library-owned computer. The library saves money because it does not need to purchase as many computers, and they don't have to worry about what you might be downloading because it stays on your computer. And, in many local libraries, the card catalog is all online; with a laptop and Wi-Fi, you can even search for the book you need.

An all-in-one printer or fax modem could be useful in asking for vital records from a courthouse miles away, so you may still use your phone line for some genealogy chores!

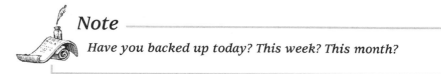

Note ──────────────────────────────────────

Have you backed up today? This week? This month?

Don't forget output. Back up your data. A CD-ROM burner is good for storing and backing up your data, which you must do on a regular basis. If you don't use CD-ROMs, thumb drives and portable hard drives are available. Use an online storage service (see Chapter 1). Use floppies you picked up at a garage sale! Whatever you have, use it to back up your data. Don't put this off for later. When you are making a lot of progress, back up at least once a month. Once a week is better, because if you lose more than a month's work to a lightning strike or natural disaster, you may be too discouraged to start again.

A good color ink-jet printer, especially an all-in-one that can scan and copy, can help you preserve images of your original documents and primary sources.

And there are other choices in hardware.

New Choices

Handheld Web-enabled devices and cell phones with e-mail access are popping up all over. The latter can offer you convenience when traveling, but cost will be a big factor. The former have some issues with connectivity, and for those with far-sightedness, those tiny screens can be hard to see!

Personal Digital Assistants

The personal digital assistant (especially those models with Internet connections) has become popular with genealogists. In addition to its usefulness in note-taking, retrieving e-mail, and, if it has the proper port, uploading and downloading information to desktop or laptop computers, some surprisingly functional software for these devices is available. Here are some examples:

♦ The Personal Ancestral File (PAF) 5.1 from FamilySearch.org has Palm capability, which is handy for storing work until you can upload it to your computer. After you download this free software from www.familysearch.org, go back to the PAF page, and scroll down until you see PAF Data Viewer for Palm Handhelds. Then download that, too.

♦ The GedStar (www.ghcssoftware.com) lets you browse a GEDCOM (see the Glossary) and could be useful for trips to the library (see Figure 2-1). The program even has its own discussion list (http://groups.yahoo.com/group/genpalm/).

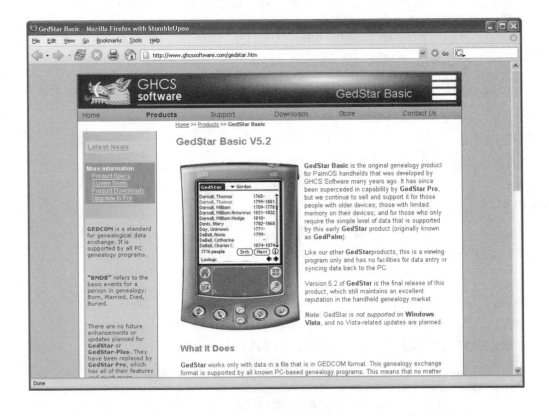

FIGURE 2-1. *GedStar from GHCS software keeps your GEDCOMs in a PDA.*

- MyRoots (www.tapperware.com/MyRoots) is a genealogical database that can be accessed using a Palm Pilot.

- A list of Palm programs is maintained at Cyndi's List (www.cyndislist.com/software.htm#Palm).

Mobile Phones

Connection to the Internet through a cell phone is slow, expensive, and hard on the eyes. This isn't something I recommend to genealogists for an everyday Internet connection. Nevertheless, while at a genealogy conference or seminar, or if you simply must keep up with a mail list while away from your computer, this is an option.

Software

Once you have your hardware in place and you know how you're going to connect, you need to look at your software. Many Internet service providers (ISPs) include software as part of the package: the communications software, browser, file transfer program (FTP), e-mail, and other programs you need.

The programs you use to access the Web are often called *clients*. These programs send signals to other computers, called *servers*, instructing them to display files and information to you or to run programs for you. The resulting display might be e-mail, a Web page, or a GEDCOM you want to download. The program the clients run might be a browser or a chat room.

Which Browser Should I Use?

I'm often asked, "Which is the best browser?" In my opinion, this is like asking, "Which is the best car?" It all depends on your taste, habits, and needs. The current leaders in the browser wars are still Microsoft Internet Explorer and Netscape's progeny, Mozilla Firefox.

Microsoft Internet Explorer: Entire books are devoted to helping you get the most out of this browser. The major online services and ISPs have lined up with one or the other for their customers to use and install automatically with their software, so you don't have to do any extra work to use it. Microsoft Internet Explorer is free, and you get it (whether you like it or not) when you buy a Windows system. It works well with Outlook, Microsoft's calendar, contacts, and e-mail program.

Firefox can also be obtained free of charge, has a nice user interface, and is easy to use. It now has a companion e-mail program called Thunderbird, which is covered in the section "RSS Readers." As of this writing, they do not have a calendar/contacts sibling, although Sunbird is in the oven, so to speak. Some sites, you will find, do not look as "clean" in Firefox as they do in Internet Explorer, especially if the site was created with a Microsoft product.

Other browsers, such as **Opera** and **Ariadne**, are less feature-packed, but they're free, easy to use, and sometimes much faster. Some of these programs are a pain for beginners because their Help files can be confusing, they have some display problems with certain web sites, and they don't offer much support. For experienced users, however, their simplicity and speed make up for that.

If you have disability issues, such as macular degeneration or arthritis, there are browsers that magnify the type on a web page, read the words out loud to you, accept spoken rather than typed commands, and so on. Check out www.w3.org/WAI/References/Browsing for a list of pointers to information and some demonstration versions of alternative browsing methods, although the page itself says it is no longer being maintained and updated.

My advice is to test-drive a few of them and see which browser suits you best if you don't like the one that comes with your service's software.

Genealogy Programs

Your most important software, however, will be your genealogy program, which is basically a database program. The output can be simply data, whole books with pictures, or wall charts. In shopping around for the right genealogy program for you, consider these factors:

♦ First and foremost, check the program's ability to record your sources. If it doesn't have a way for you to track where and when you found a fact, reject it out of hand. You'll wind up retracing your steps a thousand times without the ability to instantly retrieve the sources you've already used.

♦ Second in importance, but only slightly second, is the appearance. This may seem trivial, but it's not. Most genealogy programs have some sort of metaphor: When you open the program, the screen looks as if you are working on a scrapbook, 3 × 5 cards, or a genealogical chart. Finding one that presents the data in a way that suits your methods is important.

♦   Third, consider how you output your data. Don't use anything that can't output a good GEDCOM. A GEDCOM is a text-only file with the data formatted so that any other program can use it. This is important for comparing your research to others', but that's not the only output form for your work. For hard-copy output, think about what you want to create. A website? A book? A quilt? A giant mural for the next reunion? Look for a program that fits your output needs.

♦   Fourth, look at the package's support, and ask friends what their experience was when they needed support. Read the manual to see how much support is included with the purchase price and for how long. Understand that within a year, the software (any software) will be upgraded. Find out whether upgrades are free or available for a minimal charge. A really good program may cost from $25 to $50 a year to keep it current; some shareware gives you upgrades for $5 or less. Also, ask at the next meeting of your local genealogy club whether anyone has the program you are interested in and is willing to help you with the learning curve.

♦   Finally, consider the cost. When you find the program you want, can you afford it? If not, see whether the program comes in different versions—some less powerful but also less expensive than others. Sometimes the cost includes CD-ROMs of secondary or primary material, but perhaps some of this material is available at your local library, and you need not buy it.

The following sections provide a quick roundup of some popular programs that you can at least try for free.

Brother's Keeper

Brother's Keeper is a good program without a lot of bells and whistles. It has a learning curve, too, because it does not have a lot of onscreen cues. Nevertheless, it is a good, basic program.

With Brother's Keeper 6.2, you can attach sources to any event, person, or family; access a source to view it or modify it separately from data; and print a list of all sources (separate from data). Also, output can be GEDCOMs, a list of people with any fields you want to include, and you can output that list as a text file or as a comma-delimited file. Brother's Keeper 6.2 is shareware; you try it and then send in the $49 if you decide you like it.

You can send many reports to a disk file. In the descendant report, group sheets, and custom lists, you set up the report and then choose File | Create Text File. In the Register Book, Indented Book, and Ahnentafel Book, you set up the report and choose File | Create RTF File. Then you load the rich-text format (RTF) file into Word or WordPerfect. On the Group Sheet screen, you can also choose File | Create HTML Files.

The program has no real metaphor, unlike most genealogy software, as shown in Figure 2-2. The simple form has blanks to fill in, with tabs to click for entering details. In the edit screen shown, the user could choose one of these siblings to enter a death date, for example.

Brother's Keeper 6.2 is easy to use once you learn it, and it prints over 30 different charts and reports. This program has been around for a long time (longer even than Family Tree Maker). Also, the author is open to suggestions from users and will answer requests for help.

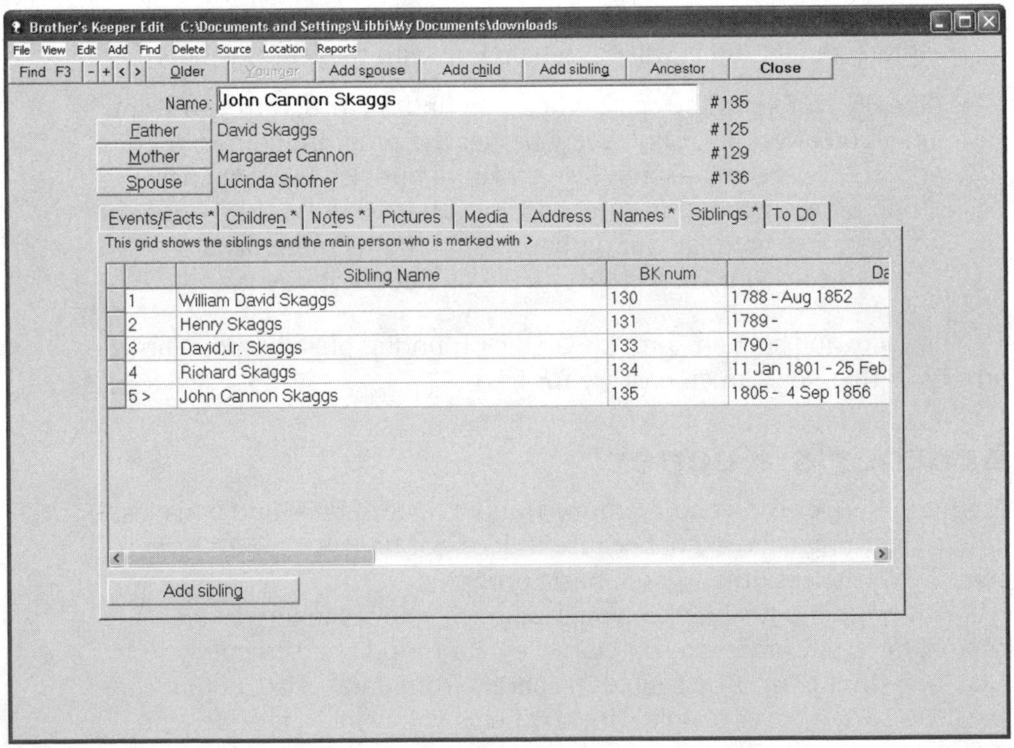

FIGURE 2-2.   *Brother's Keeper 6.2 has a plain interface.*

Personal Ancestral File

Personal Ancestral File (PAF) is the program that members of the Church of Jesus Christ of Latter-day Saints (LDS) use. Personal Ancestral File is available for free on the Internet at www.familysearch.org; click Order/Download Products, and then click Software Downloads.

PAF 5.2 can produce, either onscreen or on paper, family histories, pedigree charts, family group records, and other reports to help users in their search for missing ancestors. In the latest version, an individual record can accommodate the wide variety of naming conventions used throughout the world. This version will convert PAF 3.0 and 4.0 data files to its improved file format. PAF 5.2 is available on CD-ROM as well for a small fee. Also, for less than $7, you can download PAF Companion for more choices in printer output, including color.

PAF has fields that are of use in submitting family members for Temple use that non-Mormons will not use. However, it is designed to be simple, to output in GEDCOM and other formats so you can share your data, and is supported by several forums on the Web.

RootsMagic

This $30 program is what became of Family Origins after some software companies merged and revamped their product lines, eliminating the Family Origins name. There are two main views: Tree View and Family View. You switch between the two by simply clicking the tab for the desired view. The edit screen allows you to add an unlimited number of facts for every person (birth, death, marriage, occupation, religion, description, and so on). If you want to add a fact type that isn't in the predefined list, you can create your own. GEDCOM import and export, as well as output, are supported, and multimedia files can be included.

The program allows notes and unlimited source citations for every fact. You can add, edit, delete, merge, and print the sources of your information. Simply add the source once, then when you add a fact to a person and want to document where that information came from, you simply point to the source in the Source Manager.

Output includes pedigree charts, family group sheets, four types of box charts, six styles of books, 27 different lists, mailing labels, calendars, hourglass trees, graphical timelines, relationship charts, letter-writing templates, individual summaries, five types of photo charts, and seven types of blank charts. Your database can be output into a pedigree chart with Hypertext Markup Language (HTML) links among the individuals in the genealogy.

Family Tree Maker

This program comes in versions from $30 to $100; the more expensive bundles may include a video, subscription to online databases, CD-ROMs, and/or a book. Genealogy.com, owned by A&E Television, distributes Family Tree Maker. It connects with that site to help you begin your research, and the site has subscription databases you can search, as well as the old Family Origins 10 software.

Family Tree Maker's metaphor is a standard pedigree tree, which you fill in by moving from branch to branch by pressing the TAB key. Facts and sources are tracked; output can be GEDCOM, HTML, PDF, and other formats. It has all the features you could want, but your output may become part of the Family Tree Maker database, which they will later sell to others.

Family Tree Maker is by far the most popular program because it is easy to use.

The Master Genealogist

The Master Genealogist (TMG) does everything the previously mentioned programs will do, but more—it helps you organize your search. For $40 for the Silver edition and $80 for the Gold, The Master Genealogist is not more expensive than the other programs. You can tie many more facts and historical context to your ancestors with TMG, as it is affectionately known, as well as output in almost any format you like.

Mind you, it has a learning curve, and the program is written with professional genealogical standards in mind. That should not deter you, however. It comes with a tutorial and has much more flexibility than its easy-to-use competitors. It is designed to let the novice get started quickly and grow into the more advanced features. Wizards, "cue cards," data-entry templates, ditto keys, macros, and other features make TMG easy to learn and use.

It is this flexibility that makes people feel The Master Genealogist is worth the effort to use. The program allows for an unlimited number of people, events per person, names per person, relationships, user-defined events, free-form text, photographs, citations, and repositories. You, not the software, control the data. There are also features to help you track what you need to find and a to-do list of genealogy chores.

Referencing source data is TMG's strongest point for the serious genealogist. Each entry provides space for documenting an unlimited number of citations, including a rating scale for their reliability, which is an important point and unique to TMG. Newspaper articles, family bibles, and interviews with your relatives all have different reliability, which can be recorded with TMG.

And So On

The short list presented thus far merely scratches the surface of available genealogy programs by presenting those that are arguably the most popular. Go to Cyndi's List (www.cyndislist.com/software.htm) and poke around a few websites. Go to local meetings of your genealogy club and ask for recommendations. Go through the checklist of programs I gave you and test-drive a few that are shareware. Then you'll be ready to choose.

Additional Programs

There are other programs that are not, strictly speaking, genealogy programs. These include databases, journaling programs, and other, more mundane software, such as word- processing programs, that can be used to make your quest for family history easier. You may want to consider any combination of these.

Database CD-ROMs

You'll find that many records have been indexed and transcribed or scanned onto CD-ROMs. Some of these you can access at a local library; some you can order with software or by themselves; some are available from the Family History Centers. Census records available on CD-ROM include the U.S. federal census, various census records from Canada and the U.K., Cherokee and African-American census records, and a few local censuses. Cemetery records and death records from all over North America and the U.K. are available on CD-ROMs; so are parish records. Check out www.cyndislist.com/cd-roms.htm#Vendors for sources of these CD-ROMs.

Clooz

Clooz is not another genealogy program, but instead a database designed in Microsoft Access for systematically organizing and storing all the documents and clues to your ancestry that you have collected over the years. It is an electronic filing cabinet that assists you with search and retrieval of important facts you have found during the ancestor hunt, showing you a complete picture of what you have and what you lack. It has 35 templates for entering genealogical data from a myriad of document types, and your data can be sorted in dozens of ways. Once you have imported the individual family members from your genealogy program, you can start to assign documents to each person. Then, a report on a person will show you all the wills, deeds, birth and death certificates, diary entries, or other documents that mention him or her.

Clooz can also help you organize your genealogy to-do list and help you track what needs to be done.

Word-Processing Programs

Don't overlook the lowly word processor as one of your genealogy tools. You can use it for journaling your genealogy quest, for creating custom write-ups of your results, and even for creating a book. You can use a word processor to create and track your to-do lists, write letters for vital records, and more.

As with your genealogy program, you need a word processor that can handle all of your chores, yet isn't more trouble to use than it's worth.

Notable: A Journaling Program

Notable, available at www.startmyjournal.com, is just one example of a journaling program in which you can record your own life history for future generations. I mention it because it has excellent starter questions, not only for you, but also for people you may interview to get genealogy information. Notable is easy to use because it prompts you with ideas and helps you create a life story. The program comes in two versions: The LDS edition contains specific topics related to the religion and asks a few more questions that add topics to the user's list that are associated with religion. The regular edition is aimed at non-Mormons, but still asks a lot of questions!

The program has no export or import function; it cannot merge, for example, GEDCOM data with one of your stories. The Notable output has to be hard copy to accompany any genealogy program output you have. It is also strictly a writing program: No graphics, sound, or animation capabilities are included. However, it is a good way to record family stories, whether your own or those of your relatives.

These are minor quibbles, however, because the program is intended to be a writing tool, and it's a very good one. The prompts are pertinent, sometimes even surprising or disconcerting, but they certainly get you thinking.

Maps

Sooner or later in tracing your genealogy, you're going to need maps, and not just your handy 2008 road atlas. The boundary lines of cities, counties, states, and even countries have changed over the years; Kentucky used to be part of Virginia after all!

A dictionary or index of place names is called a gazetteer. As I mentioned in Chapter 1, a hard copy is a handy thing to have, but you can use software and Internet versions, too. I list several good map and gazetteer sites in Chapter 23. You may also want to have on hand a program such as U.S. Cities Galore, Microsoft Streets, or Pocket Streets to find current places. Check out Cyndi's List at www.cyndislist.com/maps.htm#Software for the latest in such software.

E-mail

Reading mail is the biggest part of online life. Some of the best information, and even friendships, come through e-mail. If you have an account with an ISP, a mail reader makes your life much easier. The mail readers in browsers tend to have fewer features than the stand-alone mail clients. To get the most out of electronic mail, you need to get a few things under your belt.

Filters

A filter is an action you want the mail program to take when a message matches certain conditions. For example, you can have an e-mail program reply to, copy, move, or destroy a message based on such things as the sender, the subject line, or the words found in the text. You can have the e-mail program do all that before you read your mail or even before the e-mail gets downloaded from the ISP's mail server. If you've never dealt with e-mail, this might seem like a lot of bells and whistles, but believe me, when you start getting involved in active mail lists (see Chapter 7), you'll want to sort your mail by geography, surname, and time period, at least! Furthermore, there'll be some people who you don't want to hear from. You can have your mail filters set up to delete mail from those people.

Most e-mail programs also come with built-in detectors for the unsolicited advertising e-mail and scams that circulate regularly. If you ever get an e-mail promising you riches or touting an "unknown stock," forward it to your ISP's customer service department so they can block that sender.

RSS Readers

One way to avoid the unsolicited advertising e-mail is to subscribe to your favorite blogs, genealogy columnists, and lists via RSS, Atom, or other "push" technology. RSS stands for Really Simple Syndication. Atom is the same thing using a different set of commands. They are both ways for a site to send you information, but it is much harder for a spammer to send you things you don't want.

RSS feeds are a safe, reliable, and fun way to get the latest news, techniques, releases, and information, as well as to keep up with changes to your favorite Web sites. While you can use RSS feeds to get regular updates from CNN about news or the National Weather Service about your local tides and water temperature, using RSS feeds for genealogy is just a dream come true.

In the old days, a Web surfer would have to bookmark and remember to visit a favorite site to find updates. To get information from columnists such as DearMYRTLE and Dick Eastman, the Web surfer would subscribe to an e-mail newsletter, risking unsolicited e-mail as well. Other information came to the Web surfer via an e-mail newsletter or, back in the dark ages of the Internet, a Usenet newsfeed.

Problems arose with each of these methods: viruses, unauthorized posts, and sheer volume, to name a few. While the volume problem may still apply to RSS feeds, the benefits include better organization of your information and protection from viruses, unsolicited bulk e-mail, and other ills of e-mail and newsfeeds. In addition, RSS formats for iPods,

RSS Terms to Know

RSS is a relatively new format on the Internet, but like all things online, it has its buzzwords and trade names. Here is a short list of the ones that are essential to understand.

- **Aggregator or feed reader** A piece of software to retrieve the Web feeds you want. Some can search for a special set of feeds.

- **Atom** Another form of push technology that is similar to RSS. Some feed readers can read both.

- **Push** The term for delivering content to a user automatically after a request to do so. Mail lists were an early form of push technology, but they delivered text content only. Modern push technologies can deliver any and all forms of digital content: audio, video, graphics, text, and HTML.

- **RSS** Really Simple Syndication is a method of coding eXtensible Markup Language (XML) to send text, graphics, and/or links to a special "reader" automatically.

- **Web feed or feed** Pushing content to a user by a system such as RSS. The user can be notified of new content without having to actively check for it or disclosing any personal information, such as e-mail address.

smart phones, and PDAs mean you don't have to be in front of your desktop computer to use them!

You can get a simple program, such as RSS Reader, to gather your desired information or use a mail program that also retrieves feeds, such as Mozilla Thunderbird, as shown in Figure 2-3, making it as simple as reading e-mail to catch a feed. Basically, you just cut and paste the Uniform Resource Locator (URL) of the RSS feed into whatever program you have chosen. Like e-mail, you can get overwhelmed with the volume of entries, so be choosy!

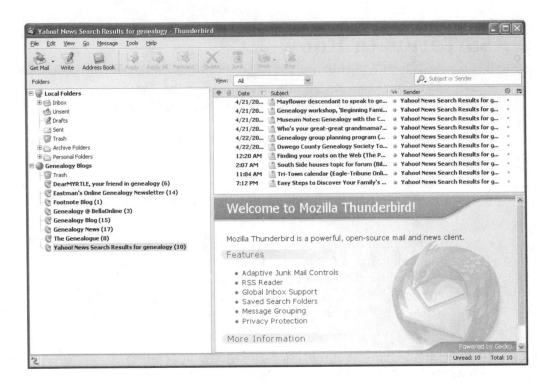

FIGURE 2-3. *Mozilla Thunderbird is an e-mail program that can also collect RSS feeds from sites.*

Audio Resources

The Internet has become a broadcast medium, and radio shows originating thousands of miles from you can stream right down to your computer over the Internet. To listen, you need a good media player, whether it is Microsoft's Windows Media Player, RealAudio, iTunes, or some other program. Most such programs have a free version and are usually easy to set up and use. Furthermore, most chat programs now allow voice and sound as well as text. AOL Instant Messenger, ICQ, and others have functions that let you speak into a microphone attached to your sound card, sending your voice to your buddy using the same program.

Viruses and Worms

No journey is without risk. Whenever you enter the jungle of cyberspace, that dreaded microorganism, the computer virus, might be lurking about. Not only that, but your activities could attract Trojan horses and worms, too, so keep a sharp eye out.

A *virus* is a program hidden on a disk or within a file that can damage your data or computer in some way. Some viruses simply display a message or a joke, while others can wipe out all the information you saved to the hard drive. Therefore, I strongly recommend that you inoculate your computer before using any mode of electronic travel.

One breed of computer virus is the *Trojan horse*. This is a program that seems to be useful and harmless when it first arrives, but secretly might be destroying data or breaking down the security on your system. The Trojan horse differs from a virus only because it doesn't propagate itself as a virus does.

A *worm* is a program that causes your computer to freeze or crash as it sucks up all of your available resources, such as system memory. A worm can make copies of itself and spread through connected systems.

Programs to detect and remove these exotic virtual creatures are available from your local computer store or various online services. Some are shareware, while others are more costly. But if the program manages to delete a virus before it harms your system, it's worth the price.

The two major virus-protection suites are Norton AntiVirus and McAfee VirusScan, which include one free year of virus updates, available to you once or twice a month. Whatever program you buy, however, be sure to keep it updated.

Even if you have virus-protection software, you need to take precautions. Make a backup of everything that is important to you—data, letters, and so on—and resave it no less than once a month. The virus-protection software may offer the ability to make a recovery disk; do so. This can save you much time and trouble later on down the line if your system needs to be restored.

Generally, when you download a file, look for an indication that it has been checked for viruses. If it's not there, reconsider downloading from that site. If someone mails or hands you a floppy disk with data, always run a virus check on the disk before you do anything else. Once a virus is copied to your hard disk, removing it can be a major headache. In addition, make sure that you run a virus check on your hard drive at least twice a month, just to be certain. This should be part of your computer's regular tune-up and maintenance.

Virus protection is good, but if you opt for a high-speed, continuous connection, such as DSL or cable Internet, you also need a firewall to help protect you from hackers, Trojan horses, and worms. A firewall is a piece of software, hardware, or combination of both that forms an electronic boundary, preventing unauthorized access to a computer or network. It can also be a computer whose sole purpose is to act as a buffer between your main computer and the Internet. A firewall controls what goes out and what comes in according to how the user has it set up.

Examples of firewall programs are ZoneAlarm by Zone Labs, BlackICE Defender from NetworkICE, and Internet Security 2000 by Symantec Corp. A detailed description of how firewalls work can be found on Shields Up, a website devoted to broadband security created by programmer Steve Gibson, head of Gibson Research Corp. (www.grc.com) of Laguna Hills, California. Run the tests. You'll be surprised.

Publishing on the Internet

As I noted in the previous chapter, you can use several free sites to publish as well as search your genealogy. I noted several sites that let you post your facts in HTML; there are other options, as well.

Turning a GEDCOM into HTML

Several methods can help you turn your information into a static Web page: Translators, HTML editors, and Web sites allow you to place your information in their predesigned pages.

Translators

Some programs are available that take a GEDCOM from any program on the market and turn it into HTML. An inexpensive program ($10), such as GedPage (www.frontiernet.net/ ~ rjacob/gedpage.htm), shown in Figure 2-4, turns GEDCOM files into attractive HTML files.

You can choose a version for Macintosh or Windows (versions 3.1 and later). The output is formatted as family group sheets. Using this program is simplicity itself. First, create a GEDCOM. Then change the files HEADER.HTM and FOOTER.HTM to say what you want—generally, this is your contact information. (You can do this in any text editor. Simply replace the text and leave anything within the < and > brackets alone.) Start GedPage, and fill in the blanks for the URL and the e-mail address; then choose colors if you like. Click Create Page. In a few seconds, a set of pages for the database is created. Then you use

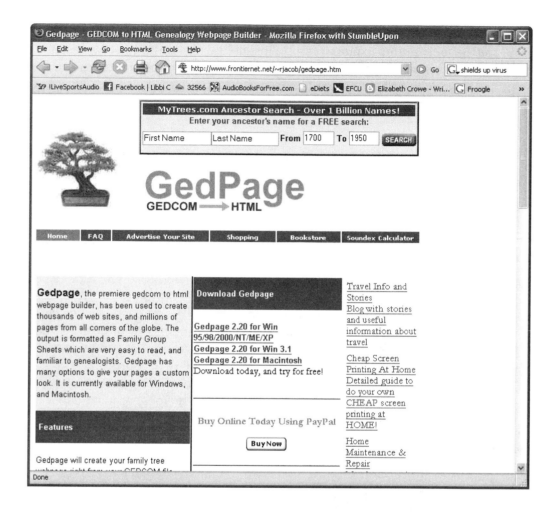

FIGURE 2-4. *GedPage creates family group sheets in HTML for posting to a website.*

an FTP program to upload the pages to your site. This program is only one example; others are out there. Check out Cyndi's List for a current list of programs (www.cyndislist.com/software.htm).

HTML Editors

For the real do-it-yourselfer, HTML editors can help you create your own site from the ground up. Most modern HTML editors work just like word processors; in fact, Word 2000 can save any document file in HTML format, complete with links and graphics. Microsoft Internet Explorer and Netscape both come with simple, useful HTML editors as part of the package. Internet Explorer can be installed with Front Page Express, and Netscape with the Composer module. Both are fairly easy to use.

Once you finish, the programs can post the results for you. On the File menu, simply choose Publish.

Web Sites

Ancestry.com, ROOTSWEB.com, Genealogy.com, FamilyTree.com—the list of sites where you can upload your genealogy for free or nearly free are numberless. You'll learn how to use these sites in later chapters.

Blogging

Another way to publish is to keep a "web log" or "blog." You don't have to learn HTML, FTP, or any other arcane computer language. You simply log on to a site such as FaceBook or Blogger.com and follow several, easy onscreen prompts within your browser to create your blog.

These sites provide for easy typing or copying and pasting your data from then on. You add bold, italics, and underline in the same way you do in e-mail or using your word-processing program. As soon as you click the Publish button, the item is added to www. < yourtitle > .blogspot.com (you can find mine at http://ecwriter.blogspot.com), Just record your family history, anecdotes, and recipes, or just keep a journal of your progress. In fact, DearMYRTLE is using hers to preserve stories she told her daughters when they were children (www.dearmyrtle.com).

Wrapping Up

To get online, you need the following:

- A computer (with lots of hard disk space!)

- An Internet service provider

- A browser

- A genealogy program

- A program that can play podcasts, sound files, etc.

- A way to post your results on the Web

Chapter 3

Genealogy Education

A lot of genealogy is learn-by-doing, but that's no reason to reinvent the wheel. Workshops, seminars, reading, and courses can help you start climbing that family tree efficiently and effectively.

"I always stress education, especially for those who are new to genealogy and think that everything is on the Internet," said Liz Kelley Kerstens, editor of *Digital Genealogist* and the National Genealogical Society's *NewsMagazine* (see Figure 3-1). "I'm always telling people about the NGS courses and conferences because it's hard to learn in a vacuum. The courses and conferences fill your head with so many ideas that you have to take something away from them."

Kerstens said that she herself, a genealogist of note, is currently pursuing a Master's degree in history, pacing her studies around pursuing her own genealogy and her work. She recommends the system of melding work, study and research.

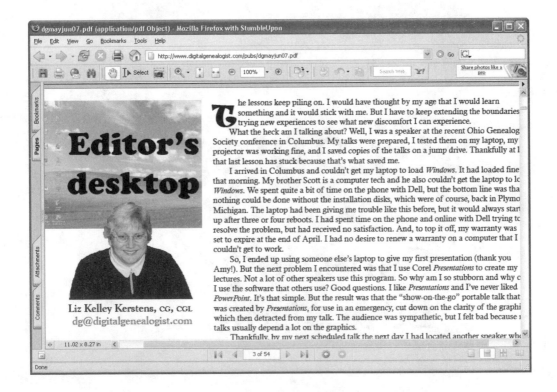

FIGURE 3-1. *Kerstens' magazine,* Digital Genealogist, *is only available online and via e-mail in PDF format.*

"Even one course can be overwhelming with my life's pace, but I finish them because I made a commitment," she said. "And when I'm taking a course, I try to give it as much attention as I can because, first, I'm paying a lot for graduate tuition, but also the whole point of taking the courses is to learn. It's so much more fun to learn when you're doing it for fun and not worrying about getting a fabulous job or the next promotion. I already have a fabulous job and can't think of anything I'd rather be doing (other than sleeping)!"

You have many choices when it comes to learning about genealogy. You can read books like this one, take college-level courses, read genealogy blogs and Really Simple Syndication (RSS) feeds, or read "how-to" articles on websites. You can learn about one aspect or study to become a Certified Genealogist. You can go to a class or have a class come to you over the Internet. If you decide to go to a class, you can still sign up for it online if you want. It's all up to you!

Books, magazines, and online articles, such as in blogs and RSS feeds, are ways to teach yourself about genealogy. The advantage of this method is that you can choose to learn at your own pace and choose the topics according to your needs at the moment.

However, if you want to learn from someone else, you can find resources for that, too. Online courses allow you to learn at your own pace, create your own experience, and keep the rest of your life going. There are courses that you simply read; in other online courses, you interact with the instructor and/or other students. This chapter will show you several online courses that are free; others may involve fees, but will also confer education credits of one sort or another.

"Offline" classes, seminars, and conferences are also worthwhile. Amateurs and professionals, beginners and experts all benefit from them. Most conferences and seminars have tracks for the beginning, intermediate, and advanced levels, and even the most experienced genealogist can learn a thing or two. Plus, there is an indescribable joy in meeting new friends who share your passion (which many family members may not yet understand!).

Most of the time, if someone else is teaching you, fees are involved—sometimes modest and sometimes more substantial—but if you share travel and lodging with a genealogy buddy, it need not be prohibitively expensive. And, often with a little research, you can find good conferences and classes right in your own backyard!

> **Note**
>
> *Institutes are week-long courses of study on a specific area, usually held at the same site every year, with class size ranging from 15 to 30 students, allowing more personalized instruction. Conference formats are usually speakers and panel discussions over a few days, where attendance for each session can be in the hundreds, and the site usually changes every year. Seminars are somewhere in between with regards to duration and group size.*

Teaching Yourself: Columns, Podcasts, and Blogs

Here are some resources to help you continually hone your genealogy skills and knowledge. In general, these are all some form of periodical, though the distribution method changes.

Roots Television

Roots Television (www.rootstelevision.com) is a site where you can learn genealogy by watching videos produced by and for avid genealogists and family history lovers of all stripes. Some of it is pay-per-view, but a lot of it is free. The difference between this and your regular television is time: You can watch the show in three- to eight-minute chunks or all at once, and you watch when you choose, not when a network has scheduled it.

This excellent site has information on archives and libraries, scrapbooking, genealogy travel, Civil War reenactments, DNA genealogy, reunions, sepia-toned photos, Internet sites, different aspects of history and old country traditions, story-telling, multicultural food, flea markets, nostalgia and mystery solving. You'll find interviews, lectures, presentations, and their delightful "Who Do You Think You Are?" series. Do not miss the clip "A Psychic Roots Tale!"

I know folks who simply listen to the clips as they weed out spam from the e-mail inbox!

DearMYRTLE

DearMYRTLE's daily genealogy blog has free news and tips, problem-solving and other discussions, and much more. It's a must-read for any beginner. You can visit her site www.DearMYRTLE.com to subscribe by RSS feed and have her writing come to you (see Figure 3-2).

On her site, you can also find older columns, especially her Beginning Genealogy Lessons. DearMYRTLE's Lessons, at www.dearmyrtle.com/lessons.htm, are 12 how-to articles on specific topics, such as keeping dates straight and using government resources.

Finally Get Organized is her series of columns on not letting the work you've done get lost in the shuffle. If you've been at genealogy for more than a year, you are probably feeling a little overwhelmed by what you've collected, what's still on your to-do list, and what to do with both. This list takes you through a checklist for each month of the year, with goals for each week and tasks to reach each goal.

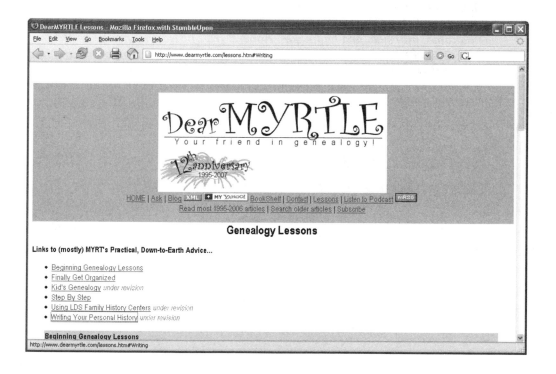

FIGURE 3-2. *DearMYRTLE is a great resource for teaching yourself some genealogy basics.*

The site also has links to other sites, such as Kid's Genealogy, a list of links to help you find lesson plans, mailing lists, and school projects to teach young people about genealogy.

Success Story: Using Message Boards Solves a Mystery

Betty Krohn took one of DearMYRTLE's classes on Internet genealogy research, where it was recommended that the students go to www.rootsweb.com and check out the message boards. Betty decided that her first task was to find information on Robert Suiters, Sr., an uncle of Betty's who had left Ohio in 1929 and lost touch with his family.

"The very first message to pop up when I entered the name of Suiters (my maiden name) was from a person who was looking for any family of Robert Suiters. Until that time I had been unable to locate any trace of Robert Suiters. We knew he existed, but didn't know if he was still alive or where in the world he would be living. So you can imagine my excitement when I read that message," Betty said. "We learned that Robert had gone to Oklahoma, married, and had a son, Robert, Jr., but that marriage ended in divorce, and Robert, Sr. left again, leaving the son and never contacting him again." Robert was alive, and he was soon on the phone with Betty's father. Through the message board, Betty was able to reunite much of the family.

Dear MYRTLE also has podcasts, which will be discussed later.

Eastman's Online Genealogy Newsletter

Eastman's Online Genealogy Newsletter (see Figure 3-3) is one of the oldest and best sources of information for the amateur and professional genealogist alike. Dick Eastman actually has five different RSS feeds available:

- **Eastman's Online Genealogy Newsletter (EOGN)** http://blog .eogn.com/eastmans_online_ genealogy/index.rdf
- **EOGN's Other News** http//othernews.eogn.com/index.rdf
- **EOGN's Genealogy Announcements** http://announcements .eogn.com/index.rdf

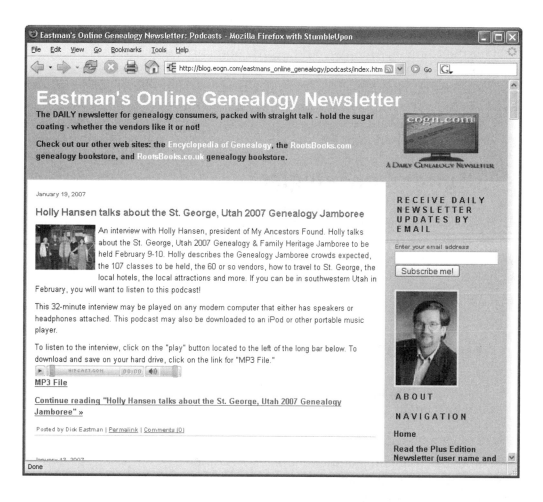

FIGURE 3-3. *Dick Eastman offers a blog, podcast, and more at his site.*

♦ **All three of them in one RSS news feed** http://www.eogn.com/all-the-news/index.rdf

♦ **RSS Feed of Podcasts** http://www.eogn.com/rss/eogn.xml

The daily blog will have interesting articles on new products, sites, and online resources, as well as discussions on techniques. Like DearMYRTLE's blog, the site allows comments by readers, which are sometimes even more interesting than the original article. The free blog will often have news updates, such as Ancestry.com's newest databases or the National Archives and Records Administration (NARA) newest workshop. The main value of the daily blog is that Dick is so good at keeping up with the latest news and releases. The "Plus Edition" has more detailed articles, most of all his thoughtful and honest reviews of sites and software. The "Plus Edition" is about $20 a year, or you can try it for three months for about $6.

Digital Genealogist

The *Digital Genealogist,* published and edited by Liz Kelley Kerstens, is a bi-monthly magazine in .pdf format. It comes right to your e-mail inbox, or you can read it online. You can subscribe for $20 a year at www.digitalgenealogist.com. The magazine focuses on the use of technology in genealogy and all its various applications. A sample issue of the magazine is available on the website, as well as the table of contents of the current issue and two articles at any given time.

Genealogy Gems

"Genealogy Gems: News from the Fort Wayne Library" is a monthly electronic newsletter published by the Genealogy Center of the Allen County Public Library. This public library is recognized as having one of the best genealogy departments in the United States outside of Salt Lake City. Their collection includes more than 332,000 printed volumes and 362,000 items of microfilm and microfiche.

Each issue gives updates on special events in the department; provides descriptions of department collections, resources, and services; and highlights lodging facilities, travel directions, and lecture opportunities. There are two ways to subscribe if you are interested in receiving the issues as they are published. Send an e-mail message to GenealogyGems_subscribe@FriendsOfAllenCounty.org or go to www.FriendsOfAllenCounty.org and fill out the subscription form toward the bottom of that webpage.

Other Blogs and Feeds

It is entirely possible to spend your entire day reading interesting, informative, and entertaining genealogy blogs. But if you did that, when would you do your genealogy? So, out of the hundreds of blogs and feeds out there, I'll point out the ones you should start with, and let you explore further to discover others that fit your schedule and needs:

- **Del.icio.us Genealogy Sites**   has an RSS feed of new and changed pages with "genealogy" in their tags that have been submitted by readers. Put http://del.icio.us/rss/tag/genealogy in your RSS reader.

- **DistantCousin.com**   recently added a newsfeed of new documents on this online archive of genealogy records and scanned images of historical documents from a wide variety of sources, such as newspaper obituaries, city directories, census records, ship lists, school yearbooks, military records, and more. In all there are more than 6 million genealogy records from more than 1,500 sources online. There are no fees or memberships required to use the records at DistantCousin. Add http://distantcousin.com/RSS/rss.xml to your reader.

- **Eats Like A Human (http://eatslikeahuman.blogspot.com)**   This is the blog of a programmer who has worked with the Mormon Church and pursues genealogy with a software engineer's perspective. "Taking Genealogy to the Common Person" is the subtitle of his blog. His introduction says: "A clear majority of people on this earth want to know more about their ancestors. In spite of their innate interest, they are often overwhelmed at the complexity of the process and underwhelmed by the experience. This blog is a forum for promoting innovation that will help to take family history to the common person." His recent challenge to the genealogy industry to make source citation easy and natural is great.

- **Everton Publishers Genealogy Blog**   is at http://genealogyblog .com.

- **FamilySearch Labs**   at http://familysearchlabs.blogspot.com/ index.html chronicles the newest software for FamilySearch.org (see Chapter 14). Great for the geeky genealogist!

- **MSNBC.com Genetic Genealogy**   is a regular feature of the news site about how science is filling out family trees. Go to http://www .msnbc.msn.com/id/3038411.

- **Random Genealogy (http://www.randomgenealogy.com)**   picks up news stories involving genealogy that other blogs haven't seemed to mention.

♦ **Renee's Genealogy Blog (http://rzamor1.blogspot.com)** started in September 2005 and uses AtomFeed to syndicate it to readers. She started doing genealogy at 15, and is now the secretary for the Utah Valley PAF Users Group and a Family History Consultant at the Alpine Family History Center. Renee is an old hand at genealogy and generously shares her insights and news. Her blogs are thoughtful and eclectic. A good read!

♦ **BlogFinder** at http://blogfinder.genealogue.com is a good way to keep on top of the newest blogs, but again, be careful not to let blogs substitute for genealogy!

Podcasts and Streaming Audio

Podcasts are like radio shows that you can play whenever you want. You can listen to them live as they happen with any program that plays sound files: Microsoft Media Player, QuickTime, RealPlayer, iTunes, etc. With the same program, you can download the file and listen to it at your convenience, either while sitting at your computer or on your MP3 or WMA player (e.g., iPod).

Here is a quick list of some of the best genealogy podcasts out there. Most of these programs can be sent to your computer via RSS or similar "push" feed, or you can get them from the sites listed, either live or archive versions:

♦ **Eastman's Online Genealogy** Dick Eastman offers interviews with many of the world's leading genealogy experts on an occasional basis. Download them at http://blog.eogn.com/eastmans_online_genealogy/podcasts/index.html.

♦ **Family Roots Radio** This podcast broadcasts live at 1:00 p.m. Pacific Time on Thursdays (see Figure 3-4). Kory L. Meyerink answers general questions from listeners, spotlights important family history news, and provides research tips from professionals. The show often has guests. You can find it at http://www.familyrootsradio.com; you can download podcasts of past shows as well.

♦ **Genealogy Gems** Lisa Cooke provides inspiration and techniques to help family researchers get the most out of their research time. You can download the podcast at http://genealogygemspodcast.libsyn.com; the shows are posted about six times a month.

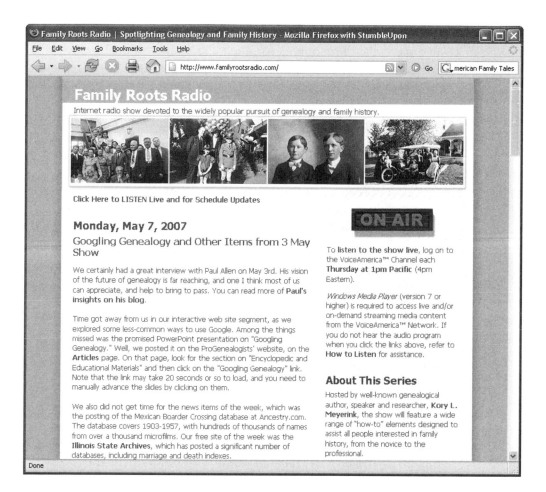

FIGURE 3-4. *Family Roots Radio is live on Thursdays, but you can download the sound files to listen to whenever you like.*

♦ **Genealogy ON DEMAND** Shamele Jordon offers quick weekly tips to motivate you and your ancestral search. Johnson is a researcher, lecturer, and writer; she is a researcher for the PBS series *African American Lives*; a family reunion expert on *Ebony* magazine's Black Family Reunion Tour; an advisory board member of the Family Reunion Institute of Temple University; the former president of the African American Genealogy Group in Philadelphia, PA; and a lecturer at the Institute of Genealogy and Historical Research at Samford University in Birmingham,

Alabama. Her site, http://genealogyondemand.wordpress.com, also has a list of resources for each show, and all past shows are available.

♦ **Irish Roots Cafe**   Michael C. O'Laughlin hosts a Monday podcast on Irish genealogy and family heritage on Mondays at http://www.irishroots.com/podcast/rss.xml.

♦ **Relatively Speaking**   This is a live radio show from KSL News Radio that airs on Sundays at 4:00 pm Central Time. Jackie McKay and Mary Slawson share tips on how to find members of your family and interview genealogists, historians, and other experts. The podcast file is at http://www.ksl.com/?sid = 640045.

♦ **The Genealogy Guys Podcast**   George G. Morgan and Drew Smith discuss genealogy each week and answer e-mail questions from readers. You can subscribe to and download the podcasts at http://www.genealogyguys.com. The show is posted at their website most Sundays, occasionally on Monday.

♦ **The Teapot Genies**   These are three women with a passion for genealogy with a United Kingdom emphasis. The site (http://www.bananatv.com/default.asp?program = genealogy) is where they post videos as they do their detective work. Kaye Vernon, Billie Jacobsen, and Wendy Dzubiel are the hosts.

♦ **The Seeker Magazine Radio Hour**   This airs at 11:00 a.m. Eastern Time on Saturdays as streaming media over the Internet. Linda Hammer, a former private investigator and process server, talks about finding missing friends and relatives live on the air from WTMY in Sarasota, Florida. Tune in over the Internet at http://www.the-seeker.com/radio.htm.

Note

Streaming media differs from podcasts in that it is more like radio and television: You have to either catch it as it happens or set up a system to record it for later playback.

♦ **Under the Tree**   Located at http://underthetree.libsyn.com, this is a weekly podcast by Meredith C. Williams. She features genealogy research from an African-American perspective.

> **Note**
>
> *For several years, DearMYRTLE (http://podcasts.DearMYRTLE.com) hosted a weekly Tuesday Internet radio show (and later podcasts) on genealogy, with tips, interviews, and her special "mighty mouse" tours of interesting websites. In late 2006, family obligations forced her to suspend the regular shows, but you can still download shows from 2005-2006.*

Online Courses

In some cases, you can have the education come to you—that is, learn by independent study. Genealogy societies and even universities have such courses, and in some cases, you can take the class over the Internet.

> **Note**
>
> *A good listing of both resources and education in genealogy, and a site that was quite up to date as of this writing, is at www .academic-genealogy.com; look for the topics and regions you need.*

Family History Live Online

Tex and Lynne Crawford offer lectures, classes, and even seminars, live over the Internet, with software called ReGL. The classes, with topics such as Hispanic Research and Indexing, are presented by experts and certified genealogists. Some are fee-based, but many are free.

With the software, the lecturer's voice is transmitted live over the Internet, as are charts, pictures, and whiteboard displays. You type in your questions and follow along. It's as exciting as being at an "onsite" class, with the added advantage that you are at your own computer and can try out the techniques, websites, etc. right away.

One of the most enjoyable things about the site is the occasional "fair." This is a free, day-long series of interactive lectures on varied topics, usually on a Saturday. DearMYRTLE explained blogging, and Justin Schroepfer explained FOOTNOTE in just two of the eight sessions of a recent fair (see Figure 3-5). The fairs are free. Check out www.familyhistoryliveonline.com for the current schedule.

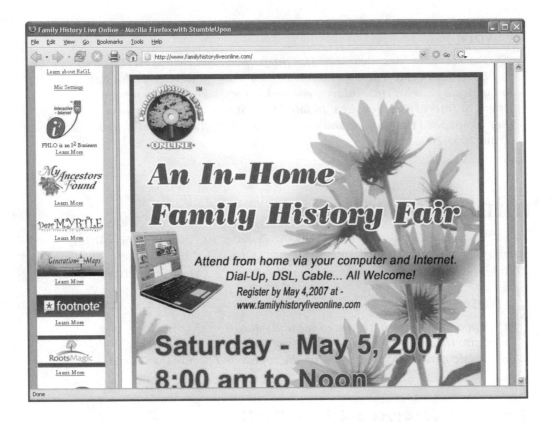

FIGURE 3-5. *Family History Live Online offers free and fee-based courses on many genealogy topics.*

Genealogy.com

Genealogy.com has several free, self-paced courses to help you get started in genealogy. Click Learning Center on the home page navigation bar to find them. The Learning Center has the following articles:

- ♦ Begin Your Research at Home
- ♦ What's in a Name?
- ♦ Collaborating with Others
- ♦ Finding Existing Research
- ♦ Outfitting Your Genealogy Toolkit

Brigham Young University

Brigham Young University (http://ce.byu.edu/is/site/courses/freecourses
.cfm) has a series of free, self-paced online tutorials on family history
research (see Figure 3-6). Among the courses are Finding Your
Ancestors, Introduction to Family History Research, Helping Children
Love Your Family History, Family Records, Vital Records, Military
Records, as well as courses on researching in France, Scandinavia, and
Germany.

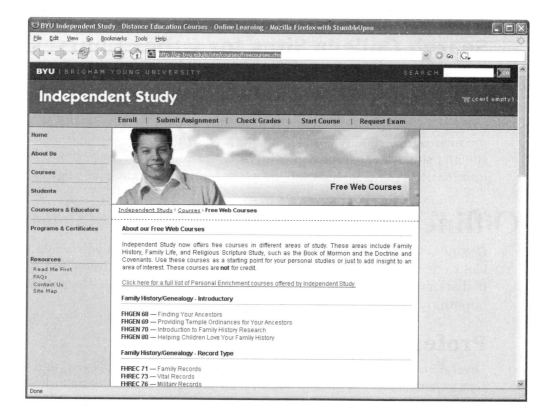

FIGURE 3-6.   *BYU, an accredited school, offers college-level genealogy courses through
its independent study program over the Web.*

National Institute for Genealogical Studies/University of Toronto

At www.genealogicalstudies.com you can find The National Institute for Genealogical Studies, which has joined forces with the Professional Learning Centre, Faculty of Information Studies, University of Toronto, to provide Web-based courses for both family historians and professional genealogists. Countries included are the United States, Canada, England, Germany, Ireland, and Scotland. There are also certificates in librarianship and general methodology.

Search College Sites for Other Courses

Search any major search engine for "genealogy courses independent study" or "genealogy courses distance learning," and you will come up with many smaller colleges and institutions that offer at least a course or two, and sometimes continuing education units. Also, go the site of the nearest community college, junior college, or other higher-learning site and simply search for "genealogy." Often library science and information science majors will include a course or two in genealogy.

Offline

Getting your genealogy education online is fun, but perhaps you would like some face to face (or F2F) time with others who are learning, too. In that case, you might investigate the following ideas for some educational opportunities in the real world.

Professional Organizations

Several institutions accredit the services of professional genealogists and researchers around the world. One of their primary goals is to establish a set of standards and a code of ethics for the members. Often, the accrediting body will offer courses, instruction, and testing. You don't have to be accredited to do family history research for hire, but it does offer clients assurance of a level of standards and professionalism that is accepted within the profession.

Genealogy Pro (http://genealogypro.com/articles/organizations .html#GRINZ) has a list of several such organizations in English-speaking countries.

Wholly Genes Genealogy Conference and Cruise

The publishers of Wholly Genes software came up with the idea of a late-year, educational cruise of the Eastern Caribbean with a series of speakers and workshops on genealogical research methods, tools, and technologies from some of the most popular speakers and authorities in those fields. The third annual cruise was scheduled for October 2007 as of this writing, with speakers on topics from "Barking Up the Wrong Tree" and "Heraldic Detective Work" to "Reverse Genealogy."

Check out www.whollygenes.com for the next cruise.

NGS

At www.ngsgenealogy.org, you can find many resources for online and offline learning (see Figure 3-7). Figure 3-7 shows the education page at the NGS site, which lists courses for genealogy studies. This page is at http://www.ngsgenealogy.org/edu.cfm.

American Genealogy   For many years, NGS has offered a home-study correspondence course entitled "American Genealogy: A Basic Course." The NGS recommends that you take the online introductory course first and then move on to the home-study course, which covers some of the same topics in more depth and includes many more besides. Those who successfully complete the online introductory course will receive a discount coupon that can be applied toward the home-study course. Check the NGS website for the current fees.

The package includes lessons, resource materials, government publications useful to genealogists, help request forms, and the envelopes and postage needed to mail in your lessons.

The 16 lessons are "hands on" and require trips to libraries, courthouses, and other sites, as well as the ability to write well about your research. The NGS website, however, has online resources to help you with this. Most people take 18 months to complete the course, although extensions are granted.

Youth Resources   Teachers can find lesson plans; suggested books; articles on genealogy as a tool in teaching social studies, writing, literature, and research skills; a list of websites; and other materials for teaching

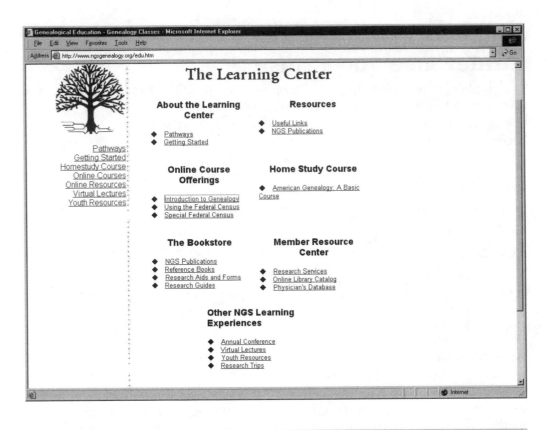

FIGURE 3-7. *The NGS has a good selection of courses for beginning, intermediate, and advanced genealogists.*

young people about genealogy on the NGS page at http://www
.ngsgenealogy.org/youth.cfm. You can also find information on the
Rubicam Youth Award, a $500 prize for eighth through twelfth graders for
original genealogy work.

Introduction to Genealogy "Introduction to Genealogy" is a
six-lesson, online course for those who have done little, if any, research
on their families, open to anyone who wishes to enroll. Members of the
National Genealogical Society (NGS) receive a tuition discount. The six
lessons cover genealogy basics, and though online resources may be used
as examples, online research is not emphasized. The lessons cover basics

such as recording your findings, getting information from published sources and your own family, and getting vital statistics on 20th-century people.

Federal Population Census Schedules   "Using Census Records in Genealogical Research" is an online course designed for genealogists who want to learn more about the information that can be found in the federal population census records (from 1790–1930) and how that information can be used in their genealogical research. It is open to anyone.

The course teaches you to identify the types of information found in the federal population schedules; to interpret and evaluate that information; to use the online census microfilm catalogs; to use the Soundex indexing system; to use online census images, transcriptions, and indexes; and to use proper citations for census records.

Special Federal Census Schedules   Beyond the standard names, ages, and other information, each census has collected special data, and the nature of that data has changed over the years. "Special Federal Census Schedules" is a three-lesson course that covers the census schedules for special populations, the mortality schedules, and other special schedules. On completion of this course, you will be able to identify the types of information provided in these schedules, interpret and use that information, identify the availability of the schedules, use National Archives online microfilm catalogs, and write citations for the special schedules.

BYU

Brigham Young University (BYU) offers a college-level, 18-credit-hour certificate program in genealogy, which can be taken as an independent study off-campus (what used to be called a "correspondence course"), except for a proctored exam. It is not a degree program, but it gives a solid background in fundamental family history research principles, coupled with specialized genealogical training in a particular geographical area.

The required courses are "The Family and the Law in American History," "English Language Paleography," and "Special Topics in Family History Research." In addition, the student chooses two source courses and one elective course from the North American option or the British option.

Details can be found at http://ce.byu.edu/is/site/.

University of Washington Genealogy and Family History Certificate

A nine-month evening certificate program for teachers, librarians, amateur researchers, and others interested in researching their families, this on-campus program is described at http://www.outreach .washington.edu/ext/certificates/gfh/gfh_gen.asp. Participants develop a completed family history project as part of classes that meet one evening per week on the UW campus in Seattle.

Through lectures, discussions, readings, and field trips, students learn how to use the resources and methods necessary to develop a family history and to examine such topics as the migration of ethnic groups, population shifts, and the differences in urban and rural lifestyles. Students have access to the resources of the University of Washington libraries while enrolled.

Participants get nine Continuing Education Units (CEUs) and a certificate when they complete the program. Check the website for fees.

Genealogy Events

Finally, you can learn about genealogy at events such as seminars, workshops, and even ocean cruises! You can search for them on the following websites:

- About.com Genealogy Conferences (http://genealogy.about .com/cs/conferences)

- Cyndi's List (http://www.cyndislist.com/events.htm)

- Genealogy Forum (http://www.genealogyforum.com/gfaol/ events/Conference.htm)

- Geniespeak (http://www.geniespeak.com/event.html)

- Genealogy Events Web Ring (http://k.webring.com/ hub?ring = gencon)

FGS Conferences

The Federation of Genealogical Societies (www.fgs.org) holds a national conference each year for genealogists of all levels of experience. The conferences spotlight management workshops for genealogy organizations, genealogical lectures by nationally recognized speakers and regional experts, and exhibitors with genealogical materials and supplies. Check the website for fees, which historically have been under $200.

National Institute on Genealogical Research

Information on this oldest of genealogy institutes can be found at www.rootsweb.com/ ~ natgenin. The National Institute on Genealogical Research started in 1950 and is sponsored by the American University, the American Society of Genealogists, the National Archives, and the Maryland Hall of Records. The National Archives provides strong support, including meeting space. The cost for this week-long event is usually around $350.

The institute's program takes an in-depth look at federal records of genealogical value located primarily in the Washington, D.C. area. The program is for experienced researchers (genealogists, historians, librarians, and archivists) and is not an introductory course in genealogy. For example, sessions for 2003 included "Advanced Census Research Methodology," "Federal Land Records," and "Cartographic Records."

Institute on Genealogy and Historical Research

Held at Samford University (Birmingham, Alabama) every June, this five-day event is for intermediate to advanced genealogists. Small classes are held during the day. Each evening of the institute features a dinner with a speaker as well. Details and registration information can be found at www.samford.edu/schools/ighr/ighr.html. Check the website (see Figure 3-8) for fees, which historically have been under $400.

The Salt Lake Institute of Genealogy

Held at the Family History Library in Salt Lake City, Utah, by the Utah Genealogical Society, this is a week-long, hands-on event, usually held early in the year. Check the Utah Genealogical Association website at http://www.infouga.org/site/ for fees, which historically have been

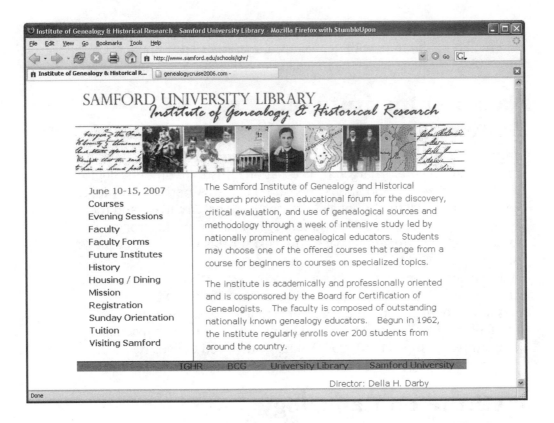

FIGURE 3-8. *IGHR in Birmingham, Alabama, is an intensive five-day event.*

under $400. In 2003, attendees could choose from ten different courses of lectures, including topics on American, Canadian, and German research.

Regional and Local Workshops and Seminars

Many state historical societies hold seminars. An example is the Wisconsin State Genealogical Society, which has two events each year—one in conjunction with the annual meeting in the spring and one in conjunction with the fall meeting. Events are open to the public for a nominal registration fee. Each one features a nationally known expert, speaking on a facet of genealogical research of particular interest to

Wisconsin researchers. The Spring Gene-A-Ramas are held at various locations around the state, whereas the fall seminars generally alternate between the Madison and Milwaukee areas. Details and registration forms can be found at http://wsgs.org/index.php.

Success Story: Learning to Plat at a Conference

Ann Lusk, attending a beginning genealogy course in her hometown of Huntsville, Alabama, learned about platting deeds. To plat a deed, you draw a picture of a piece of land from the description on the deed. Taking what she learned from the class, Ann worked with two Tennessee deeds, described in meets and bounds, a method that notes adjoining land. By platting two deeds for land owned by men with her husband's surname, cutting them out, and laying them on the table together, she saw the two pieces fit together "like hand and glove." This helped her show that the two men were father and son, and from that she could look for the original family plat. This information not only helped her Daughters of the American Revolution (DAR) application, it also qualified her for the First Families of Tennessee (www.east-tennessee-history.org/index.cfm/m/18).

Finding a local class, seminar, workshop, or other event near you is the best way to start. Query a search engine for "genealogy" and the name of the town you live in or will be visiting. Also, check Cyndi's List page (www.cyndislist.com/events.htm), Dick Eastman's weekly newsletter, and DearMYRTLE's sites often for announcements.

Wrapping Up

To summarize, you can learn about genealogy at all levels online and offline, and both are enjoyable.

- Taking beginners' courses can save you some time and effort in your research.

- Seminars, conferences, and courses are a good way to meet other genealogists and expand your skills.

- Local, regional, and national programs give you a wide choice of how to learn about genealogy.

Chapter 4

Online Communities

 My mother once said the online friends she made in researching her genealogy were among the nicest people she knew. She found her whole Crippen line on a Prodigy group; she helped many folks she never met with the data she had gathered on Spencers and Powells.

To some people, the online community is more "real" to them than their physical community. From Facebook to YouTube, from Blogspot to Yahoo!, people are exchanging their knee-jerk reactions and deepest thoughts.

In the earliest days of the Internet, people felt anonymous when they posted messages, data, and pictures on the World Wide Web. So few people were using it, and mainstream media paid it little mind. A common adage went, "On the Internet, no one knows you're a dog."

Times have changed. Here we are well into the first decade of the online century, and the Internet has *become* the mainstream. Further, we all realize that what goes online stays online. Perhaps, forever. ROOTSWEB (see Chapter 17) has mail list messages dating back to 1987; employers routinely "Google" applicants; people have been fired for what they write in their blogs. And as Gen. Oliver North learned, "erasing" an e-mail does not mean it is really gone.

Manners Matter

by Kevin Kelly

Sit up straight, folks—Miss Manners is here. She has mastered her voice mail, got control of her cell phone, and now she's logged on to the Net.

In real life, Miss Manners' true name is Judith Martin. For years, she's written about excruciatingly correct behavior for all those moments when the modem is not on; now she has a few interesting things to say about the wired life. For example, people who don't give a hoot about sending thank-you notes are suddenly bent out of shape when they get an e-mail message typed in ALL CAPS. *Wired* spoke to Miss Manners and asked her, very politely, how etiquette is bringing civility to the online frontier.

Wired: What is it about cyberspace that has rekindled interest in etiquette?

Miss Manners: Freedom without rules doesn't work. And communities do not work unless they are regulated by etiquette. It took about three minutes before some of the brighter people discovered this online. We have just as many ways, if not more, to be obnoxious in cyberspace and fewer ways to regulate them. So posting etiquette rules and looking for ways to ban people who violate them is the way sensible people are attempting to deal with this.

Wired: Do you find online etiquette rules parallel the rules of etiquette offline?

Miss Manners: Yes. Spamming is the equivalent of boring people or mixing in business. Flaming is the equivalent of being insulting. You may not realize how annoying it is when you ask an obvious question to a group that has been meeting for a while. So etiquette refers you to an FAQ file. I'm delighted people are doing a good job on the Net.

Wired: To sort out the correct behavior when corresponding through technology, you suggest the body is more important than any disembodied communication. Somebody sitting in front of you should take precedence over just a voice—like a phone conversation. And a voice takes precedence over a further disembodied e-mail. The more disembodied the communication is, the less precedence it has. Is that fair?

Miss Manners: Yes. And it is disobeyed flagrantly. The interesting thing is why people think that someone who is not present (a phone ringing) is more important than someone who is. Generally, it has taken a person a lot more effort to come to see you than to call you on the telephone.

Wired: Let's see. I need some advice. E-mail has an alarming proclivity to be copied. What are the rules for passing on private e-mail?

(Continued)

Miss Manners: For e-mail, the old postcard rule applies. Nobody else is supposed to read your postcards, but you'd be a fool if you wrote anything private on one.

Wired: Most people are not writing their e-mail that way.

Miss Manners: That's their mistake. We're now seeing e-mail that people thought they had deleted showing up as evidence in court. You can't erase e-mail. As that becomes more commonly realized, people will be a little wiser about what they type.

Wired: You're very much of a stickler for keeping one's business life from intruding upon one's social life. That distinction online is coming more blurred all the time. There seems to be a deliberate attempt to mix these two up—working at home, for example. Is this the end of civilization as we know it?

Miss Manners: Blurring the two is not conducive to a pleasant life, because it means that the joys of being loved for yourself and not for how high-ranking you are or what you can do for other people quickly disappear. People who are downsized, for instance, find they've been dropped by everyone they know because they don't have real friends. They only had business acquaintances. One of the big no-nos in cyberspace is that you do not go into a social activity, a chat group, or something like that and start advertising or selling things. This etiquette rule is an attempt to separate one's social life, which should be pure enjoyment and relaxation, from the pressures of work.

Reprinted with permission from *Wired* magazine, November 1997 issue

Even if you have been online for years, I strongly recommend that you read *Netiquette* by Virginia Shea, an online book of proper online behavior. You can find it at www.albion.com/netiquette (see Figure 4-1). In my opinion, it should be required reading similar to the driver's education handbook you had to read to get your license.

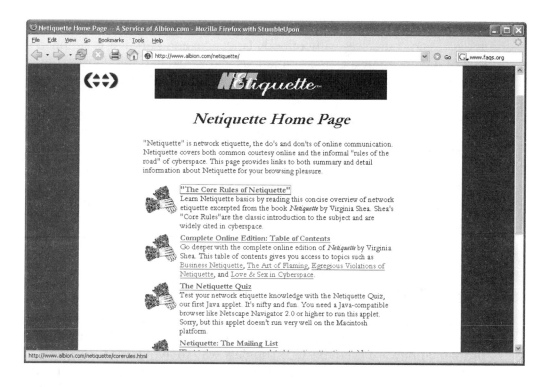

FIGURE 4-1. Netiqutte, *an online book, details proper online behavior.*

Civil Discourse

Always remember that you cannot hide behind your modem. If you would not say something at a party or in church, you probably should not say it online. Besides, you catch so many more flies with honey!

Flames

A flame is an argument on a message system in which people type insults and angry messages back and forth. No matter how you converse online—e-mail, chat, or instant messages—things can sometimes get tense. Shea's book *Netiquette* posits that flames are sometime necessary to prevent rudeness from running amok. That may be, but I still do my best to avoid flaming.

Flame wars happen. Part of it is human nature, part of it is the difficulty in expressing ourselves without body language, and part of it is simply a lack of patience. Always be as patient as you would like someone to be with you. Help the newcomer, and try not to click Send until you have read your text—twice.

Often, these arguments are the result of a misunderstanding, where one person misinterprets another, who, in turn, takes offense. Flames accomplish nothing. They never change any minds, and they hurt feelings.

If someone flames you, the best course of action is to: a) inform the moderator of the group, list, or chat room that you've been flamed and b) don't respond to the flamer. Indeed, you might even want to set up your e-mail program, chat program, or newsreader program to filter out all messages from the flamer. If it happens on a message board, simply stop opening messages from that sender.

The Rules

No, we're not talking about dating, but rather about conversations online. Sometimes you get flamed because you broke a rule—a rule you were probably unaware even existed. The best way to avoid this is to keep yourself informed of the standards and traditions of the group. You can do this in two ways: One way is to lurk until you get the lay of the land, so to speak. To lurk is to read the messages without responding to or posting any messages yourself. This isn't considered rude. With the exception of chat, most message systems won't alert others to your presence until you post something. Lurking before you leap is completely acceptable in online genealogy.

Another way to familiarize yourself with online rules is to read the rulebook. Name a topic, and someone who has dealt with it for years has written a file of frequently asked questions (FAQs) on it, which has become a de facto rulebook. You can find many of them at www.faqs .org. The home page of this site has a Search box. Type **Genealogy** in the Search box, click Search, and you get a list of FAQ files for various groups, as shown in Figure 4-2. You might also want to search the FAQ archive for adoption, family history, and ancestry FAQs for related groups.

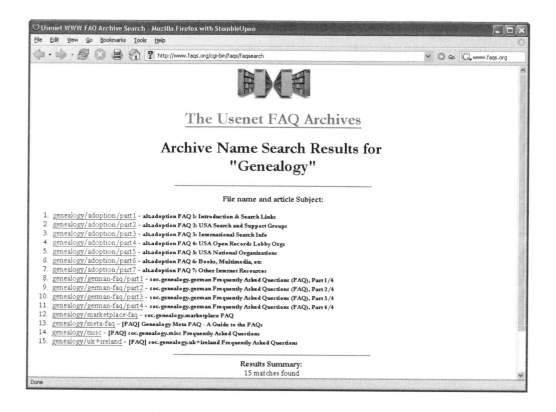

FIGURE 4-2. *The FAQ archives have answers to many beginners' questions.*

Mail lists often store their FAQ files on a website and also send it to you as your first message after you subscribe to the list. Save the message as a text or document file for future reference.

Getting Along

Try to stick to the topic being discussed in a chat room, newsgroup, mail list, or message list. Again, the FAQ should list the acceptable topics. Ads are usually verboten. A product announcement is typically okay, but an outright sales pitch isn't. Straying off the topic commonly leads to flames. Generally, whether you are posting a comment to a blog or answering a query on a message board, you need to stick to the topic at hand.

Remember: What you send is posted exactly as you send it, unless the site, group, or mail list (such as soc.genealogy.surnames) has a moderator who edits all incoming messages. On chat, when you press ENTER, it is sent off—mistakes and all.

Participants in genealogy groups want the topics of discussion to relate directly to genealogy or family history. In some groups, however, the tacit agreement is that anything a subscriber thinks is appropriate is appropriate, as long as it relates to genealogy. To discern these tacit rules at a particular site, lurk for a while to discover if it tends to be more lax about off-topic posting.

> ## Note
>
> *Lurk: To read messages in a discussion without posting any yourself.*

Assume an attitude of courtesy among subscribers and readers. Remember, your postings and comments might be seen by as many as 20,000 readers on different networks throughout the world.

Read carefully what you receive to make certain that you understand the message before replying. Read what you've written carefully to ensure that your message won't be misunderstood. As a matter of fact, routinely let a reply sit overnight and then read it again before sending. This can prevent that sinking feeling of regret when you realize that what you posted wasn't what you meant to say.

Avoid sarcasm. If humor seems appropriate, clearly label it as such. A smiley face should indicate humor. It is easy to misunderstand what's being said when no tone of voice, facial expression, or body language can guide you. A corollary: Give others the benefit of the doubt. Perhaps what you understood to be rude was meant to be funny. Communicating online is a fine art!

Know your audience and double-check addresses. Make sure the person or list of people you're sending your message to is the appropriate one.

Be tolerant of newcomers, as you expect others to be tolerant of you. No one was born knowing all about the Internet or Usenet. Don't abuse new users of computer networks for their lack of knowledge. As you become more expert, be patient as others first learn to paddle, swim, and then surf the Net, just like you. Be an active participant in teaching newcomers.

Avoid cluttering your messages with excessive emphasis (**, !!, > > > >, and so on). This can make the message hard to follow.

Also, know how your mail program answers messages. Many mail programs default to copying the entire message over again into the reply. When you respond to a message, either include the relevant part of the original message or explicitly refer to the original's contents, but delete the unimportant parts of the original message. People commonly read your reply to the message before they read the original.

In responses, don't quote more than necessary to make your point clear, and please never quote the entire message. Learn what happens on your particular system when you reply to messages. Is the message sent to the originator of the message or to the list, and when is it sent? When you're responding to another message, your subject line should be the same, with RE: at the beginning.

Always include a precise subject line, with a surname, in your message. This should be something that attracts attention, and the only way to do this is to make sure that the subject line describes the main point of your message. Don't put "Looking for..." as the subject line with no surname. People will scroll right past your message and never read it.

If you're seeking information about a family, include the surname in uppercase letters in the message's subject line. Many readers don't have time to read the contents of all messages.

Here's an example of a bad subject line:

```
Wondering if anyone is looking for JONES
```

And here are some examples of good subject lines:

```
Researching surname ENGLE 1700s
SPENCER: England>MA>NY>OH>IN>MS
Delaware BLIZZARDs pre-1845
Civil War Records
```

In the good examples, note these conventions: Surnames are in all caps, but nothing else is. A greater-than sign (>) is used as an arrow to denote migration from one place to another. A date is always helpful. If your message is a question, indicate this in the subject line. Although passages in all uppercase are considered shouting, the exception to this rule in genealogy is that surnames should be in uppercase, just as in any query. Limit a message to one subject. This allows readers to quickly decide whether they need to read the message in full. Second subjects within a single message are often missed.

Questions are often the exception to this rule. You might need to post a message that's full of questions on a subject. When you ask a question within such a message, end it with a question mark (?) and press ENTER. This should be the end of that line. This makes it much easier for people to reply, because most newsreaders quote the original message line by line. Be specific, especially when you ask questions. If you ask about a person, identify when and where the person might have lived. In questions concerning specific genealogical software, make clear what sort of computer (PC/MS-DOS, PC/Windows, Apple Macintosh, and so forth) is involved. The folks reading message boards are helpful but busy, and are more likely to answer if they don't have to ask what you mean.

A good idea is to put your name in the text of your message, along with your best e-mail address for a reply. You might want to disguise your e-mail address, though, to prevent its being harvested for unsolicited bulk e-mail (see Chapter 2). A good convention is:

```
Please reply to libbic "at" prodigy.net.
```

The end of the message is a good place for your name and e-mail address.

Sometimes, the message systems get absolutely clogged with messages, for example, if rotten weather, an earthquake, and a national holiday all converged on a certain Monday, and many people were at home online because they were unable or not required to go to work. In this case, you must choose what to read based on the subject line or sender because it is impossible to read everything posted to the group that day. This is when an RSS reader and e-mail program that lets you filter the messages for the subject headings is invaluable.

Chat Etiquette

Chat and instant message programs are discussed in detail in Chapter 7. Chat boards might not have formal FAQ files, but the following are some general rules for chat.

Generally, you will find helpful, polite people in genealogy discussions. Often, especially if you have one of the instant message programs such as AOL Instant Messenger, you'll be chatting with people you've at least contacted before. And, of course, if you're taking an online course, specific rules are going to be in force as to who can "talk" and when. Nevertheless, in all these scenarios, you must meet certain etiquette standards in chat.

All of the etiquette rules covered earlier in this chapter apply to chat. Using all capital letters, except to mention the surnames you're researching, is considered shouting. Flames are useless and annoying; you should show respect for everyone. And make certain that you aren't taking offense when none was intended.

Note

A handle, screen name, or display name is simply the identification for you that appears to other users. It is often best to use something other than your real, full name.

Stay on topic or, if you get sidetracked, create a separate room to follow your tangent.

Lurk before you leap into sending messages: Check out the room and see if the topic is what you're looking for.

You can send your e-mail address by private message, but don't post it in the message system, because if you do, the spammers will flood your mailbox. If someone refuses to give you an address, don't be insulted—it is probably just a security measure.

Smileys will be common, as will all sorts of acronyms. Refer to the Glossary for a list of smileys and acronyms used in online chat.

Many Internet Relay Chat (IRC) servers and most of the instant message programs enable you to send sound files, pictures, and even programs. Be wary of this feature for two reasons: First, it represents a security risk to receive files from someone you don't know well; second, this adds to the traffic on the server and slows down everyone's interaction, not only that of the sender and the receiver.

Chat and instant message programs have some limit to the number of characters that can be sent in one chunk. If your thoughts run longer, type the message in parts, each ending in an ellipsis (...) until you finish. Don't be surprised to find that, as you do this, other messages are popping up between your lines. Those paying attention can follow your train of thought better if you take advantage of a feature many programs have: the capability to send your text in a specific color and/or typeface.

Don't Pass It On!

For some reason, people delight in spreading myths, legends, and hoaxes through every online medium in existence. Your mailbox will often be clogged with these, from text to video to carefully edited pictures. The proper online etiquette here: First, do not respond to scams and hoaxes. This only encourages the scoundrels. Second, when you receive e-mail chain letters, virus warnings, and "true stories," don't send them on. That just clogs the bandwidth.

Always check out such "forwards" at The Urban Legends page, www.snopes.com (see Figure 4-3), which keeps daily tabs on the various urban legends going around.

Most importantly, please just delete them! You'll be doing a lot to make the online world a better place!

FIGURE 4-3. *Never pass on a warning, chain letter, or story. Always check them out on Snopes.com.*

Wrapping Up

Let's sum up the rules of online life this way:

- ◆ To be polite, stay on topic.

- ◆ Read the FAQ files for any group you participate in.

- ◆ Use filters and chat commands to track the conversations that interest you, and ignore those that don't.

- ◆ Use the right formats: Don't use all capital letters except for surnames; do use symbols and acronyms to keep things brief.

- ◆ Don't clog up everyone's mailboxes with the latest urban legends.

Chapter 5

Ethics, Privacy, and Law in Genealogy

Genealogy has a long history of legal and ethical connections. From the settling of estates, to the eligibility of soccer players for national teams, to the very course of a nation's history, genealogy has had a role to play. The validation of genealogical information and the publishing of that information, online and otherwise, will also have legal and ethical ramifications. Ethics, privacy, and copyright are important to consider when you pursue your genealogy.

Say, for example, you find an illegitimate birth, an ethnic surprise, or a convicted criminal in your family history. If the information is only one or two generations back, you would want to treat the facts differently than if the events happened over 100 years ago.

Note

Disclaimer: I am not a lawyer, and this chapter is not meant to be legal advice, but merely information.

You will have three basic issues to confront in genealogy: accuracy, privacy, and copyright. These issues are just as important in the "real world" as they are online. Happily, it isn't hard to be on the right side of all of these issues!

Note

Keep these three principles in mind:

1. *Do not publish vital statistics about living persons, because the data can be used in identity theft.*

2. *Do not use anything you find in a book, a magazine, GEDCOM, or online without proper attribution and permission. Facts are not copyrightable. The presentation and formatting of facts are copyrightable.*

3. *Be aware that not everyone in the family will be thrilled to see family skeletons published. In fact, you may find that some relatives have emotional reactions to what you find; be prepared.*

Privacy

"Genealogists are sharing, caring people, and most of us think nothing of handing over all of our genealogical data to distant cousins, even strangers," says Myra Vanderpool Gormley, Certified Genealogist (CG), editor of *RootsWeb Review* and a nationally syndicated columnist. "However, we should start thinking about the ramifications of our actions. The idea of sharing genealogical information is good, and technology has made it easy. However, technology is not exclusively a tool for honest people. If detailed personal information about you and your living relatives is on the Internet, crooks can and do find it, and some scam artist might use it to hoodwink your grandmother into giving out the secrets that will open her bank account. It has happened. If your bank or financial institution still uses your mother's maiden name for a password, change it," Gormley said.

Remember that your living relatives have the same rights to privacy that you do, and among these rights are:

♦   The right to be free of unreasonable and highly offensive intrusions into one's seclusion, including the right to be free of highly objectionable disclosure of private information in which the public has no legitimate interest

♦   Appropriation of one's name or likeness by another without consent

♦   False light in the public eye—the right to avoid false attributions of authorship or association

"Publishing private genealogical information—and the important word here is private—about a living person without consent might involve any or all three aspects of their right to privacy. Publishing is more than just printed material or a traditional book. Publication includes websites, GEDCOMs, message boards, mailing lists, and even family group sheets or material that you might share with others via e-mail or traditional mail. They might be able to seek legal relief through a civil lawsuit. It is okay to collect genealogical information about your living relatives, but do not publish it in any form without written permission," Gormley said.

"We should exercise good manners and respect the privacy of our families—those generous relatives who have shared personal information with us or who shared with a cousin of a cousin," Gormley added. "Additionally, there is another and growing problem—identity theft. Why make it easy for cyberthieves to steal your or a loved one's identity? But, identify theft involves much more than just your name, address, or phone number. This idea that one's name, address, phone number, and vitals fall into the area of privacy laws is a common misconception by many people. In reality, the facts of your existence are a matter of public record in most instances. However, personal information, such as health issues, a child born out of wedlock, spouse abuse, how much money you have in the bank, etc.—those are things that are not general public knowledge, and these are personal things that if you publish them about your living relatives, there could be an invasion of privacy involved (but I'm not a lawyer)," Gormley says.

Note

"When you post public messages (on message boards and mailing lists, for example) about your research, it is sufficient to say you are researching a Jones or a Cynthia Jones line. You don't have to reveal relationship by saying she is your mother or maternal grandmother. In the pursuit of our ancestors, let's not inadvertently hurt our living family members or ourselves. Think twice before you post or share any data about the living."

—Myra Vanderpool Gormley, CG

"The concept is simple, although it is far more complicated in execution. In short, ask yourself repeatedly: 'Is there anyone who will mind if I publish this information?' There are legal issues as well with living individuals and with publishing info about people within the past 72 years in the U.S., 100 years in Canada and the U.K.," says Dick Eastman, editor and publisher of one of the most popular genealogy columns online. Eastman's genealogy tips have helped thousands of online genealogists over the last 15 years. His weekly *Eastman's Genealogy Newsletter* has been a treasure trove of news and tips for years.

"Protecting the privacy of living individuals and the issue of whether or not to publish sensitive family information (such as a great-great-aunt's child born out of wedlock) are big concerns," Eastman says. "Those can

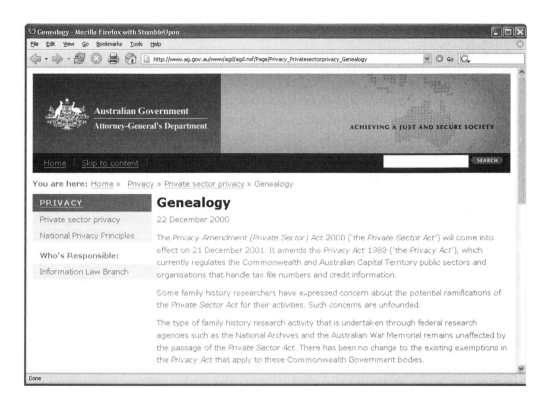

FIGURE 5-1. *The Australian Attorney General has a page explaining privacy and genealogy in that country which can helpful in researching family history.*

become legal issues if a distant (or not-so-distant) relative takes exception to your publishing such information. Lawsuits have been launched because of these things." Indeed, Australia recently amended its privacy laws, and the Australian Attorney General has a page explaining privacy and genealogy in that country (see Figure 5-1). The webpage is www.ag .gov.au/www/agd/agd.nsf/Page/Privacy_Privatesectorprivacy_Genealogy.

Copyright

A sad fact of Internet life is that some have come to believe that the entire Internet is "public domain"—that is, free for the taking. It just isn't so. Copyright applies equally to online material and offline material.

Just because the material is online changes nothing. Copyright laws are not, however, the same all around the world, and that's where online copyright becomes complicated.

As a genealogist, you should educate yourself about copyright laws (not just U.S. copyright laws) and understand what is "fair use" of another's work and what is copyrightable in the first place. A good start is the publication "Copyright Basics" from the Library of Congress, available online at http://www.copyright.gov/circs/circ1.html and in hard copy (see Figure 5-2). Be aware that if you take copyrightable material without permission, not only are you stealing, but you also may be plagiarizing. In most instances, however, genealogists will share some or all of their material with you, if you ask first.

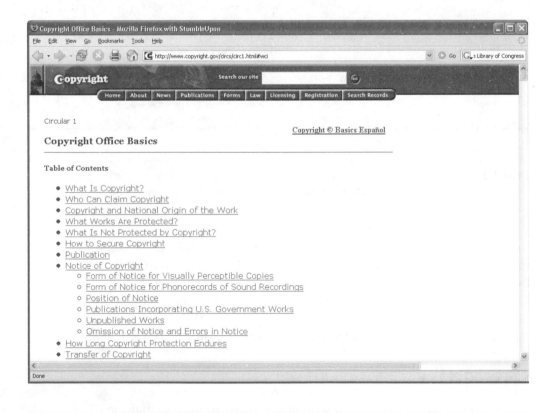

FIGURE 5-2. *"Copyright Basics" is a good place to start educating yourself on copyright law.*

Copyright laws vary by country, but for most countries, the basic premises are the same:

♦ Facts and data cannot be copyrighted.

♦ Narration, compilations (that include a genealogy database), and creative works can be copyrighted.

In other words, the presentation of facts can be protected by copyright, but not the facts themselves. When you present data in your own distinctive format, such as a book, then that presentation of the material is protected by copyright, even though the facts are not.

Gormley says, "If you do not want to share your genealogical research, that is fine, but you cannot claim copyright to facts, and a great deal of 'online genealogy' is nothing more than compiled facts—although seldom verified or even referenced as to the actual source of the information. If you don't want to be 'ripped off'—and if you mean by that that you do not want others to use genealogical facts you have compiled—then don't share your genealogy with anyone: Put it in a vault."

> *Note*
>
> *Just as bad as stealing another's work is posting your data with certain facts changed, such as a date, to "protect" your information. Posting what you know is not to be true does not advance the art and science of genealogy in any way. Don't ever do it.*

DearMYRTLE, the daily genealogy columnist, says, "Fortunately, I know of only one person who has stated she is unwilling to share her compiled genealogy data and documentation with others because she plans to print a book. I suspect, though, that the individual in question most certainly benefited from previously compiled research in books, websites, and CD databases. It would be impossible to avoid the use of these items as clues leading to the discovery of original documents. For example, one would even have to consider a clerk of the court's marriage indexes as previously compiled research. Such an index is indeed one step removed from the original creation of marriage licenses and marriage returns."

"I wish I knew!" says Dick Eastman when asked how to protect data you have carefully collected. "There is no foolproof method [to avoid] being ripped off. Of course, you should always add copyright claims. But that only stops the honest people and maybe a few unknowledgeable ones who never thought about copyrights until they read your claim.

"I used to recommend technical solutions: I recommended Adobe Acrobat PDF files. However, a free program appeared that does a great job of converting PDF files back to useable text, so now even that recommendation has been weakened. I do not know of any other way."

Eastman says there are no easy answers, only guidelines. "The person who is to publish the information needs to ask himself: 'Am I sure that I have a legal right to use this information?' If you have any doubts, don't publish! However, determining whether or not you do have a legal right to publish a piece of information can become very complex. I spent a lot of time discussing this with a lawyer who works for a Boston legal firm that specializes in intellectual properties issues. She is also an experienced genealogist and a member of the advisory board for a prestigious society. The more she talked, the more confused I became. At the end of our conversation, she said, 'Well, there really is no easy way,'" Eastman concluded.

Other Matters

Be prepared for relatives to be sensitive about certain family history, as my husband's grandfather was (see Chapter 1). A long thread on the Ancestry.com ethics discussion board described one researcher's problems in tracing her husband's line. Her in-laws became angry and insulting when asked a simple question about her husband's grandfather. She then researched discreetly, without asking her in-laws any more questions. When she came across a fact that may have been what upset her in-laws, she resolved to keep the data private.

In such a case, you may even want to put the information aside in something to be opened with your will, and ask your descendants to add it to the family tree after everyone involved is gone.

Success Story: DearMYRTLE Helps Analyze Data

Tracy St. Claire of BibleRecords.com, recently came across a potentially delicate problem: Her transcribing of a set of diaries and letters from a mid-19th-century man. The writings could possibly be interpreted as circumspect homosexual love letters and diary entries. Or not, as her mother-in-law did not get the same feeling from reading the materials. Perhaps the man was simply purple in his prose. Still, the question occurred to her: Is she "outing" not only the author, but also the correspondent?

She posed the question to DearMYRTLE, who pointed out that if the materials are transcribed, not abstracted, then full context allows not only honesty, but also tools for objective analysis. Family historians are not judges, but conveyors of facts.

As the materials are over 100 years old and the family did not file extension of copyright at the end of 75 years, copyright does not apply. So, in being both transparent and accurate, the transcription of the materials and posting them on the Internet do meet the criteria for ethical genealogy, and the age of the material means copyright does not apply.

"Traditionally, genealogists have been a kindly, sharing group of individuals," says Pat Richley, also known online as DearMYRTLE. "After all, no single researcher has every piece of the ancestral puzzle. We need to share research back and forth among those with common ancestors. Successful genealogy research does not exist in a vacuum where one works totally alone. It is then only a matter of common sense to cite the source of each piece of the puzzle, to leave a wide audit trail for those that follow, and to give credit where credit is due.

"That wide audit trail is essential for others to be able to evaluate the reliability of our research in our absence. Given such source citations (author, title, call number, microfilm number, publication date, etc.), it would be possible for a great-great-grandchild to obtain photocopies (or whatever they'll be using) of original documents relating to his family tree. Should additional documentation come to light in the meantime, that distant great-great-grandchild should compare it with our old compiled genealogy to see if the new information supports or refutes the lineage assumptions we've made."

Genealogies will improve over time, as one generation takes what others have compiled before and gathers additional documentation—perhaps distinguishing between two John Smiths in an area where it was previously thought there was only one individual by that name. In such a case, it isn't necessary to denigrate the work of the previous researcher. Merely point out the expanded list of documents proving the distinctions and bring the family puzzle into a new light. But in doing so, cite all sources!

There is also a need for individuals who merely photocopy 25 pages of their personal recollections at the local office supply store and send them in manila envelopes to their distant family members. Wouldn't we each give our eyeteeth to have such a write-up from our Civil War or Revolutionary War ancestor? But, as always, family lore must be proved before incorporating it into our pedigree charts. Looking at documents created at the time our ancestors lived are eyewitness accounts of life as they knew it.

For further reading, DearMYRTLE recommends *Evidence! Source Citation & Analysis for the Family Historian* by Elizabeth Shown Mills (Genealogical Publishing Company, 1997) available at www.genealogical.com.

Note

"In a perfect world (online or off) everyone would cite their sources properly and give credit to all who have shared research and information with them. Alas, there is no such place—never has been. Even basic good manners—such as saying "thank you"—are rare. But the genealogist with good manners is far more likely to be rewarded with a wealth of material and help than those without."

—Myra Vanderpool Gormley, CG

Give Back

Finally, it is at least as good to give as to receive. Once you have some experience, you should consider contributing to the amount of good, accurate information available online. For example, on www.familysearchindexing.org, you can volunteer to be part of their indexing project. In the first quarter of 2007 alone, volunteers indexed nearly 30 million names by simply reading scanned documents and typing the names and page numbers. This was done by thousands of volunteers, some of whom can only spare one hour a month. But in that hour, you can probably index 50 or so names. Multiply that by the hundreds of thousands of people who use www.familysearch.org, and you can see what an impact that can make!

Similarly, most of the USGenWeb and international GenWeb sites are thrilled to have volunteers help them index and transcribe wills, deeds, letters, tax rolls, or any other primary source you can get your hand on. Again, give an hour a month, and you can be of great help to many other researchers! Check out www.usgenweb.org, drill down to the states and counties for which you have data, and contribute.

Join a local historical or genealogical organization, and share your findings with the membership in their publications and online sites. For years, my mother edited *LeDespencer*, the Spencer Historical and Genealogical Society (www.shgs.org) newsletter, which was mostly transcribed original materials from letters and diaries to narratives about ancestors. She indexed each volume herself, too. She learned a lot about our branch of Spencer ancestors as well as lots of other branches in the process!

Sites about Copyright, Ethics, and Privacy

The following are some good online articles on these topics:

- "Copyright Basics" from the Library of Congress (http://www.copyright.gov/circs/circ1.html)

- 10 Myths about Copyright Explained (http://www.templetons .com/brad/copymyths.html)

- Association of Professional Genealogists' Code of Ethics (http://www.apgen.org/ethics/index.html)

- Board for Certification of Genealogists' Code of Ethics (http://www.bcgcertification.org/aboutbcg/ code.html)

- Can You Copyright Your Family Tree? (genealogy .about.com/od/writing_family_history/a/copyright.htm)

- Copyright Fundamentals for Genealogy (http://www.pddoc .com/copyright/genealogy_copyright_fundamentals.htm)

(Continued)

- ♦ Creating Worthwhile Genealogies for Our Families and Descendants: Genealogical Standards (http://www .ngsgenealogy .org/comstandards.cfm)

- ♦ Genealogist's Code of Ethics (http://www.rootsweb.com/ ~gasaga/ethics.html)

- ♦ Horror on the Web by Myra Vanderpool Gormley (http://www .ancestry.com/columns/myra/Shaking_Family_Tree10-29-98. htm)

- ♦ Nolo.com (http://www.nolo.com)—click the Patents, Copyright & Art tab.

- ♦ The United States Copyright Office (http://lcweb.loc .gov/copyright).

Wrapping Up

Ethics, privacy and copyright are the three concerns with genealogy legalities. To sum up:

- ♦ The first rule: Do not publish anything about living people, on the Web or otherwise. This helps prevent someone from getting a name, birth date, and birth place to create a false identification or to steal an identity. On the other hand, do not publish anything you know to be untrue to avoid having bad data become part of the Internet forever.

- ♦ The second rule: Be sensitive about publishing information on those who have passed on. You may find it fascinating that your great-great-grandfather was illegitimate and a pirate; perhaps your cousins won't be so enthralled.

- ♦ The third rule: Cite your sources, both to protect intellectual property rights and to leave a wide audit train for future genealogists.

- ♦ The fourth rule: Contribute to the collection of good, accurate data on the Internet by becoming involved with indexing, transcribing, and discussing original sources.

Part II

General Genealogy

Chapter 6

Revving Up Search Engines

Throughout this book, I will try to point you to the best genealogy resources on the Internet as I know them at the time I am writing. However, by the time you read this, untold numbers of sites may have been created, or deleted, or changed from wonderful to not-so-much, and vice versa. Keeping track of all of this is made much easier by search engines and portals.

It's a fact of Internet life that new sources of genealogical information appear daily, so you might miss an important new resource if you don't do your own searches once in a while. Search engines and portals offer ways to send changes and news stories that match certain keywords to you via e-mail or push technology, and I will show you how to take advantage of that.

Finally, as a genealogist, you've experienced the thrill of discovering things for yourself—it can be quite a kick to find a website or blog none of your friends know about. To do this, you need a way to find genealogical resources on the Internet on your own. That's where search sites come in.

Defining Terms

Search engine is an all-purpose label used to describe anything that will let you search for terms within a group of data. That data could be on a single site or on billions of pages on the Internet, or on some subset in between the two. Just about anything that lets you search gets called a search engine, but some other terms are more accurate for specific sites.

Note

If you are interested in search engines, how they work, and how they compare to one another, check out Search Engine Watch (http://searchenginewatch.com) and Search Engines.com (http://www.searchengines.com).

A *spider* is a program that looks for information on the Internet, creates a database of what it finds, and lets you use a Web browser to run a search engine on that database for specific information. As noted, this can mean billions of pages or only the pages on one site. A search site might have one or more search engines and can claim to search "the whole Web," but, in reality, most probably cover about 15 percent of the Web at any given time. This is because pages quickly appear and disappear on the Web. That's why you might want to use several different search sites when you are searching for specific information or for general types of sites. Or, you might want to try one of the many meta-search engines that try several search sites at once.

A search site called a *directory* or a *catalog* uses a search engine to let you hunt through an edited list of Internet sites for specific information. The value of these sites is that in a directory or catalog, websites are sorted, categorized, and sometimes rated. Most often, the directory is included in a *portal*, which pulls together searches of news, information, text, pictures, and whatever into one page, which you can modify to your liking. And this is what an online genealogist needs.

Yahoo! (www.yahoo.com), shown in Figure 6-1, was one of the first catalogs or directories established online; it is also a good example of a portal, which offers other services, such as chat, news, forums, and more.

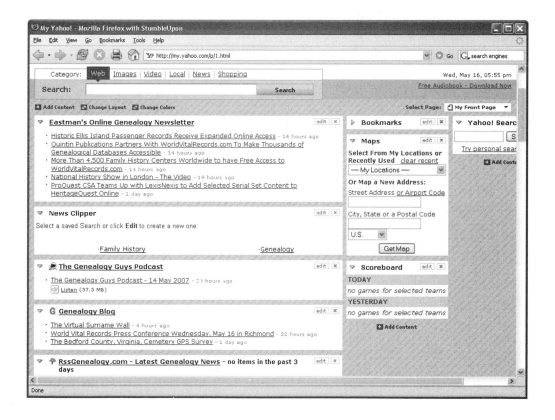

FIGURE 6-1.   *A portal allows you to set up a page that tracks news and sites pertaining to any topic you choose. Here, I chose genealogy for the My Yahoo! page.*

A portal is a little bit of everything: a search engine for the Web at large, a catalog of sites the owners recommend, and usually a group of other features, including stock prices, Web-based e-mail, shopping, and so on.

In the figure, you can see that I have personalized My Yahoo! to pull genealogy information onto the portal for me. To do this is simple. First, establish a Yahoo! account and password. Then click the Add Content button. On the Add Content page, search for "genealogy," and add the modules that interest you. Save the changes. Then, choose Add Content again, and browse the News section. You can create news clippers that post or e-mail you a notice when a story appears on any topic from "genealogy" to "Kentucky basketball." I added the modules to the portal page; you may choose to have it e-mailed to you or picked up by a Really Simple Syndication (RSS) reader.

You can add additional pages and access them by tabs, so you could have one for general genealogy, one for surnames, and so on. Google, MSN, AOL, Excite, and even my Internet service provider (ISP), Bellsouth.net, all offer similar capabilities. Once you have the portal set up the way you like it, you can make it your home page.

A *meta-search* engine submits your query to several different search sites, portals, and catalogs at the same time. You might get more results, and you will usually be able to compare how each one responded to the query. These searches may take longer, however, and getting millions of results is almost more trouble than getting one. There are genealogy-specific meta-search engines, and you will find information on some of them later in this chapter. Examples of general meta-search sites are Dogpile, Mamma, Profusion, and others.

Searching with Savoir Faire

Now, searching can be as easy as typing "Powell Genealogy" and clicking the search button, yet that might also get you so many hits that you feel you are drinking from a fire hose. You can make the spiders boogie if you just speak their language. Thankfully, search algorithms have come a long way since the days when search engines could not tell the difference between a blind Venetian and a Venetian blind!

Here are some general search tips:

♦ Use phrases instead of single words in your searches. Type several words that are relevant to your search. Typing `Spencer genealogy Ohio` will narrow a search well.

♦ Enclose phrases in quotes. Searching on the phrase `Spencer family history` without quotation marks will match all pages that have any of those three words included somewhere on the page, in any order, and not necessarily adjacent to each other. Searching with the phrase `"Spencer family history"` (with quotation marks) will return only those pages that have those three words together.

♦ The more specific you are, the better. Searching for `Irish genealogy databases` will give you fewer, but closer, matches than searching for `Irish genealogy`.

♦ Use plus and minus signs in your searches. A word preceded by a plus sign (+) must appear on the page to be considered a match. A word preceded by a minus sign (–) must not appear on the page to be considered a match. No spaces can be between the plus and minus signs and the words they apply to. For example, entering

```
+Spencer -royal genealogy
```

would ask the search engine to find pages that contain the word "Spencer," but not the word "royal," with the word "genealogy" preferred, but optional. Most search engines would get some Spencer genealogy pages but leave out those that include Lady Diana, Princess of Wales. More about this type of search can be found in the following section about Boolean searches.

♦ Every now and then, search for "geneology" instead of "genealogy." You will be amazed at how many pages out there use this misspelling!

Note

Narrow your searches if you get too many matches. Sometimes, the page with your search results will have an input box to allow you to search for new terms among the results. This might mean adding terms or deleting terms and then running the search again only on the results from the first search. You can also run searches within search results to help narrow down choices. This is the easiest way.

Using Boolean Terms

Searching the Internet is no simple matter. With literally billions of sites, some of them with millions of documents, and more words than you can imagine, finding exactly the right needle in all that hay can be daunting. The key, of course, is crafting a precise query.

Boolean operators are handy tools for honing your searches. Named after George Boole, the 19th-century mathematician who dreamed up symbolic logic, Boolean operators represent the relationships among items using terms such as OR, AND, and NOT. When applied to information retrieval, they can expand or narrow a search to uncover as many citations, or hits, as you want.

The Boolean OR

When you search for two or more terms joined with an OR operator, you get back hits that contain any one of your terms. Therefore, the query

```
Powell OR genealogy
```

will retrieve documents containing "Powell" or "genealogy," but not necessarily both. Note that nearly all search pages default to OR—that is, they assume you want any page with any one or more of your terms in it.

You can see it makes good sense to use OR when you search for synonyms or closely related terms. For example, if you're looking for variations on a name, search for

```
SPENCER SPENCE SPENSER
```

The average search engine will assume the OR operator and find any page with any one or more of those terms. However, the average search engine will also sort the results such that the pages with the most relevance appear at the top, using all your search terms to score that relevance.

The Boolean AND

In the Boolean boogie, joining search terms with AND means that all terms must be found in a document, but not necessarily together. The query

```
George AND Washington
```

will result in a list of documents that have both the names "George" and "Washington" somewhere within them. Use AND when you have dissimilar terms and need to narrow a search. Usually, to use AND in a search, you type a plus sign (+) or put the term AND between the words and enclose everything within parentheses, like so:

```
(Spencer AND genealogy)
```

Note

Remember, a simple AND doesn't guarantee that the words will be next to each other. Your search for **George AND Washington** *could turn up documents about George Benson and Grover Washington!*

The Boolean NOT

When you use NOT, search results must exclude certain terms. Many search engines don't have this functionality. Often, when you can use it, the syntax is to put a minus sign (–) in front of the unwanted term.

The query

```
Powell NOT Colin
```

will return all citations containing the name "Powell," but none including "Colin," regardless of whether "Powell" is there. Use NOT when you want to exclude possible second meanings. "Banks" can be found on genealogy surname pages as well as on pages associated with finance or with rivers. Searching for

```
banks AND genealogy NOT river
```

or

```
banks +genealogy -river
```

increases the chance of finding documents relating to the surname Banks (the people, not riversides). In some search engines, the minus sign often takes the place of NOT.

The fun part is combining Boolean operators to create a precise search. Let's say you want to find documents about the city of Dallas, Texas. If you simply search for "Dallas," you could get copious hits about Dallas County in Alabama (county seat: Selma), which might not be the Dallas you want. To avoid that, you would use AND, NOT, and OR in this fashion:

```
(Dallas AND Texas) NOT (Selma OR Alabama)
(Powell AND genealogy) NOT (Colin AND "SECRETARY OF STATE")
```

Note that parentheses group the search terms together.

Beyond AND/OR/NOT

In most Web search engines, unless a phrase option is specifically offered, the capitalization or order of the terms isn't important: A Venetian blind is the same as a blind Venetian. However, some search engines enable you to fine-tune a search further.

The WITH operator, for example, searches for terms that are much nearer to each other. How "near" is defined depends on the engine. Some would look at `"George WITH Washington"` and deliver documents only containing the words "George Washington" next to each other. Others might consider words in the same sentence or paragraph to be near enough.

Check the search engine's Help files to see if it uses wildcards or word stemming (for finding all variations of a word, such as ancestry, ancestral, ancestor, and ancestors).

Using these techniques, you can search the Web much more efficiently, finding just the right document on George Washington Carver or a genealogy site on the right set of Powells. Learn the steps to the Boolean boogie, and you'll soon be Web dancing wherever you please!

Search Sites

Lots of search sites are out there, some of which are more useful to genealogists than others. The following is a list of genealogy-related catalogs, portals, and search engines, in alphabetical order.

Access Genealogy

At this site, www.accessgenealogy.com, you can read and search free of charge for many different types of records for genealogy research, including newspapers and periodicals; emigration and immigration forms; census reports; voting records; and archives from libraries, cemeteries, churches, and courts (see Figure 6-2).

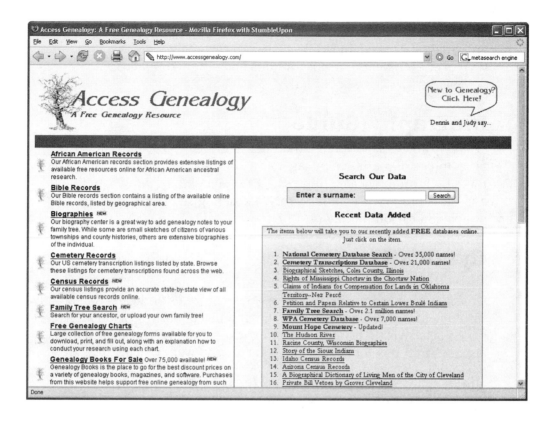

FIGURE 6-2. *Access Genealogy is a meta-search site specifically for family history researchers.*

Ancestor Hunt

This site is an edited catalog, and it is wonderful. With this meta-search site at www.ancestorhunt.com, you can search for ancestors and locate surnames in some of the best and largest databases of genealogy records online. The site has unique searches, such as the Surname Search Portal and the Obituary Search Portal, both of which search several sites at once.

Two of the exceptional pages are Genealogical Prison Records and Past Sheriffs of the US. You will find these, along with many other search engines and free genealogy resources, in the Genealogy Search Engines and Contents menu, which is located on each page.

One of the most popular sections is the Bible Records Transcriptions and Images. These family bibles are completely indexed by surname, with over 200 pages of transcriptions and scanned images.

This site is one to bookmark!

Biography Guide

Was any ancestor of yours a member of Congress? Search for biographies of members by last name, first name, position, and state at this site: http://bioguide.congress.gov/biosearch/biosearch.asp. If your ancestors are in the database, this fascinating site can add a new dimension to your family history.

Cyndi's List

The site www.cyndislist.com catalogs about a quarter-million genealogy websites. You will find links to the genealogy sites and sites that simply would help a genealogist. This is the *first* place many new online genealogists visit. The links are categorized and organized, and there's also a search box for finding the subjects you want quickly.

Cyndi Howells works on the list every day, updating, deleting, and adding sites. Each new or updated link will have a small "new" or "updated" graphic next to it for 30 days.

The main index is updated each time activity occurs on Cyndi's List. Check the date under each category heading to determine when the last update was made for that category. The date is also updated at the bottom of each category page.

Genealogy Pages

A collected catalog of genealogy sites, the website www.genealogypages .com also offers you a free e-mail inbox and a browser-based chat site, so it qualifies as a portal.

You can browse the collection of links by category or search the entire collection. Because it's all about genealogy, you don't have to put that term in the search box. For example, a search for "South Carolina Powell" in the regular search box turned up nothing, even though in the advanced search box I could choose between AND (the default) and OR. And even if it was recognized as a phrase, I couldn't get a match on all three. Searching on "South Carolina" got good results, however, as did searching on "Powell."

Genealogy Search Help for Google

This page (http://www.genealogy-search-help.com/) puts in Google advanced search terms for you. So, you type your ancestor name and as many parents, grandparents, etc. as you can, and the site codes in the Boolean parameters. Fast, easy, and some targeted hits.

GeneaSearch.com

This portal, www.geneasearch.com, is along the lines of Genealogy Pages. Several search options exist, but searching by surname is your best bet. GeneaSearch gives results similar to those of Genealogy Pages. They will both return submitted GEDCOMs from users that will be secondary sources for genealogy.

The site's services include free genealogy lookups, free genealogy sites, family surname newsletters, data, books from genealogy societies and individuals, surname queries, female ancestors, new site announcements, a beginner's genealogy guide, and free clip art. Other genealogy resources include tools, links, and lists of societies. Also, there are free genealogy databases and genealogy resources for each state.

Genealogy Research Resources

At www.misbach.org/resources.html, you can find input boxes for some of the most popular search engines on the Internet for doing genealogical research. When you enter your search criteria in any of the fields, it will take you to the labeled website and show you the results of your query. You have to navigate back to Genealogy Research Resources to do the next search, however, so you may want to bookmark this page.

GenGateway

Another version of a catalog of websites organized into categories for genealogists is www.gengateway.com, by Steve Lacy. It indexes thousands of webpages and sources. Choose the category you want to search, such as surname or obituary, and you'll get well-sorted results.

To navigate the site, use one of the many useful gateways listed in the navigation bar on the left of the home page. If you're new to the site, first try the Beginners Gateway or the Search Pages.

GenServ

An all-volunteer effort, GenServ, at www.genserv.com, is a collection of donated GEDCOMs with a sophisticated set of search commands. The database has over 25,000,000 individuals in more than 19,000 databases. All this family history data is online and available by search and reports to subscribers. You can search a limited amount of the data in a free trial (see Figure 6-3). GenServ has been online since 1991 and on the Web since 1994. To access the system, you have to at least submit your own GEDCOM. If you pay the optional yearly fees, you can perform many more searches per day than the free access allows.

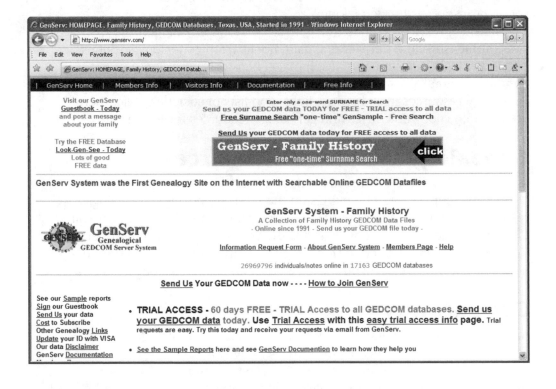

FIGURE 6-3. *GenServ offers one free search.*

> **Note**
>
> *GenServ is submitted GEDCOMS. Therefore, it is all secondary source material. When you seem to have a match, you need to contact the submitter to determine what primary source material he or she might have, and offer to exchange what data you have.*

The capability to do complex searches on the databases means a real learning curve exists. Furthermore, only the "surname count" search can be done from the Web; all the rest are done via e-mail messages. This has the advantage of letting you input your terms and then surf on to other sites. The results, meanwhile, come back by e-mail (and quickly, too!).

Uploading your data and learning how to query this set of databases is worth your time.

GenSource

The specialized genealogy directory site www.gensource.com provides the online genealogist with three databases to assist with research online.

The first database is called Search Common Threads, which will help you find other genealogists researching your family name. If you're at a "dead end" finding information on an ancestor, add an entry to Common Threads so other family members can find you.

Search the second database, I Found It!, to locate genealogy sites on the Internet. You can use the I Found It! search engine to locate pages on surnames, one-name studies, ship passenger lists, genealogical societies and associations, researchers, software, books, family mailing lists, online records of churches, census data, cemeteries, and more.

Search the third database, the IFI (I Found It!) Archives, for sites containing actual historical records. Many people have taken the time to transcribe records and place them on the Net for your use, all of which are indexed for research purposes.

NedGen

This is one example of a beyond-U.S.–based search engine aimed at genealogists. At www.nedgen.com, you can Search over 60,000 genealogy websites in the United States, Canada, Europe, France, Germany, Italy, Ireland, Netherlands/Belgium, Scandinavia, the United Kingdom and other European countries, Australia and New Zealand,

Asia, and African and Jewish genealogy. You can also use the page navigation bar to search ship and passenger lists, adoption records, census records, online databases, vital records, and Ellis Island records. Search migration, military, personal homepages, Genealogy software, Origins, Ancestry, and Classmates from here, too! Trace your roots in Europe with this genealogy and ancestry search engine dedicated to indexing family history and roots on personal homepages with online family trees in Europe.

ROOTSWEB Search Thingy

Go to www.rootsweb.com, click Searches, and click Search Thingy. Then put in your search terms. The meta-search goes through all ROOTSWEB pages and databases. The disadvantage to Search Thingy is that OR is the only Boolean operator you get, so a search for James Reason Powell will get any page with any one of those terms.

Surname Web

Located at www.surnameweb.org, Surname Web has a database of names submitted by users, as well as pages from other websites. Simply input the surname you are looking for.

WorldConnect

WorldConnect (http://worldconnect.rootsweb.com) is a division of ROOTSWEB. ROOTSWEB's motto is "Connecting the world, one GEDCOM at a time." People can upload to and search this collection of GEDCOM databases for free. All you need to do is fill out the form with name, place of birth and death, and dates of birth and death. You can choose an exact search if you're sure of your facts, or a range of 2 to 20 years for dates, and Soundex searches for names and places. It's fast, but the results depend entirely on the uploaded GEDCOMs. If you have no hits, consider uploading your information for others. If you already uploaded your information, you can exclude your own database from future searches.

Like GenServ, WorldConnect is all-volunteer, amateur information. You must contact the submitter of a database to find out the primary sources for the data. However, unlike GenServ, you can do the searches via the Web.

General Search Sites

Many Web-wide search engines and portals can help you find genealogy resources. Using the search techniques previously mentioned, you'll probably have good results trying these general search engines. Some of them have catalogs of genealogy sites. For those that do, information on how to browse them is listed, in the list below. On all of them, though, searches as described in the beginning of this chapter will work:

+ **Search** (www.search.com) is a mega-search engine.

+ **Dogpile** (www.dogpile.com) is a mega-search engine. One search will query several other search engines. It also uses the + and – Boolean searches. Don't bother with the Dogpile "Web directory," because it's simply a listing of their paid advertisers. The search function, however, is fast and gives good results.

+ **Google** (www.google.com) provides the obvious search of your surnames and ancestors' hometowns, as well as many tools to help the genealogist.

Google announced in 2007 that it has partnered with four states—Arizona, California, Utah, and Virginia—to remove technical barriers that kept its search engine, as well as those of Microsoft Corp. and Yahoo! Inc., from accessing some public records. This means that deeds and other vital statistics can become accessible through a Google search in time. Google hopes to ultimately persuade federal agencies to employ the same tools, but first will have to overcome privacy concerns.

Google has a news search, as shown in the previous Yahoo! example, and can send an RSS feed, an e-mail, or post it on your personalized Google site when your keywords are found in a news story. I keep a "genealogy" one going, and often use it to read newspapers' genealogy columnists from around the world.

Another important feature is page translations. Click Language Tools on the main Google page. You have a choice of putting in a page you already found or simply pasting in a block of text to be translated. Also, if a regular Google search turns up non-English pages, one of your choices will be Translate This Page—great for when you get beyond the boat to the "old country!"

Google Book Search can make you feel like a kid in a toy store. On the Google page, click More and then click Books. Now type the genealogy information you're looking for, such as a surname or a location, or just "genealogy." The Google Book Search looks in the full text of thousands of books, and within seconds returns hits based on relevance (see Figure 6-4).

The fun doesn't stop there. Click a book title, and you'll see basic information about the book similar to a card catalog. You might also see a few sentences with your search term in context. If a publisher or author has granted permission, you'll see a full page and be able to browse within the book to see more pages. If the book is out of copyright, you'll see a full page, and you can move forward or

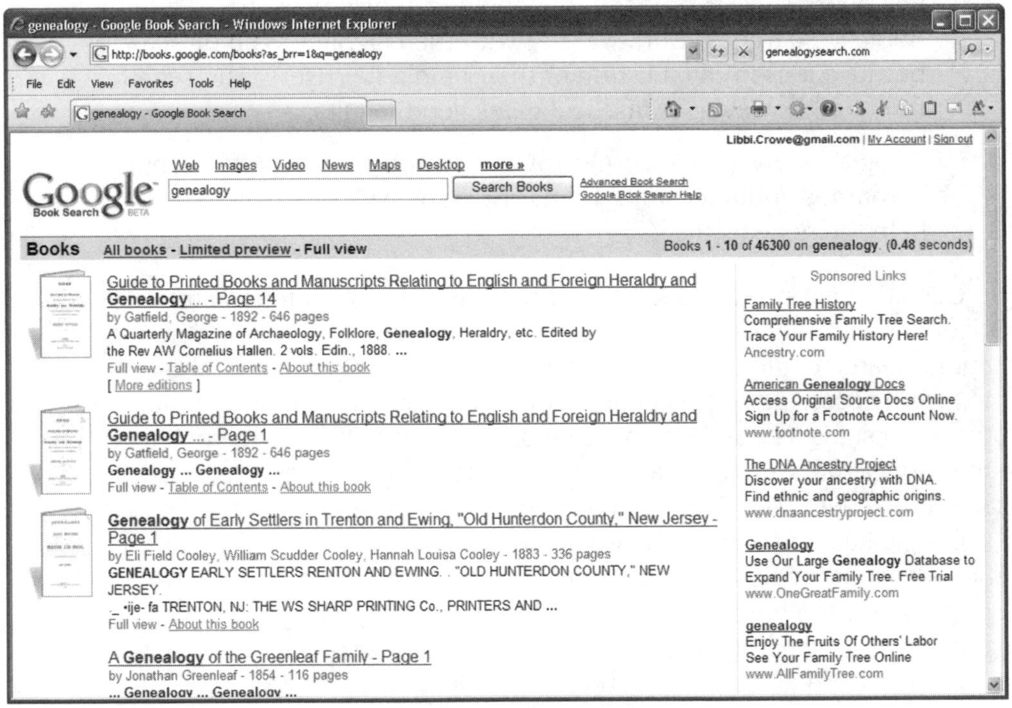

FIGURE 6-4. *Search the full text of books on Google, and perhaps find a published genealogy on your surname.*

backward to see the full book. Clicking Search Within This Book, allows you to perform more searches within the book you've selected. Clicking Buy This Book connects you to an online bookstore where you can buy the book. For some books, you will see a Find This Book In A Library link: this goes to a local library where you can borrow it.

Yahoo! (www.yahoo.com) enables you to search the whole Yahoo! catalog by typing "genealogy" and/or the surname and/or the location in the search box, or choose Arts | Humanities | History | Genealogy. Yahoo!'s new search engine is faster than before, and it gives you a choice of opening a link in a new window to make browsing through your results easier. Also, you can now search news, pictures, and U. S. maps as well as webpages.

Obituary Search Pages

Several pages enable you to search recent and older obituaries:

♦ Legacy.com (www.legacy.com/Obituaries.asp) has a page called ObitFinder that searches recent obituaries by name, keyword, and location.

♦ Obituary Links (www.obitlinkspage.com) searches cemetery records, obituaries, and other pages from sites such as Ancestry.com, ROOTSWEB, and so on. This is a meta-search engine that focuses on death records.

♦ Origins.net (www.origins.net) is a fee-based genealogy search site; you can try a sample search for free. Users pay a license fee for use of the Origin Search software at $5 for 24 hours or $15 for 14 days. Origins.net provides access to databases of genealogical data for online family history research in the United Kingdom, Canada, Australia, New Zealand, and the United States. Origin Search (www.originsearch.com) is a new service from Origins.net that allows searching, via a single search request, of millions of webpages containing genealogy data. By entering a surname and any other relevant information, such as forename, year, place of birth, or residence, the search engine will link you directly to sites where that name and information appears.

The free Irish Origins service is based on the same software and functionality as the overall service. If you are considering using Origin Search, you can check thoroughly the functionality and quality of service you will receive before committing to pay for it. The site has 11 categories of data available for searching, ranging from birth and death records to military and immigration records. Origin Search does not hold any primary data, such as the General Register Office for Scotland records that used to be held on Scots Origins. Nor is Origin Search an interface for databases, but rather a specialized genealogical search engine that saves users time and ensures that they find information that may not be found on general search engines such as Google, Excite, and so on.

White Page Directories

So far, you've looked at search engines and directories for finding a website. But what if you need to find lost living relatives? Or what if you want to write to people with the same surnames you're researching? In that case, you need people search engines, called White Page directories. Like the White Pages of your phone book, these directories specialize in finding people, not pages. In fact, all the search engine sites mentioned previously have White Page directories.

The AT&T site (www.att.com/directory), shown in Figure 6-5, has an excellent set of directories for people and businesses, with a reverse phone number lookup (put in the phone number; get the name). It's basically a White Pages for the whole United States.

Switchboard (www.switchboard.com) is one of many White Pages services on the Web. It's free, and it lists the e-mail addresses and telephone numbers of millions of people and businesses, taken from public records. It's also a website catalog. If you register as a user (it's free), you can ensure that your listing is not only accurate, but also has only the information you want it to reveal.

Bigfoot (http://search.bigfoot.com/en/index.jsp) is another such effort to catalog people, with the same general rules: Input your information, and you get searches that are more specific. Bigfoot also has postal addresses in addition to e-mail and telephone information.

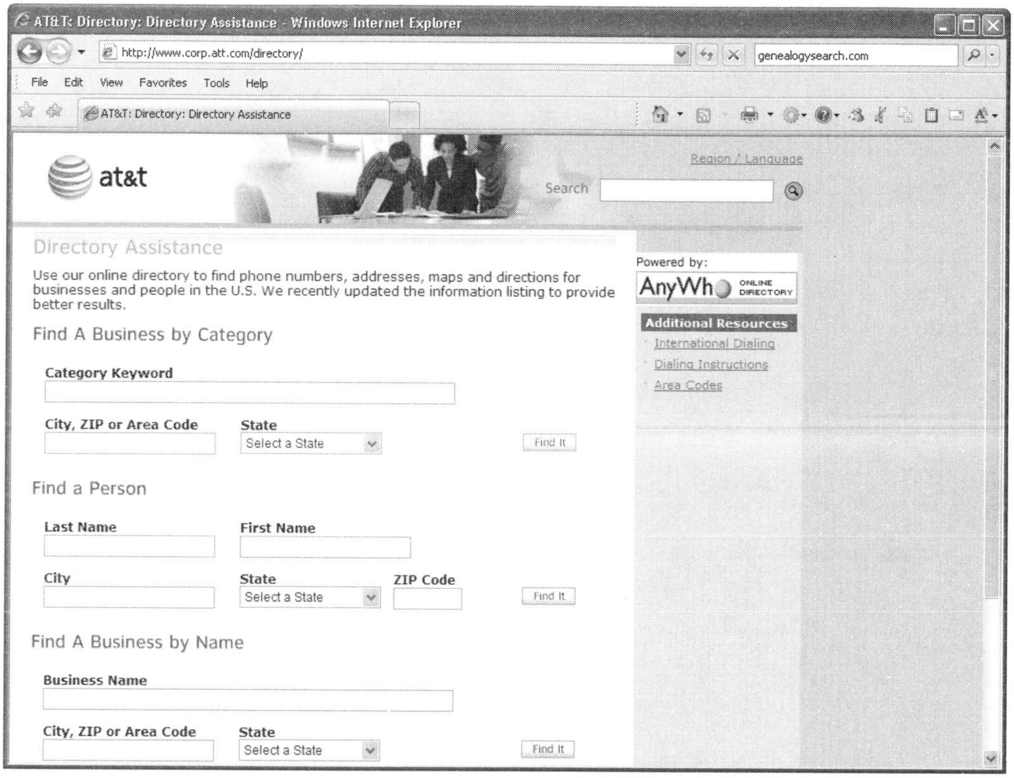

FIGURE 6-5.   *White Page sites are like online phone books.*

Wrapping Up

+ Learn to use Boolean search terms to target your Web searches.

+ Use genealogy-specific sites to search for surnames and localities.

+ Use general search sites and catalogs that gather news and links about genealogy.

+ Use White Pages search sites to find living people.

Chapter 7

Chat

Sometimes you might want to talk to a fellow genealogist to resolve problems you're encountering in your research. The online world can help you there, too, with chat.

Chat is not nearly as common as it was even five years ago. Certainly Internet Relay Chat (IRC) has fallen into disuse. The increasing attractiveness of instant-messaging programs, text messaging on phones, and blogs combined with spammers' bad habit of using contact info in chat rooms to blast the online world with spam have left IRC looking like an old downtown pub that lost its clientele to a pre-fab chain restaurant down the road. Only the die-hard addicts remain.

And yet, some genealogy chats continue, mostly in Web-based form, and generally as a moderated format where a leader answers typed questions with either text or Voice over Internet Protocol (VoIP). For the most part, chat rooms are now Java-based and do not require a separate chat program. Many genealogists also use instant-messaging programs for scheduled or impromptu one-on-one communication on brick walls, recent finds, and new resources.

The modern chat is useful for education: chat as online classroom. With sound capabilities, that metaphor becomes much closer to reality. In addition, some chat rooms are still just a fun place to hang out and discuss the weather, your health, and computer problems when you take a break from genealogy.

Success Story: Where's Amos?

I wandered into Uncle Hiram's Chat Cabins at www.bhocutt.com. I thought it best to familiarize myself with my new "digs" before the following night's grand opening and my hosting debut. Thinking I'd be alone to try this and that, I was surprised to find three chatters in a deep genealogical discussion. They told me that DearMYRTLE's newsletter had guided them to this corner of cyberspace. I could tell by their conversation that they were veterans in the field, but I pressed on and asked if there was anything I could do to help them with their research. One chatter stepped forward and presented his brick wall.

The ancestor's name was Amos HURLBUT. He had recently found him in the 1870 census in Iowa and was looking for his parents. The census told him that he was born in New York and was 36 years old. He already knew that Amos and wife Sarah POTTER were married in New York and that Sarah was from Franklin County, New York. He ended by telling me that

Marvin HURLBUT was also found in the same part of Iowa as Amos and may be related. Eager to please, especially on my first "unofficial" day, I told him I would look to my resources and see what I could find. I always feel it best to start with the facts, so I pulled up the 1870 census to see what the chatter saw. With ease I found Amos in the Iowa 1860 and 1870 census, and I saw the Marvin HURLBUT he was speaking about. But this didn't get me any closer to Amos's parents. I thought, hmmm, if Sarah was from Franklin County, New York, maybe Amos was as well. So I decided to search the 1850 census with Soundex for HURLBUTs in that county, but all matches came up empty. Not an Amos to be found. I turned to other facts in the case. Who was this Marvin fella? I decided to search for his name to see what I could find. To my surprise, Iowa cemetery records showed a Marvin HURLBUT born in 1826 in Onondaga County, New York. This seemed to match the age of the Marvin previously found on the census. My next thought: If Marvin was born in 1826, he just might be a head of household in 1850. A search produced a Marvin HERLBUT in Chautauqua County, New York, matching the age and wife of the Marvin I've been seeking. Marvin seemed to be found, but where's Amos?

Assuming Marvin was related and that families moved in packs, I decided to give a look in 1850 for other HURLBUTs in Clymer, Chautauqua County, New York. And it was there in the index where I found Daniel HERLBUT. When I viewed the census for Daniel, I let out a yell, for there was a son named Amos at home at the age of 17. Perfect match! I could have ended there, but my curiosity took over. I then found Daniel in the same town in the 1840 census. Then I found a Daniel in 1830 in Onondaga County (yes, the same county in which Marvin was born). Although I have a strong feeling, I cannot prove that Amos and Marvin are related or that Marvin is Daniel's son. But the information I found on Marvin led me to find Amos. It just goes to show you that any piece of information found can be vital to your research.

— GenHostMike

Can We Talk?

Online chat has been around for a long time. From the earliest days of The Source and CompuServe to the present, chat has been a staple of online communication. Chat is useful, whether you're collaborating on a genealogy project, sending digital reunion memos to your extended family, or discussing your hobby with a large crowd.

Chatting Up the Internet

The most popular form of chat today is instant messaging, thanks in large part to America Online's Instant Messenger program, known to users as AIM, and MSN Messenger. In this form of chat, a select, invited list of people (from two to a whole "room") exchange typed messages in real time. This feature has become so popular that instant messaging is used 200 million times a day, according to AOL PR people. Another example is ICQ (I-seek-you), a different instant-messaging program that AOL recently bought out; it gets hundreds of new users a day.

The other most common chat program is a Java-based chat that shows in your Web browser. As long as you have the latest version of Java on your computer, nothing else is needed to participate.

Different programs enable you to have one-on-one and multiperson conversations with people. Some require you to sign on to a chat server, where the program you use doesn't matter. Others only let you chat with people using the same program and who have allowed you to put them on their "buddy list." The former lets you connect with more people; the latter gives you more security. A few will let you do both.

All forms of chat are addictive. You start typing messages with your buddy in Omaha, or your son at college, or your sister-in-law and suddenly you discover an hour has slipped by. Beware!

AOL Instant Messenger

You can find AOL Instant Messenger (known as AIM) at www.aim.com. It is a free service of AOL, like XDrive, which was discussed in Chapter 2. AIM is the most widely used instant-messaging program. The software gives Internet users the capability to send instant messages and create chat rooms with other AIM users, whether or not they use AOL. AIM also supports voice chat through VoIP.

MSN Messenger

This program comes already installed on many computers running Windows, and it works very much like AIM. You register as a user for free, choosing a screen name and a password. If you already have a Passport account, you can use that login information. MSN Messenger has a link to chat rooms on MSN. In the chat rooms, you have to scroll through long lists of role-playing and other topics to find one on genealogy.

Success Story: GenPals Solves a Mystery

Charlene Hazzard, CharAH1@aol.com (NY "G" families), and Mary Martha Von Ville McGrath, marymarthavonville@ hotmail.com (Ohio "G" families), solved a mystery through GenPals (www.geocities.com/genpals2002/ChatAndCommunity .htm).

"When new to the Internet, I found a message on Guenther/Ginther/ Gunter/Gunther (from Charlene Hazzard), and when I finally figured out how to write a message, got an answer from her. She had my line into what is now a different country in Europe and had it back two generations from there!"

Mary Martha had a town name of Herstom in Germany. Charlene knew that this was the common nickname for Herbitzheim, which is now in France. Charlene had communicated directly with the Herbitzheim (aka Herstom) town historian until he died in 2000. "I had only a nickname for the town of origin, and Charlene explained the real name of the town. By the way, her message was from 1999, and she is the only one who had info from Europe," said Mary Martha. "What an answer to a 30-year-old prayer. Thank you, God!"

Mary Martha and Charlene became the coordinators on GenPals for the descendants of this family who settled in New York and Ohio (many are still in both states). Mary Martha found Charlene's message four years after it was saved, truly a miracle in their book.

Yahoo! Messenger

Yahoo! Messenger works just like MSN and AIM. Go to www.yahoo.com, click Chat, click Genealogy, and pick a room for Web-based chats, or you can download Yahoo! Messenger to set up your own private chat room. Join the Yahoo! group Genealogy Chat Friends http://groups.yahoo.com/ group/genealogychatfriends to view the calendar of chats and transcripts of past chats.

ICQ

ICQ (available at www.icq.com) is a system similar to AIM that's free of charge. ICQ is a one-on-one or multiple-person chat in the instant-messaging model. When you're online, it registers your presence with the secure ICQ server so that other ICQ users can "see" you. You can keep a buddy list and be informed when your buddies log on. You can send messages and files, even talk by voice or send live video. All the while, the program runs in the background, taking up a minimal amount of memory and Net resources, so you can continue to surf the Web or run your genealogy program. You can start ICQ and then look for ongoing genealogy chats, as shown in Figure 7-1, at www.icq.com/groups/browse_folder.php?tid = 717 (or go to www.icq.com, click Groups at the top, and click Genealogy under the Family And Friends subheading).

Chat and instant-messaging programs have their own interfaces, but share many of the same functions. Let me urge you to read the Help file for your program. Most of the time, the Help file is a mini-manual that will tell you how to best use the client.

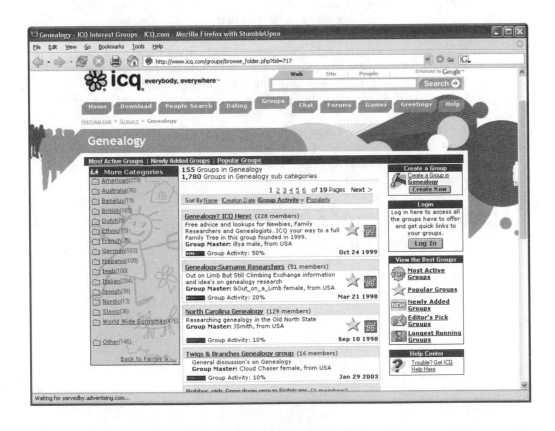

FIGURE 7-1. *ICQ has several regular chats on genealogy.*

Where to Chat

When you are ready to type or talk over the Internet, several sites have regularly scheduled chats.

About.Genealogy.com

About.Genealogy.com has a list of regularly scheduled chats at http://genealogy.about.com/library/blchatsched.htm. Monday nights are topical, how-to chats moderated by Kimberly Powell, the about .genealogy.com leader. The topic changes each week, often reflecting user suggestions. On Friday nights, the chats are simply open and, as of this writing, unmoderated. If you would like a chance to be the moderator, there is a link to volunteer!

Acadian-Cajun Chat Room

Every evening at 7:00 p.m. Eastern folks meet for scheduled chats to discuss Acadian/Cajun genealogy at www.acadian.org/chat.html. Most are unmoderated, although users may volunteer to moderate one on a certain topic. The site uses a Java window that takes IRC-style commands.

AfriGeneas Chat

At www.afrigeneas.com/chat, you can take part in nightly moderated and unmoderated chats on African-American genealogy. AfriGeneas will be profiled in-depth in Chapter 13.

Genpals Chat and Community

This group, located at www.geocities.com/genpals2002/ ChatAndCommunity.htm, formed when MSN started to charge for its original Genpals chat room. While an MSN Community Group chat room remains, it a private chat room for members of the GenPals Community Group and requires membership to log in. Membership to the GenPals MSN Community is free.

Browse the community pages; look through the photo albums, recipe pages, jokes, and success stories; and above all, visit the surname posting boards. While the primary language spoken in the GenPals Chat Room is English, GenPals does boast members fluent in Dutch, French, German, and several other languages.

Genealogy.com Chat

At http://chat.genealogy.com, you can discuss any and all surnames you like. This chat is not the place for newbies looking for techniques or learning experiences. It is unmoderated—that is, there are many conversations going on at once. Read the rules and tips before you try it; though browser-based, it works much like the old IRC programs, with commands preceded by a forward slash (/). Do not use your e-mail address as a login name, as spammers do lurk!

Genealogy Lookup Chat

At www.rootsweb.com/~genealogylookup/genchat.html, you will find a great group of people who help each other out with genealogy chores, as well as conducting nightly chats on topics such as German genealogy and the Daughters of the American Revolution. All the chats are moderated, and there are at least four chat rooms every night. All times posted on the site are Eastern Standard Time.

IIGS Chat Rooms

One of the last IRC holdouts, the International Internet Genealogy Society's chat rooms at www.iigs.org/irc/index.htm.en (see Figure 7-2) have two advantages: an international emphasis with many languages and many experts. The disadvantages: You must download an IRC client (the site has links to several simple, free ones) and learn the commands, such as /join and /block. Still, this is one of the few places where you can discuss German genealogy in German!

Looking 4 Kin

At www.looking4kin.com, you can find an all-surname chat from JustGen. The chats have a Canadian emphasis, but not exclusively.

New Brunswick Chat Line

At http://new-brunswick.net/chat/index.html, the Java-based chat rooms emphasize Canadian maritime history and genealogy. Events are moderated; unmoderated chats happen on the fly.

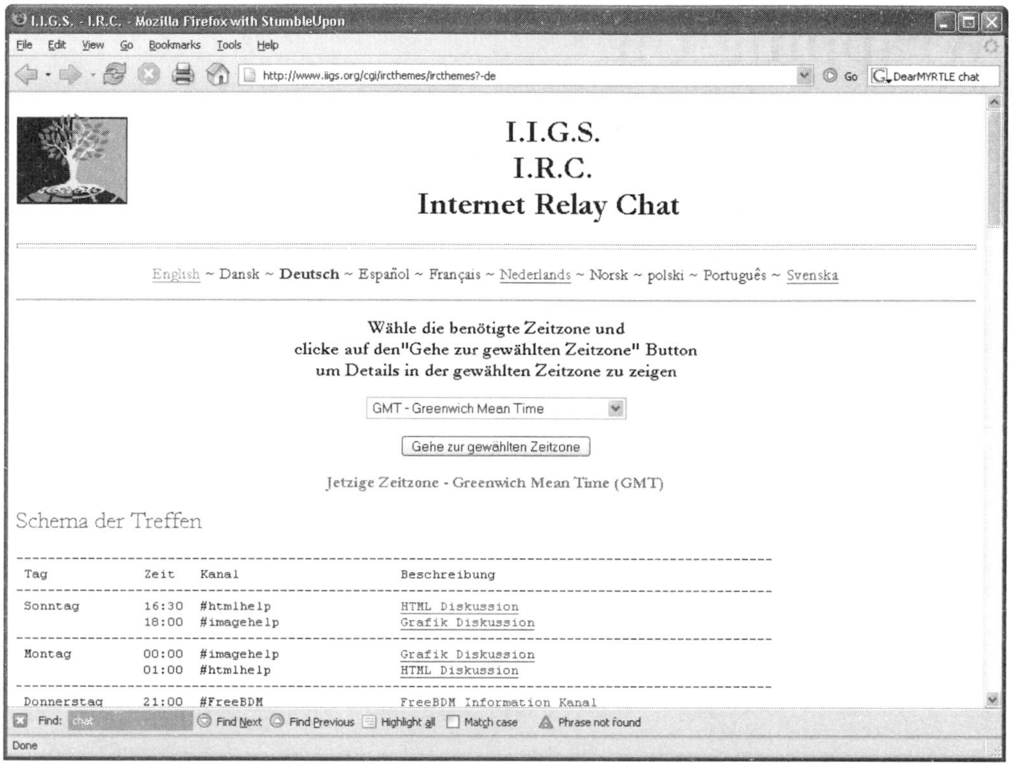

FIGURE 7-2. *IIGS chat rooms have regular sessions in German and other languages.*

> **Note**
>
> *As with any online genealogy topic, search your favorite portal (Google, Yahoo!, MSN, Excite, etc.) for "genealogy chat" (or "geneology chat"), and see what comes up!*

Wrapping Up

♦ Moderated chats are like online classes, with exchange of information or a question-and-answer format.

♦ Instant messaging is the most common form of chat.

♦ All chat forms can be addictive—handle with care!

Chapter 8

Genealogy Mailing Lists and Forums

With blogs and Really Simple Syndication (RSS) feeds, you can learn from experts. With mailing lists and forums, you can learn from other genealogists like you.

Electronic mail (e-mail) lists are discussion groups based on e-mail messages. All subscribers can send and receive e-mail from the list. Messages sent to the mailing list get forwarded to everyone who subscribes to it. Replies to messages from the list get sent as well, where they are forwarded to all participants. And so it goes.

Mailing lists can be completely automated, with a program taking care of subscribing people to the list, forwarding messages, and removing people from the list. Or, people can get into the loop, handling any and all of the mailing list functions that programs can do. Such "moderated" mailing lists can take two forms: They might have restricted memberships, where you need to be approved to subscribe, or a moderator (or moderators) might let anyone join but would review each incoming message before it gets distributed, preventing inappropriate material from getting on to the list.

Forums are message-based systems where the messages are held on a website, waiting for you to come read them. Most forums are divided into topics, which are general categories of messages. Within the topics are more specific messages called threads.

Some may have an option to e-mail you a notice when a message is posted that you have an interest in. Others may have the option to e-mail you all new messages one by one or in a collection called a digest, which makes them like a mailing list to the user. Some forums are moderated; most genealogy ones are.

Many mailing lists and forums focus specifically on genealogy. In addition, many more lists and forums, although not specifically for genealogists, cover topics of interest to genealogists, such as ethnic groups and historic events.

General Tips

With a decent mail program, participating in mailing lists is easy. You simply have to figure out how to subscribe, manage, and unsubscribe to a list. Often, the instructions are included in the mailing list's home page.

Subscribing to Mailing Lists

Say you want to know more about genealogy in the Mobile, Alabama, area. Sure enough, there's a mailing list. Searching for `Mobile Genealogy Mail List` in Google, you find the Genealogy Resources on the Internet page with this listing:

```
AL-MOBILEBAY. A mailing list, sponsored by the Mobile
Genealogical Society (http://www.siteone.com/clubs/mgs/), for
anyone with a genealogical interest in the Mobile Bay, Alabama,
area -- specifically Mobile and Baldwin Counties in Alabama
plus the bordering counties in Mississippi (George, Greene,
Jackson), Alabama (Clarke, Escambia, Monroe, Washington), and
Florida (Escambia). Topics for the list include genealogical
queries and discussions of resources having to do with the
above counties and various time periods in the area's history
such as the Louisiana Purchase (Mobile was the first capital of
Louisiana), Spanish West Florida, the Confederate period, the
Mississippi Territory, etc. In addition, "press releases" from
genealogical societies and libraries in the aforementioned
counties are welcome. To subscribe send "subscribe" to
al-mobilebay-l-request@rootsweb.com (mail mode) or
al-mobilebay-d-request@rootsweb.com (digest mode).
```

Now you know how to subscribe. As you are sending this message as a command to a mailing list program, it's best to put "END" on the line below "subscribe" (see Figure 8-1). That way, should your automatic signature slip in, it will be ignored by the list program. If you do not do this, it's possible you will get a message back describing all the different ways the program does not understand what you sent.

You will receive a welcome message, which you should save to a text or document file. It will tell you how to manage your subscription to get off the list, suspend it temporarily, and prevent your own messages to the list from coming to you from the server.

Most mailing lists have two e-mail addresses. You use one address to subscribe or change how you use the mailing list and the other to post messages to the other people on the mailing list. Some mailing lists might have a third address to use for certain administrative chores, such as reporting some violation of the list's rules to the moderator. One of the most common and annoying mistakes one sees on mail lists is when someone posts `"unsubscribe"` to the message's address, instead of the same address used to subscribe. Some folks simply *[screenshot of an email message window — "Untitled - Message (HTML)" with To... field "al-mobilebay-l-request@rootsweb.com", empty Cc and Subject fields, and message body reading:]*

Subscribe
END

FIGURE 8-1. *If you're in doubt whether an automatic signature might slip into a message to a listserv program, put "END" after the subscribe command line.*

refuse to look at the directions and continue to post `"unsubscribe"` messages to the message address over and over until someone flames them. Don't be one of these people.

Note that in some mailing list programs, you can send a command—`who` or `reveal`—to find out who is subscribed to a certain list. To prevent your address from being listed in the `who` command, you often have to send a specific command to the list server. The welcome message will tell you how, but it's usually the command `conceal`.

Success Story:
Board Leads to Reunion

The most meaningful success I have had was because of posting to boards. I found an aunt I never knew I had. Got to go meet her. She lives about 40 miles from me. I was adopted, so finding a biological relative was great. It was from an old posting, so keep posting everywhere. You never know when you will see results!

—G.F.S. Tupper,
host of Maine Genealogy chat, Beginners Chat,
and Beyond Beginners Chat on AOL

Mailing List Example: ROOTS-L

Imagine a worldwide, never-ending conversation about genealogy, where novices and experts exchange help, information, ideas, and gossip. Now imagine this conversation is conducted by e-mail, so you needn't worry about missing anything. You've just imagined ROOTS-L, the grandparent of genealogy mailing lists on the Internet.

ROOTS-L has spawned entire generations of newer genealogy mailing lists—some large, some small—but this is the original. The mailing list page at http://lists.rootsweb.com hosts over 30,000 mailing lists about genealogy and history (see Figure 8-2). ROOTS-L is the oldest and still the largest.

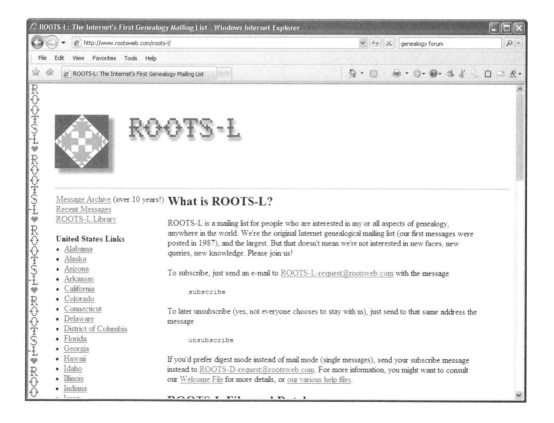

FIGURE 8-2. *ROOTS-L is the grandparent of all genealogy mailing lists.*

To subscribe, you need to do two things:

1. Make sure your e-mail inbox is large enough to hold the volume of messages you'll receive. If you have limited space, use digest mode, if available, and check your inbox more than once a day.

2. Send an e-mail message to roots-l-request@rootsweb.org, with the message "Subscribe." You don't need to include anything else in the message—no signature block, no name or address.

Some ROOTS-L Rules

ROOTS-L clearly states its rules in its welcome message. It would be wise to apply these rules to every mailing list you join, whether or not they're explicitly stated:

- The list isn't a place to bring up wars of the past or to discuss religion or politics.

- Advertising or selling a product is not, in general, acceptable. You can, however, post a new-product announcement, as in "I have a new genealogy software product" or "I have just published my genealogy."

- Make sure that you spell the word "genealogy" correctly in all your messages.

- Don't post messages longer than about 150 lines, unless you're sure they'll be of general interest.

- Don't include a "surname signature" in your messages. These are lists of surnames that appear at the end of every message some people send. The surnames play havoc with the list's archive searches, so don't use them.

- Don't post copyrighted material, such as newspaper articles or e-mail messages sent to you by other people.

- Quote only enough of previous messages to be clear about what the discussion is about. Never quote previous messages in their entirety, because this bogs down the list.

- You should search all the archives of the ROOTS-L mailing list for keywords, such as your surnames and places. Sometimes, you'll find someone posted years ago something that you wanted to know.

Success Story: The Web Helps a Mobility-Challenged Genealogist

Being mobility-challenged and on a very limited income, I have to depend mostly on the Internet at this time for my genealogy work, and I've had some success.

I had a query on an Irsch surname board for my great-grandfather and the fact he had married a Pitts in Noxubee, Mississippi, in 1860. I just happened to decide to go to the Pitts surname board and posted the same query for a Lucretia Emmaline Pitts, who had married a Frank Irsch.

I received a tentative confirmation from someone whose great-grandfather had a sister who had married an Irsch about that time. A few back-and-forths later, we thought we might have a connection; I asked if she had ever heard the names Aunt Em and Uncle Henry Hill. I had heard my grandmother speak of them, but didn't know if they were blood relatives.

We both knew we had established the connection. "Aunt Em" was the sister of her great-great-great-grandfather, Lafayette Newton Pitts, and another sister, Lucretia, had married Frank Irsch. Their father's name was James W. Pitts and their mother's name was Mary. We still haven't discovered her maiden name.

She had a picture of some of the Irsch family that Lizzie Eaton/Bennett had identified for them as her brother and family and Grandma Pitts. She wasn't sure if the older woman was her Grandma Pitts, but she didn't think so. Lizzie Eaton/Bennett was my grandmother, and if she identified the older woman as Grandma Pitts, it would have been her grandmother, Mary ?-? Pitts. I remember my mother telling me of Aunt Annie Irsch and Grandma Pitts sending Christmas gifts when she was little. Now we proudly know we have a picture of our shared great-great-great-grandmother. We are working on other shared lines, but I would call this a wonderful tale of success from the Internet!

— Louise McDonald

Losing Contact with a Mailing List

It's possible you'll stop receiving messages from a mailing list, even though you didn't unsubscribe. If this happens, it may be because:

♦   Your Internet service provider (ISP) could be having trouble with their e-mail service. Any service can have intermittent problems. Sometimes, a whole section of the Internet might be out of order for a few minutes or even for hours. In fact, AOL has had such problems in the past, as have many other online services. If all your e-mail stops coming in—not just mail from a mailing list—this could be the cause. Your mailing list may be sharing an IP address with a known spammer, through no fault of the list owner. Contact your ISP to tell them to let your mailing list through as legitimate mail.

♦ You're using a different e-mail address than the one you used to subscribe the mailing list. Most e-mail server programs will only send to the return address of the subscribe message.

If all else fails, subscribe to the mailing list again. That should get the messages flowing for you.

Forums of Interest to Online Genealogists

Forums are message exchanges on a website or portal. You can visit the forum often to see if there are new messages, but many forums now have a notification option. You can specify that you want to know when someone posts to the "SPENCER" board, for example, and an e-mail message will be sent to you when that happens.

Genealogy forums abound on the Internet. Genealogy.com has 14,000; ROOTSWEB/Ancestry.com has 161,000 message boards. The best way to find what you want is to use a search engine for the topics.

For example, I would like to discuss Powells in South Carolina. In Google, I could search:

```
Powell genealogy forum
```

That gets about 248,000 hits, the top ones from Genealogy.com, Genealogy.About.com, etc. Now I can narrow that by clicking Advanced Search in Google and adding South Carolina to the terms. That cuts the results to 69,000.

Another good technique is to use a search engine to search for the name, date, and place you are looking for. This will result in hits from both forum and mailing list archives. Or visit some of the top sites listed in Chapter 19 and search those forums.

Finally, search the portals mentioned in previous chapters. A short sampling:

- **JewishGen (www.jewishgen.org)**   The Jewish Genealogy site hosts two or three dozen groups based on geography, projects of the site, and other interests. Go to the home page, and scroll down to Discussion Groups; then click the link for Special Interest Groups (SIGS) for a current listing.

- **USRoots/Rootsquest (www.rootsquest.com)**   This site has surname-based mailing lists. You can e-mail the site owners to start your own mailing list. Of course, before you start one, check ROOTS-L, FamilySearch, and other sites to be certain that you aren't replicating an existing list.

- **Yahoo! (http://groups.yahoo.com)**   Yahoo! has thousands of discussion groups based on surnames, geography, and ethnicity. Some are public, which means anyone can post to them, and some require you to sign up before you can post to them. Go to the Yahoo! Groups page, and search for "genealogy" and/or the surnames you need.

Finding More Mailing Lists

Even though it may seem like we've covered more mailing lists than you can shake a stick at, many more exist. To find more, first check out the ROOTSWEB website for their ever-growing list. If you point your Web browser to www.rootsweb.org/ ~ maillist, you'll have access to the hundreds of mailing lists hosted by ROOTSWEB. Also, John Fuller maintains a categorized directory of genealogy mailing lists at www.rootsweb.com/ ~ jfuller/gen_mail.html (see Figure 8-3).

Cyndi's List (www.CyndisList.com/magazine.htm) is a good site to visit to keep up on the latest in mailing lists and newsletters.

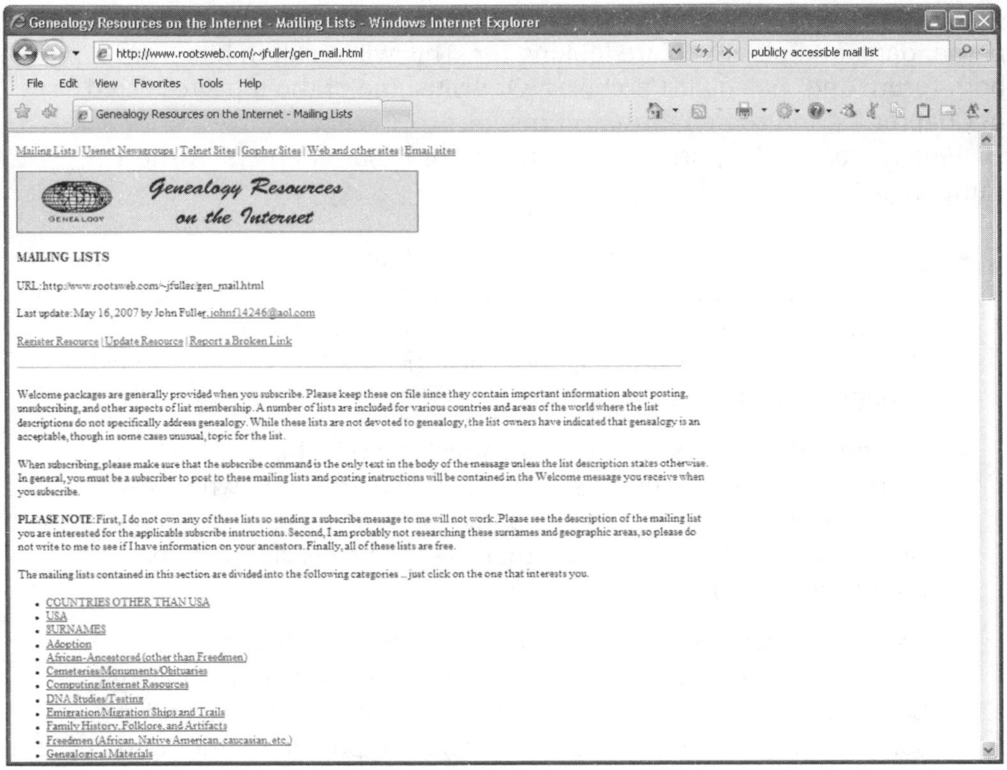

FIGURE 8-3. *John Fuller maintains a good catalog of genealogy mailing lists.*

Wrapping Up

- ◆ E-mail discussion lists bring other genealogists right to your e-mail inbox.

- ◆ When you subscribe to a mailing list, always save the reply message, which usually has the "unsubscribe" instructions as well as the rules of the list.

- ◆ Forums are usually associated with websites. You can go to the site to read the latest messages or have them e-mailed to you.

- ◆ Most mailing lists are interactive and have one address for subscribing and another for posting messages.

Part III

The Nitty Gritty: Places to Find Names, Dates, and Places

Chapter 9

Vital Records and Historical Documents

Vital records are the milestones of life: birth, marriage, and death. Other important records are naturalization, census records, and land ownership. More and more, you can find at least clues to these records online; in some cases, you can get digitized versions of the records themselves.

Historical documents, such as censuses, diaries, wills, court cases, and government publications, can put flesh on the bones of our ancestors, so to speak, when they mention individuals. These are often held at archives and libraries. In this chapter you'll learn that some things can be found online, while others can be ordered online, and still others you have to visit in person or ask for by mail, but you might be able to print the form you need from an Internet site.

Among the best of the online sites maintained by the United States federal government are the Library of Congress (LOC) and the National Archives and Records Administration (NARA). Both the LOC and NARA sites have been revamped recently, with links to genealogy guides, tips, and resources gathered together for easy access. You'll find these sites useful to help you decide what to ask for by mail or if you should visit in person. You'll eventually want to visit a NARA branch or the LOC in person because, although many resources are online, not every book or document is available that way.

Other important federal records online are the Bureau of Land Management records of original land grants and patents, immigration records, and naturalization records. Some states and counties also have certain vital records and censuses—sometimes online and sometimes just the contact information for ordering a copy.

This chapter gives you a short overview of what's where and how to access the resources of these sites.

Vital Records

In the United States, most birth, adoption, death, divorce, and marriage records will be at the state level, although some counties can help. Usually, you have to write to the organization that has the records and enclose a check to get a certified copy. You have to have a date and a place to go with a name in order to find where an ancestor's vital records are.

In rare cases, you can find the actual document online, unless it is more than a century old and some volunteer group has scanned or transcribed it to be uploaded to the Internet. Furthermore, as discussed in Chapter 1, professional genealogists insist on a certified copy, if not the original document itself, for proof of genealogy.

To get a certified copy of any these records, write or go to the vital statistics office in the state or area where the event occurred. Addresses and fees are often found online at the state's website. Usually, a fee for each document will cover copying and mailing. Each time you request a record, include a check or money order payable to the correct office and in the correct amount for the number of copies requested; sometimes, a credit card will be accepted. Don't send cash.

When you find information on an office, a phone number is usually included. Before you send off your request, be sure to call to verify that the rates haven't changed. Also, in many cases, you can find an online page with the address for obtaining current information, and sometimes you can even order the records online by credit card. Often, you will have to include something like a photocopy of your driver's license as well.

Other steps to take:

- Type or print all names and addresses in the letter.

- Give the following facts when writing for birth or death records:

  - Full name of person whose record is requested

  - Sex

  - Parents' names, including maiden name of mother

  - Month, day, and year of birth or death

  - Place of birth or death (city or town, county, and state; and name of hospital, if known)

  - Purpose for which copy is needed

  - Relationship to person whose record is requested

  - Daytime telephone number with area code

- Give the following facts when writing for marriage records:

  - Full names of bride and groom

  - Month, day, and year of marriage

  - Place of marriage (city or town, county, and state)

- ◆ Purpose for which copy is needed
- ◆ Relationship to persons whose record is requested
- ◆ Daytime telephone number with area code
- ◆ Give the following facts when writing for divorce records:
  - ◆ Full names of husband and wife
  - ◆ Date of divorce or annulment
  - ◆ Place of divorce or annulment
  - ◆ Type of final decree
  - ◆ Purpose for which copy is needed
  - ◆ Relationship to persons whose record is requested
  - ◆ Daytime telephone number with area code

Note

Don't include your whole genealogy; simply include the pertinent data for the record you want. County clerks aren't going to read through a long narrative to find out what they need to do.

- ◆ VitalRec.Com is a great place to start. This site has information not only on all U.S. states and territories, but also on Canada, Australia, New Zealand, and several European nations.
- ◆ The National Center for Health Statistics has a good how-to site at www.cdc.gov/nchs/howto/w2w/w2welcom.htm.
- ◆ Use your favorite search engine to look for the terms `vital records` and the geographical area you need. In Figure 9-1, I found the Bedfordshire/Luton, UK, archives site with just such a search at http://www.bedfordshire.gov.uk/CommunityAndLiving/ArchivesAndRecordOffice/ArchivesAndRecordOffice.aspx.

These sources are great for 20th-century records. However, if you need information on earlier centuries, city, regional, and national archives may be your best bet.

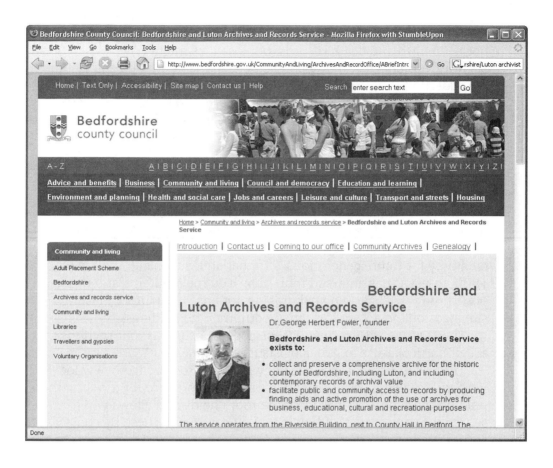

FIGURE 9-1. *The county of Bedfordshire has a site with details on what you can ask them to copy for you, what fees are charged, and how long it might take.*

For example, in the state of Tennessee, many vital records, such as births, deaths, and marriages, were not recorded by the state before 1908. Four cities—Chattanooga, Knoxville, Nashville, and Memphis—did keep local records that are now available through the Tennessee State Library and Archives. Searches of these records can be requested by mail, if you know the year of the event (birth, death, etc.). The website for the Memphis Public Library has an online index to Memphis death records that covers the years 1848-1945 at http://history.memphislibrary.org. You can get land grant records, too. The fees for these services range from $5 to $20. Go to the Tennessee State Archives site (www.tennessee.gov/tsla/index.htm) for the forms and links.

Tennessee is quite typical: Before Social Security, many states did not keep birth and death records, but localities might have. When Social Security was enacted, many people born in the late 19th century had to request a birth certificate be created for them; marriage records in some states were also lax until Social Security. In these cases, you must ask for a delayed certificate, that is, one that was created at the request of the person involved after the fact.

Library of Congress

The mission of the Library of Congress (www.loc.gov) is to "make its resources available and useful to the Congress and the American people and to sustain and preserve a universal collection of knowledge and creativity for future generations." To that end, since its founding in 1800, the LOC has amassed more than 100 million items and become one of the world's leading cultural institutions. The Library of Congress site gives online access to a small portion of the holdings.

The LOC Local History and Genealogy website has four sections that are of particular use to genealogists (see Figure 9-2).

The Local History and Genealogy Reading Room page (www.loc .gov/rr/genealogy) has information on how to prepare for a visit to the reading room. It describes what the room holds and allows you to search the card catalog of holdings. You can search these by subject, author, and other criteria.

Many of the items do not circulate; however, an interlibrary loan may be possible. For libraries in the United States, the Library of Congress serves as a source for material not available through local, state, or regional libraries. A book circulated this way must be used on the premises of the borrowing library; it becomes a temporary reference for that library's collection for up to 60 days. Requests are accepted from academic, public, and special libraries that make their own material available through participation in an interlibrary loan system. Participation is usually indicated by membership in one of the major U.S. bibliographic networks (OCLC, RLIN) or by a listing in the American Library Directory (Bowker) or the Directory of Special Libraries and Information Centers (Gale). So if you find an item that you feel may help your genealogy search, check with your local public library to see if they can participate. You will need the LOC call number (the LOC does not use the Dewey decimal system), author, title, and date of publication.

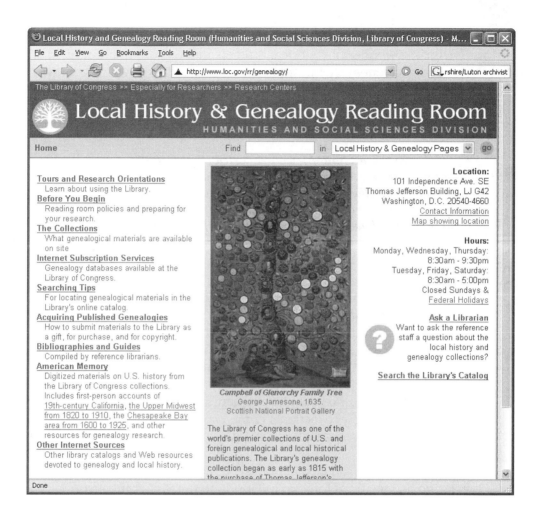

FIGURE 9-2. *The Library of Congress website has a section on history and genealogy full of useful information for genealogists.*

Other sections you will want to explore include:

♦ **American Memory** This section contains documents, photographs, movies, and sound recordings that tell some of America's story. The direct link is http://memory.loc.gov.

♦ **Research Tools** This section of the site offers many online databases and connections to resources at other sites. The direct link is www.loc.gov/rr.

- ♦ **American Treasures**   This section of the site is of interest more for the wonderful historical artifacts found there than for any specific genealogy information. The direct link is www.loc.gov/exhibits/treasures.

> ## Note
>
> *If you're researching African-American roots, you'll want to look at the African-American Odyssey page at http://memory.loc.gov/ammem/aaohtml/aohome.html. This exhibition examines the African-American quest for full citizenship and contains primary source material, as well as links to other African-American materials at the LOC.*

On American Memory home page, you can click Collection Finder to explore other primary source material. The collections are grouped by subject, then time, then place, and then library division. You can also browse by format if you want a sound file or picture. Each collection has its own distinct character and subject matter, as well as narrative information to describe the content of the collection. Whereas searching all the collections at once could leave items of interest to you "buried" in a long list, visiting a collection's home page and reading the descriptive information about the collection can give you more direction in finding what you want.

Click the Social Sciences link on the Collection Finder page, and you'll find listings from folklore in Florida to the San Francisco earthquake of 1906 to first-person narratives of the American South.

The drawbacks to the Collection Finder are that it's a catalog you browse—not an index you search—and it doesn't always list every single item in a collection, but instead gives an overview of the topic.

For instance, if only a few items in a collection pertain to the broad topic of "agriculture," the collection might not appear under that topic. Clicking a category is like saying, "I want to see a collection mainly about a certain subject." The complete list of subjects is at http://memory.loc.gov/. Say you know an ancestor owned a hotel in the early 20th century. In that case, the collection "Hotels 1870–1930" might help you research that ancestor.

You can search for phrases or keywords across all collections and look at essays, images, and primary source material, but do realize you'll get a lot of hits. Searching for the word "genealogy" across all collections gave me 168 hits, which included a genealogy of Pocahontas, letters written to Abraham Lincoln about genealogy (see Figure 9-3), and Memoirs of a Southern Woman Within the Lines (Civil War).

Some of the items you can find in the American Memory section include:

♦ Almost 200 books describing the personal experiences of individuals in and on the way to California during and after the Gold Rush

♦ Hundreds of objects dealing with the Women's Suffrage movement

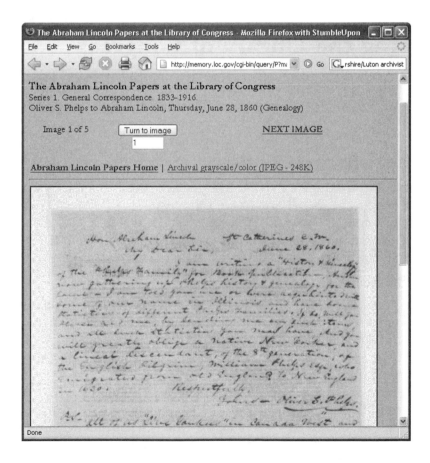

FIGURE 9-3. *You can see a scan of this entire letter on the LOC Abraham Lincoln Papers at the Library of Congress online.*

♦ Significant and interesting documents from Americans obscure to famous, as collected in the first 100 years of the Library of Congress

♦ Manuscript Division American Life Histories: Manuscripts from the Federal Writer's Project, 1936–1940

A third area of the American Memory section of the LOC for you to explore is the Maps section. On the Subject page mentioned previously, click Geography. Then you can search collections containing hundreds of digitized maps from 1639–1988. You can find city maps, conservation maps, exploration maps, immigration and settlement maps, military maps, and transportation maps, to name a few. And the amazing thing is this wealth of maps is only a tiny part of the LOC's full 4.5-million-item Geography and Map Division holdings.

Using the Library of Congress

Click Using The Library Of Congress on the home page, and you can click your way through an excellent tutorial on the ins and outs of researching the library in person. If you need to make a trip to the LOC, reading this section first can save you some time and frustration.

The Library Today

This link from the home page tells you about new exhibits, collections, and events at the LOC and its website. Visit it at least once a week, because anything new posted to the website will be announced here. The direct link is http://www.loc.gov/today/.

Research Tools

The Research Tools page at www.lcweb.loc.gov/rr/tools.html takes you to a large set of useful links of interest for researchers, both on the LOC site and on other websites. These include desk references you can use on the Web, the LOC card catalog of all materials (including those not online), and special databases.

The Vietnam Era Prisoner of War/Missing in Action and Task Force Russia Databases at http://lcweb2.loc.gov/pow/powhome.html are examples of databases. This URL takes you to a page that gives you access to a massive database of over 137,000 records pertaining to United States military personnel listed as unaccounted for as of December 1991. At the bottom of this page is a link to Task Force Russia at http://lcweb2.loc.gov/frd/tfrquery.html, a set of documents dealing with Americans who are believed to have been held in the former Soviet Union.

At the page www.loc.gov/rr/askalib/, you can click the Local History/Genealogy link. Here's what you can get here:

♦ Basic research assistance related to genealogy, local history in the United States, and heraldry

♦ Answers to queries requiring resources that are unique to the Library of Congress

♦ Response within five business days

However, you cannot get extensive research in genealogy or heraldry. If you cannot find the answers to your questions on the general links, you can e-mail your question to a librarian. Furthermore, certain topics, such as American Memory, have specific times of day when a librarian is available for a live, Web-based chat.

National Archives and Records Administration

The Library of Congress and the National Archives and Records Administration together are a treasure trove for the family historian. However, using these resources can also be like a treasure hunt!

Unlike a library, where you walk up to the card catalog computer, type a subject, find the Dewey Decimal System number, walk to the shelf, and get the book, the archive is organized by government agency. Furthermore, what you find in that catalog at the archives may be a book, a manuscript, or a government whitepaper. This complexity means that first-time archive users often need help.

At the NARA, whether online or in person, you can get that help. At many national archives, that is not the case. For example, Britain's Public Record Office has rows of volumes listing the contents of files for the Admiralty, the Foreign Office, and Scotland Yard, but the polite archivist there will simply point you to the right shelf. France's Archives Nationales and Germany's Bundesarchiv operate the same way. Though the NARA has a long tradition of helping researchers one on one, that may not be the case for long if funding woes continue (see Note).

> *Note*
>
> *Something you may want to write to your congressional delegation about: Starting in early 2007, more than a million cubic feet of documents, nearly enough to fill the Washington Monument, were in need of being organized, described, and filed. This backlog was caused by the fact that the budget for NARA has not increased in several years. This led to a shortage of qualified people to maintain the collection. Just as bad was the impact on the archivists who help researchers. Written requests for information in the past were usually answered within 10 working days 95 percent of the time, but in 2007, that dropped to 75 percent. In the military and civil branches, the backlog of unanswered letters used to be 15 to 30; in early 2007, it averaged 115 to 130. The financial squeeze has also cut off-peak hours to two nights and one Saturday each month, making research difficult for visitors from outside Washington, D.C., and for anyone who works a 9-to-5 job. The NARA is slowly being starved for funds.*

Freedman's Bureau

Archivist of the United States Allen Weinstein announced in early 2007 that the National Archives completed the five-year project to preserve and microfilm the field office records of the Bureau of Refugees, Freedmen, and Abandoned Lands (the Freedmen's Bureau). Now the LOC has 1,000 rolls of microfilm reproducing over one million Bureau field office records from the former Confederate states, the border states, and the District of Columbia. All of the microfilm series of the field office records are available free of charge for research at the National Archives Building in Washington, D.C., and at the National Archives 13 regional archives nationwide.

Following the Civil War, the Freedmen's Bureau helped former slaves make the transition from slavery to freedom by issuing food and clothing, operating hospitals and refugee camps, establishing schools, helping legalize marriages, supervising labor agreements, and working with African American soldiers and sailors and their heirs to secure back pay, bounty payments, and pensions. The records created during the course of these activities are a rich source of documentation of the black experience in late-19th-century America, and are essential for the study of African-American genealogy and Southern social history.

Included in these extraordinary records are registers that give the names, ages, and former occupations of freedmen, as well as names and residences of former owners. For some states, there are marriage registers that provide the names, addresses, and ages of husbands and wives and their children. There are also census lists, detailed labor and apprenticeship agreements, complaint registers, rosters with personal data about black veterans (including company and regiment), and a host of documentation concerning the social and economic conditions of the black family.

These are available for $65 per roll for domestic orders and $68 per roll for foreign orders—details on how to order are on the website. Also, don't miss the section of American Memory that is devoted to African-American research. It has several pages describing how to research African-American and Native American genealogy in the NARA site (see Figure 9-4) that may help you.

Other NARA Areas to Explore

You can click the Research Room link in the navigation bar to the left of the home page and go to Genealogy from there, or you can go straight to www.archives.gov/research_room/genealogy. Here you'll find information for beginners, such as the About Genealogy Research page and a list of research topics in genealogy with links to NARA resources that deal with them.

More advanced genealogists will want to read about the census catalogs, the online catalogs, Soundex indexing, and the latest additions to the collection. All genealogists should read the frequently asked questions (FAQ) file and the latest list of genealogy workshops.

After touring this general help area, you're ready to tackle the specific resources on the NARA site.

Access to Archival Databases

You can search various subsets of the NARA holdings from their Web databases, starting at http://aad.archives.gov/aad.

The Access to Archival Databases (AAD) is a searchable set of records preserved permanently in NARA. These records identify specific persons, geographic areas, organizations, and dates over a wide variety of civilian and military data, and have many genealogical, social, political, and economic research uses.

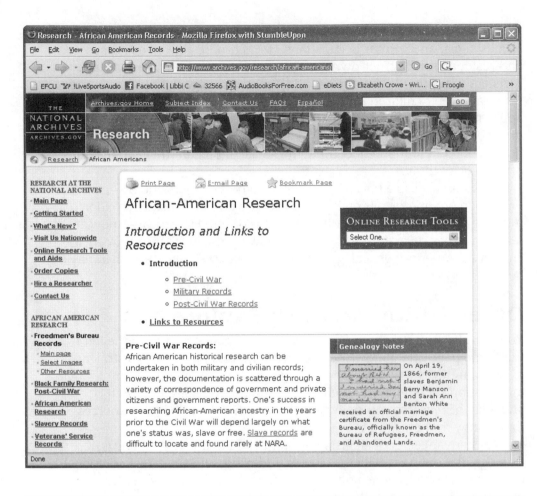

FIGURE 9-4. *At www.archives.gov/research/african-americans/, you can find a guide to researching African-American and Native American genealogy.*

The most popular of these databases are:

♦ World War II Army Enlistment Records

♦ Records for Passengers Who Arrived at the Port of New York During the Irish Famine

♦ Records of World War II Prisoners of War

♦ Central Foreign Policy Files

♦ Records of Awards and Decorations of Honor During the Vietnam Conflict

For further information about all of NARA's electronic records holdings, including those not in AAD (see Figure 9-5), see the Electronic and Special Media Records page (www.archives.gov/research/electronic-records/index.html) or NARA's online catalog, ARC.

ARC

The Archival Research Catalog (ARC) at www.archives.gov/research/arc is the online catalog of about 50 percent of NARA's nationwide holdings in the Washington, D.C. area, Regional Archives, and Presidential Libraries.

You can do keyword, digitized image, and location searches on this catalog, and in the advanced search, look for organizations, persons,

FIGURE 9-5. *The Access to Archival Databases includes some war and immigration records.*

and topics. The NARA staff is working to expand the catalog, and eventually it will reflect all the holdings. Check this site about once every two weeks to see the updates on what has been added.

Part of what is so wonderful about this updated catalog is the quick access to specific collections, such as the Guion-Miller Roll Index and the Index to the Final Rolls (Dawes)—two censuses of Native American populations from the 1800s and early 1900s—the World War II Army and Army Air Force Casualty List, and the World War II Navy, Marine, and Coast Guard Casualty List.

ALIC

The Archives Library Information Center (ALIC) is for professionals such as NARA staff and librarians nationwide. Its website is www.archives.gov/research/alic.

ALIC provides access to information on American history and government, archival administration, information management, and government documents to NARA staff, archives- and records-management professionals, and the general public.

On the ALIC page, you'll see links to quick searches of the book catalog, NARA publications on research, and special collections. On the right of the page is a set of links under What's New In ALIC For Genealogists? Here you'll find the latest additions, such as a listing of genealogical CD-ROMS.

On the left of the page, under Reference At Your Desk, you'll see a list of topics, including Genealogy and History. The former has general links to NARA pages already covered in this chapter, as well as links to other websites that can help with genealogy. The latter does the same for general history sites.

ERA

The Electronic Records Archives (ERA) will theoretically be helpful to genealogists a hundred years from now. The goal is to preserve the electronic records of the government, such as memos, e-mails, presidential speeches, and so on. As such, it has only recent records and is still a pilot program.

Microfilm Publications Search

From the NARA Genealogy page, you can click Search Microfilm Catalogs. The catalogs list the various microfilms you can purchase, rent, or view onsite from NARA; the 3,400 microfilms can be searched by keyword, microfilm ID, record group number, and/or NARA location. Most of NARA's microfilm lists and descriptive pamphlets are not online.

By searching for microfilm publications in the Microfilm Publications Catalog, however, you will be able to find out if a roll list or descriptive pamphlet is available. You will need to contact one of the NARA locations listed in the Viewing Location field(s) of the microfilm publication description to find out how to get a copy of the descriptive pamphlet or roll list.

Federal Register Publications

The *Federal Register* is a legal newspaper published every business day by NARA. It contains federal agency regulations; proposed rules and notices; and executive orders, proclamations, and other presidential documents. NARA's Office of the Federal Register prepares *The Federal Register* for publication in partnership with the Government Printing Office (GPO), which distributes it in paper form, on microfiche, and on the World Wide Web.

Prologue

The quarterly NARA magazine *Prologue* has a webpage you can link to from the NARA home page, or you can go directly to www.archives .gov/publications/prologue. Special issues, such as the 1997 "Federal Records in African-American Research," may be posted almost in their entirety, but usually a regular issue has one or two features on the website, plus the regular column, "Genealogy Notes." A list of previous columns can be found in the navigation bar from the *Prologue* page. This site is worth bookmarking.

Some Helpful Experience

Much of what is available on the LOC and NARA sites would be most helpful for intermediate to advanced genealogists. The best way to use these sites is to know what you're looking for before you start, such as a specific military record or a particular Work Projects Administration (WPA) oral history from the 1930s. The beginner will find the schedules of workshops on the NARA site and the how-to articles on the LOC site helpful as well.

Government Land Office

I just "glowed" when I found this resource, the Government Land Office (GLO) site. You can search for and view online original land grants and patents between 1820 and 1928.

> **Note**
>
> *Land patents document the transfer of land ownership from the federal government to individuals. These land patent records include the information recorded when ownership was transferred.*

Land Patent Searches

Go to www.glorecords.blm.gov, and click Search Land Patents in the navigation bar. Type the state and name you are looking for, and you'll get a list of matching records. For individual records, you can see a summary, the legal land description, and the document image (see Figure 9-6). You can also order a certified copy. In addition, you will

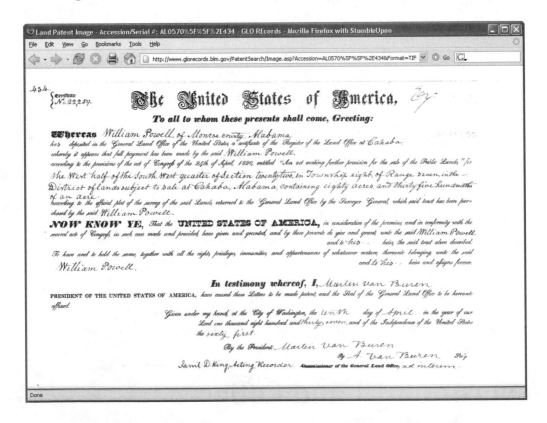

FIGURE 9-6. *A land patent to James Powell of Monroe County, Alabama, 1837*

find a link to a glossary page with details on what the search fields mean. This site does not cover the 13 colonies, their territories, and a few other states, although the site does have resource links for most states. This is because in the early years of the United States, the Congress of the Confederation declared it would sell or grant the unclaimed lands in "the West" (that is, what is now Alabama, Michigan, parts of Minnesota, Mississippi, Illinois, Indiana, Ohio, and Wisconsin). The United States could then sell this unclaimed land to raise money for the Treasury. In turn, the United States gave up its claims to any land within the boundaries of the original colonies. Not all states are available now, but they are working hard to include them.

One must remember that things were hardly organized in the first 50 years of our nation. Click the FAQ link for some good tips on what to look for.

Find Help in the FAQ

Here's a good example of the kind of help you'll find in the GLO FAQ:

Q. What is the Mississippi/Alabama and Florida/Alabama "Crossover?"

A. The St. Stephens Meridian and Huntsville Meridian surveys cross into both Mississippi and Alabama, creating situations where the land offices in St. Stephens and Huntsville, Alabama, and in Columbus, Mississippi, sold lands in both states. We suggest that anyone researching that area take a look at the databases for both states.

The original state line between Alabama and Florida did not close against the Tallahassee Meridian survey (which covered all of Florida), but rather against the earlier St. Stephens Meridian survey in south Alabama. The state line was later resurveyed, creating a situation where some Tallahassee Meridian lands fell across the border into Alabama. We suggest that anyone researching that area take a look at the databases for both states.

Survey Plats

A new addition to the site is survey plats, searchable maps of the original townships. This means that if you have a land grant like the one in Figure 9-6, which gives the boundaries, you will be able to get a small map showing the land. The drawings were created to represent survey lines, boundaries, descriptions, parcels, and subdivisions mentioned in every federal land patent.

Getting Certified Copies

With the online shopping cart, you may request certified copies of land patents, either electronically or through the mail. Hard copy will be on a letter-sized sheet of paper (8.5 × 11 inches) of your preference (plain bond or parchment paper).

Census Records

Census records are available in a variety of forms, both online and offline. For countries beyond the United States, check out Census Links, http://censuslinks.com (see Figure 9-7), which has transcriptions of censuses, such as "Roll of Emigrants That Have Been Sent to the Colony of Liberia, Western Africa, by the American Colonization Society and Its Auxiliaries, to September, 1843" and "Ecclesiastical Census of Revilla (Mexico)–1780."

Another good source is the Archives of Canada. The first census in Canada was in 1666 by Intendant Jean Talon, who listed 3,215 inhabitants. Talon is considered the "father" of modern census-taking in Canada. Regular censuses did not begin until 1841, however. Several Canadian censuses are searchable online at www.archives.ca. Use your favorite search engine to search for "census" and the country you are looking in to find other census resources. For example, Brazil's census information has an English page at www1.ibge.gov.br/english/default.php.

Note

A fire in 1921 destroyed many of the original records of the 1890 census in Washington, D.C. An account of this incident is on the NARA site at http://www.archives.gov/genealogy/census/population/1890.html.

Census Links - Mozilla Firefox with StumbleUpon

File   Edit   View   Go   Bookmarks   Tools   Help

http://censuslinks.com/

CENSUS LINKS

Users online: 25 Tell Friend Messages Add to Favorites Links: Popular New Pick TopRated Random Add Articles: Popular New

Search for [ ] in All categories ∨ All words ∨ Search Advanced

Links Categories: 3217 :: Links: 7881 :: Incoming Clicks: 0 :: Outgoing Clicks: 3510690 :: Incoming Clicks Current Month:
Clicks Current Month: 8365 :: Average rating: 2.5
Articles Categories: 0 :: Articles: 0 :: Readers: 0 :: Readers Current Month: 0 :: Average rating: 0

Good evening! ☺

Ads by Google

Search U.S. Birth Records
Birth Records
Perform an Instant
Search Right Now

U.S. Census Records
Search the U.S.
Census Collection
1790-1930. Over

Free Genealogy
Access millions of
Genealogy
records here.
Free.

CATEGORIES			
Africa (2)	Finland (0)	Newfoundland (0)	Scotland (7)
Australia (2)	France (1)	Norway (7)	Slovakia (2)
Belgium (2)	Germany (2)	Poland (0)	Surnames (165) Death Records, Marriage Records
Canada (149) Alberta, British	Ireland (26)	Portugal (0) 1893 census	Sweden (2)

Done

FIGURE 9-7.   *CensusLinks.Com is a good starting place for international census searches.*

Success Story: Stepping Back Through the Censuses

The Internet is one of the few spaces in genealogy that is friendly to people not running Windows, so instead of using CD-ROMs, I subscribe to Images Online at Ancestry.com for easy access to the handwritten census pages. Reading originals instead of relying on transcribers and indexers was part of my success in finding my great-great- grandparents. Tracking my family back through ten-year steps is what worked for me. I had inherited a genealogical chart of my male Downs/Downes line in Connecticut, showing the names of the wives but nothing else about them. So I knew only that my great-grandmother was supposed to be a Charlotte Smith. First, the 1900 census showed my grandfather living with a Charlotte Thompson, described as "Mother" and shown as being born in 1849. The step back to 1890 had to be skipped, of course, because of the destruction of those records. Then the 1880 census showed my grandfather at the age of five living in Oxford, Connecticut, with a Jane M. Burnett, who called him her grandson. This allowed me to leapfrog over the puzzle of my great-grandmother Charlotte and jump directly into the puzzle of my great-great-grandmother Jane.

I reasoned that for Charlotte to have been a Smith, it was necessary for this Jane M. Burnett also to have been a Smith when Charlotte was born, so I went to the 1850 census in search of Jane M. Smith. The 1850 schedules list everybody by name, but the index lists mostly heads of household—meaning that almost all wives and children are invisible until you read the original pages. After spending two months following the wrong Jane M. Smith with no baby Charlotte, I abandoned the index and started wading through every name in Oxford and then in the surrounding towns. In 1860 Naugatuck, I found a Jane M. Smith whose age fit that of Jane M. Burnett, but still no Charlotte.

Tracking that family back into the 1850 census, I couldn't find them in Naugatuck or in Oxford, but I did find them next door in Middlebury. And there, finally, was one-year-old Charlotte along with Jane and—for the first time with certainty—my great-great-grandfather David S. Smith. Since then, the census has helped me to solve many parts of the puzzle. The next steps—back to 1840 and beyond—will be much more difficult, because those earlier schedules do not list names of family members except for the head of household, but I am very happy with my success so far.

—Alan Downes

The U.S. Census Bureau

The U.S. Census Bureau generally provides only summary and statistical information for the first 72 years after a census is taken. The data on individuals is kept private until then. That means the 1930 census is the most recent one available for public use. The only services the Census Bureau provides related to genealogy are the Age Search Service and the counts of names from the 1990 census.

The Census Bureau does not have old census forms available. Copies of decennial census forms from 1790 through 1930 are available on microfilm, for research at the U.S. National Archives and Records Administration in Washington, D.C., at Archives Regional Centers, and at select federal depository libraries throughout the United States. In addition, these records are available at various other libraries and research facilities throughout the United States. Additional important information at the Census Bureau site is their FAQ at www.census.gov/genealogy/www/faqgene.txt.

CDs and Microfilms

Several vendors provide CD-ROMs and microfilm of census records—sometimes images of the actual census form and sometimes transcriptions. Here's a list of some of these vendors:

- AllCensus.com

- Ancestry.com

- CensusDiggins.com

- CensusFinder.com: U.S., UK, Canada, and Native American census records

- Everton.com

- FamilySearch (LDS—the abbreviation for The Church of Jesus Christ of Latter-day Saints)

- Genealogy Today

- HeritageQuest (available at many public libraries)

Your local library, LDS Family History Center, or genealogy club may also have copies of these microfilms and/or CD-ROMs with census images.

Online Searches

Ancestry.com and Genealogy.com have subscription-based services that let you search indexes of U.S. federal censuses and view the original pages. These are usually worth the money for at least a year's subscription, once you know what you are looking for.

The UK 1901 census is available for searching online at www.1901census.nationalarchives.gov.uk. This site had a disastrous beginning: When it first went online, it had over a million hits in the first hours, the server crashed, and it was months before it was back up. They finally got it all on servers able to handle the traffic, and now several UK censuses are available besides 1901: 1891, 1871, 1861, 1851, and 1841 census records and Birth, Marriage and Death (BMD) indexes.

The censuses, like U.S. censuses, ask different questions for different counts, such as occupation and place of birth. Other records are available, too, as this list shows:

- **Address search**   Find out who lived in your house in 1901.

- **Place search**   Look at who was in which enumeration district in 1901.

- **Institution search**   See who lived in hospitals, barracks, orphanages, etc. in 1901.

- **Vessel search**   Locate a naval or merchant vessel in the 1901 census.

- **Reference number**   Use this search if you know the National Archives census.

Like Ancestry.com and Genealogy.com, you can search the indexes for free, but looking at the actual record costs a fee. Unlike Ancestry.com and Genealogy.com, you can pay per record, put your subscription on hold, and buy a set of voucher lookups. Viewing transcribed data costs 50p for an individual and then 50p for a list of all other people in that person's household. Viewing a digital image of the census page costs 75p.

Transcriptions

As mentioned earlier, www.censuslinks.com is one way to find census transcriptions from around the world. Also check Cyndi's List at www.cyndislist.com/census.htm.

Some Census Sites

Other Census sites that are more local in nature are listed below.

- The Ayrshire Free Census Project (www.gavin-service.com/ ~freecen) aims to transcribe all 19th-century Ayrshire census records and upload them to a free-to-view online database. This is part of FreeCEN: UK Census Online Project.

- Massac County, Illinois History and Genealogy (www.iltrails.org/ massac/census/index.html) is an ongoing project to transcribe records of births, cemetery records and tombstones, census pages, death records, land grants, marriages, obituaries, biographies, and wills for this specific area.

♦ 1920 Yavapai County, Arizona Census Index online (www.sharlot
.org/archives/gene/census/index.html) is a local project. The
Sharlot Hall Museum in Prescott, Arizona, has posted transcriptions
of the 1870, 1880, 1900, and 1920 Yavapai County census
indexes. Genealogists can search the 1870, 1880, and 1900 census
indexes for names and partial names and also get page numbers.

♦ African-American Census Schedules (www.afrigeneas.com/aacensus)
is a volunteer project to transcribe pre-1870 census schedules.

♦ Transcriptions of censuses around the world are at the USGenWeb
project, at www.rootsweb.com/ ~ usgenweb/cen_img.htm (see
Figure 9-8). Click Census Surname Search from the USGenWeb
home page, and then use the form to search all the census
records or to narrow your search by state or year. And consider
volunteering, as the work is far from complete!

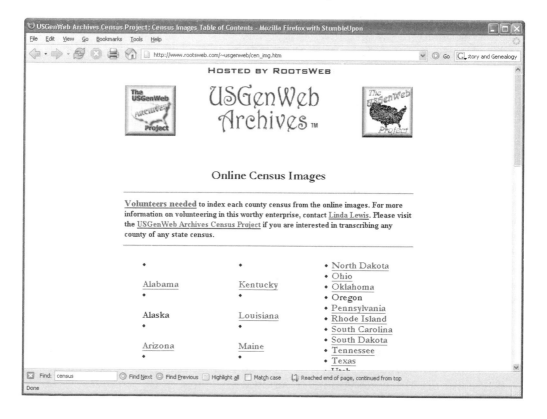

FIGURE 9-8. *At the USGenWeb census site, you can search by surname. Be part of the
project!*

As mentioned previously, an important aspect of online genealogy is giving back to the resources on the Web. A great way to do this is to participate in the Census Project. The USGenWeb Census Project was created to coordinate a U.S. federal census transcription effort. The mission is to recruit and guide volunteer transcribers in achieving the goal of providing free access to online research data for everyone. Each transcription will bear the transcriber's copyright and will be housed in the Census FTP Archives, maintained free of charge for all researchers to use. It's an ambitious project, and the 1930 census reel numbers and enumeration district descriptions have been added to the project. It will take a lot of folks to complete this project; try to be one of them!

State and Local Sources

Besides the U.S. federal census, some state and local governments took censuses for tax purposes. Such states include Illinois, Iowa, Kansas, Massachusetts, Michigan, Minnesota, New Jersey, New York, and Wisconsin, to name a few.

You can often trace the migration of families in America when state census records are used with other records, such as the federal census after 1850; family bibles; death certificates; church, marriage, military, probate, and land records; and other American genealogical sources. A major reference source is *State Census Records* by Ann S. Lainhart (Genealogical Publishing Company, 1992); also check FamilySearch or the catalog of a library under your state of interest and then under the headings "Census – Indexes" and "Census."

Search the Internet to see if state and local censuses have been indexed. See especially the AIS Census Indexes at Ancestry.com (searching Ancestry's indexes is free; seeing the original record is for paying subscribers only).

State Archives and Libraries

Many state archives and libraries have vital records and census information. For example, www.nysl.nysed.gov/genealogy/vitrec.htm is a guide to getting genealogical records from the state of New York. The Alabama Archives has a list of available census information from the state's early years at www.archives.state.al.us/referenc/census.html. Search for the state you need, along with "census" or "archives," to find such sources.

Other Sources

Sometimes you can't find a birth, marriage, or death record in the "official" sources. In these cases, you can look in county and city court records, newspapers, cemetery and funeral home records, and local libraries. These sources can give you clues to parentage, marriages, and burials, which can help you discover where the records may be located—or that the records were destroyed in some way. Some other sources—both official and private—are working to make documents available online.

Footnote

Footnote.com digitizes historical documents, and works in partnership with NARA. At Footnote.com, you will find millions of images of original source documents, many of which have never been available online before. Hundreds of the documents are free, and if you find something you know background on, you can comment on and annotate it. You can also create your own story page, pulling images from the collection to it.

Launched in January 2007, it has added about 2,000,000 items a month, most of them handwritten. You can browse or use a search box (you can do a Boolean search) to find military records, naturalization records, and more. As of this writing, only U.S. documents are being scanned and indexed, but Justin Schroepfer of Footnote said that soon more countries will be included. American Milestone Documents, Project Blue Book, Pennsylvania Archives documents from 1664–1880, and all indexed information and previews of all of the images are free. You are also invited to scan and upload your own historical documents, whether they are photographs, diaries, bible records, and so on.

Access to other documents is by subscription: $8 a month, $60 a year, or $2 an image.

Some of the free collections available include:

♦ The Ratified Amendments XI-XXVII of the U.S. Constitution

♦ Copybooks of George Washington's Correspondence with Secretaries of State, 1789-1796

- Naturalization Petitions of the U.S. District Court for the District of Maryland, 1906-1930

- Naturalization Petitions for the Middle District of Pennsylvania, 1906-1930

- Naturalization Petitions for the Eastern District of Louisiana, New Orleans Division, 1838-1861

- Presidential Photos of Coolidge, Eisenhower, Truman, and Roosevelt

- World War II Japanese Photos

- The Case File of the *United States v. The Amistad*, 1841

Bible Records Online

Bible Records Online is a site dedicated to transcribing and digitizing the contents of records inside family bibles and in other important documents from as early as the 1500s through today. Often, these were the only written records of births, marriages, and deaths of a family, but they are usually inaccessible, except to the person who owns them. At www.biblerecords.com, you can browse or search by surname. The results will be a transcribed page like that shown in Figure 9-9.

To submit your own family bible records, go to www.biblerecords .com/submit.html. Tracy St. Claire, the site's administrator, has a standard format for the transcriptions to make them easy to read and compare. If you can submit a scan of the original, that is wonderful, but she will take a transcription alone. The site also has a forum and a place for scans of photographs or other items people typically slip into the family bible as keepsakes.

Internment.net

This is another volunteer site, full of free, uploaded burial records. Volunteers transcribe and upload records of every bit of data they can find from a local cemetery. The records include the official name of the cemetery; the location of the cemetery (town, county, state, country, etc.), including the street address of the cemetery or driving directions, the date the transcription was compiled and how (tombstone inscriptions, sexton records, previous transcriptions), how complete the list is, and

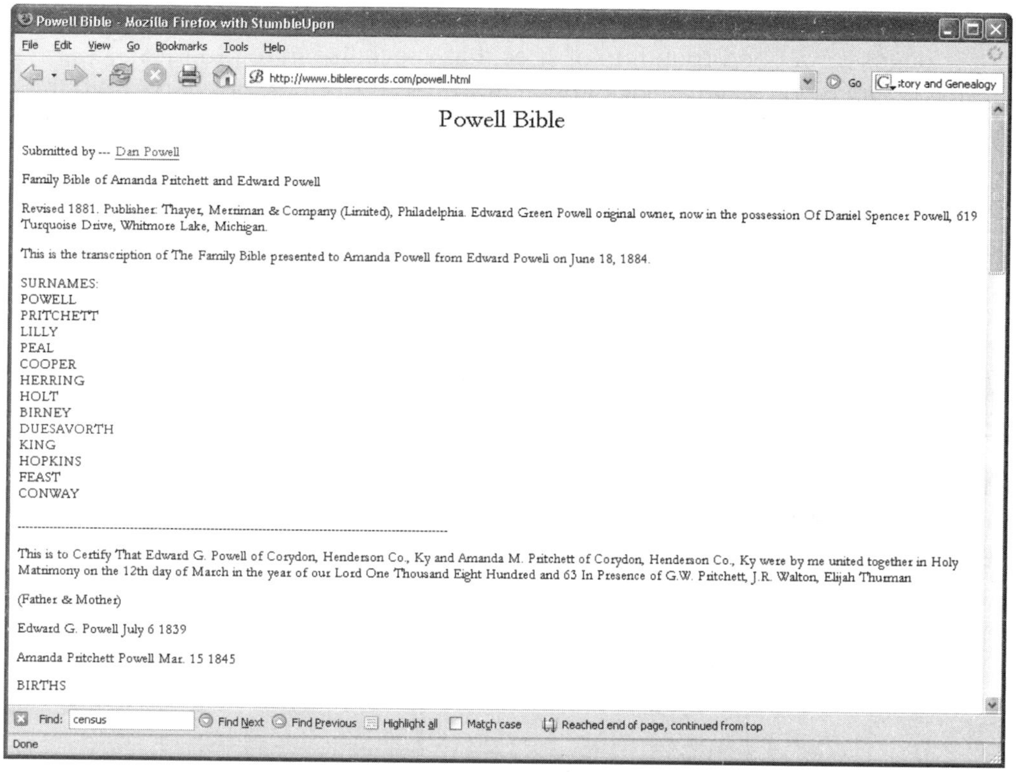

FIGURE 9-9. *A search at Bible Records Online will display a transcribed family page with an e-mail link to the person who submitted it.*

the names of the compilers. As of this writing, almost four million records were available for searching or browsing.

Obituaries and SSDI

Sometimes you can find good clues to vital statistics in obituaries, although one must be cautious. My own parents' published obituaries had minor errors because the family was not thinking clearly at the funeral home. I suspect that is the case with many death notices. Still, the parents and progeny were correct, even if some other particulars were not.

Go to Cyndi's List and look at the Obituaries and Death Notices pages for a good round-up of sites that specialize in obituaries.

Once you have a place and year of death from an obituary, if your ancestor died in the 20th century, you should look at the Social Security Death Index (SSDI) as a more reliable source for data. This is public record, and you can search it for free at http://ssdi.rootsweb.com. The results will give you the official birth date, death date, where the Social Security number was issued (usually the place of residence at the time), and where the last payment was made (usually the place of death at the time). With this information, you can use the state's vital statistics department to get a copy of birth and death certificates, which are primary sources.

Wrapping Up

♦ Vital statistics are the milestones of life: birth, marriage, sometimes divorce, and death.

♦ Most states have good vital statistics starting from 1938 (the beginning of Social Security). Prior to that, you may have to get creative.

♦ The Library of Congress and National Archives and Records Administration have several resources, guides, and databases to help genealogists.

♦ Many sites have transcribed and scanned original documents, indexed for searching by surname: bibles, cemetery records, and so on. Some are free and some are subscription-based.

Chapter 10

Online Library Card Catalogs

Despite all the wonderful things appearing online, many of your genealogical expeditions will still be in libraries. However, the online world can help you here, too. One of the wonderful things about the online world is the plethora of libraries now using online card catalogs (OCCs). This greatly speeds up your search while you're at the library. Not only can you perform an instant search of all of a library's holdings (and, sometimes, even place a hold on the material), but also, with many terminals scattered throughout the building, you needn't look up your subject, author, or title on one floor and then repeatedly run to another floor to find the referenced material. If your local library hasn't computerized its card catalog yet, it probably will soon.

And, oh, the joys of looking in the card catalog before you actually visit the library! You know immediately whether that library owns the title. With a few more keystrokes, you can find out whether the title is on the shelf, on reserve, on loan to someone, or lost without a trace. You can find out whether the book is available by interlibrary loan or found in a nearby branch library.

You can connect to most online card catalogs through the World Wide Web with a browser interface. In many cases, it will look exactly as it does in the library itself.

Note

Don't forget the Google Book Search mentioned in Chapter 6! It can show you if a library has a book that matches your search terms.

Connecting to OCCs by Web Browser

Modern libraries use computerized card catalogs all around the world. In fact, the site LibWeb (http://lists.webjunction.org/libweb) has links to over 7,500 different library pages in Europe, the Caribbean, and Asia. Similar sites are at:

♦ **UK Higher Education and Research Libraries**, maintained by Ian Tilsed of the University of Exeter, at http://www.library.ex.ac.uk/internet/uklibs.html.

♦ **The Australian Libraries Gateway**, at http://www.nla.gov.au/libraries, maintained by the National Library of Australia.

♦ **Lib-Web-Cats**, at http://www.librarytechnology.org/libwebcats, is a research listing of library pages, catalogs, and system profiles, maintained by Marshall Breeding of Vanderbilt University.

♦ **A2A**, at http://www.a2a.org.uk, is a searchable collection of archive catalogs in England and Wales from the eighth century to the present. Type a word or exact phrase into the box; you can limit the search to specific archives or to English or Welsh counties, as well as specific dates.

♦ **Catalogue Collectif de France**, at http://ccfr.bnf.fr, will let you use one interface to query the three largest online library catalogs in France, including the printed and digitized holdings of the national Library of France, the University SUDOC System of Documentation of French universities, and local libraries across France. It includes books printed from 1811 to the present in more than 60 public or specialized libraries.

Of course, some of those libraries are more concerned with engineering or agriculture or biology than they are with genealogy. The following is a tour of U.S. libraries that have extensive genealogy collections and are worth searching.

Don't Miss These Library Sites

The Birmingham Public Library (Alabama) has the best genealogy and local history collection in Alabama, and it includes major holdings for Georgia, Mississippi, Tennessee, North and South Carolina, Virginia, Louisiana, and other Southern states. Also in the collection are U.S. censuses (1790–1900) for all Southern states; selected military records of the American Revolution, the War of 1812, and the Civil War; and a large collection of abstracted records. Native American censuses for the Eastern Cherokee and Creek, The Freedman's Bureau Papers for Alabama, records of the Superintendent of Education for the State of Alabama (1865–1870), final rolls of citizens and freedmen of the Five Civilized Tribes in Indian Territory, and volumes of the American State Papers are also among the collection. The Rucker Agee Map Collection, which has about 500 atlases and over 4,500 maps of Alabama, showing its history as part of Georgia, Florida, and then Louisiana, is essential for early 19th-century research in Alabama. The Rare Book Collection includes many books published in Alabama, works on travel in the South from the 18th and 19th centuries, and major works on Native Americans and Native American affairs in Alabama. The Web site is www.bplonline.org/sou (see Figure 10-1).

You can also search the entire **Jefferson County Library System** catalog at www.jclc.org/services/opacmenu.html; it has several volumes on local history.

Samford University Library (Alabama) does not have quite the scope of the Birmingham Public Library with regards to Alabama history, but because of the annual Institute of Genealogy and Historical Research held here, has quite a collection of all things Alabama. The Web site is http://library.samford.edu.

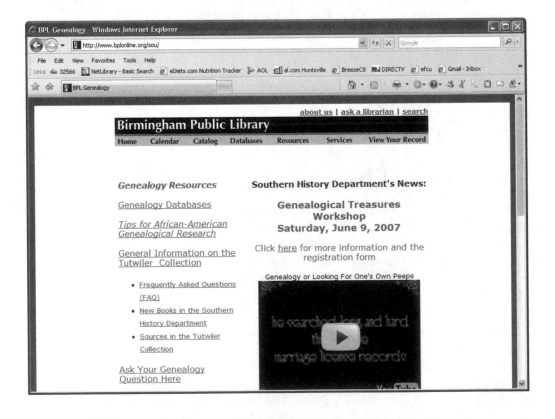

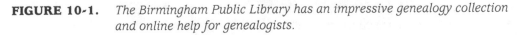

FIGURE 10-1. *The Birmingham Public Library has an impressive genealogy collection and online help for genealogists.*

The Daughters of the American Revolution Library (General), at www.dar.org/library has over 160,000 books on American genealogy, and it's open to the public.

The New England Historical and Genealogical Society Lending Library (General), at http://www.newenglandancestors.org/rs3/ libraries/circulation/Default.asp, is available to members only. Consider joining if you have any New England ancestors!

The Sons of the American Revolution Library Catalog (General), at http://sar.library.net, can tell you if this collection has genealogies of interest to you. The SAR Library maintains a non-circulating collection of genealogy and American Revolutionary War history and military records. It is located at 1000 South Fourth Street, Louisville, Kentucky, 40203. The Library Collection includes family genealogies, state and county history, and vital statistics, with many New England records; federal census records; (complete through the year 1860 for every state; some records through 1920); Revolutionary War pension applications; and a special George Washington collection containing books, journal articles, and manuscripts.

The Newberry Library (Illinois) in Chicago, at http://www.newberry .org/genealogy/collections.html, has over 17,000 genealogies. Search the catalog to see if you need to make a visit!

The University of Illinois at Urbana-Champaign Library Catalog (Illinois), at www.library.uiuc.edu/catalog, offers an outline of the UIUC online catalog, describing its major collections.

The Allen County Public Library (Indiana), at www.acpl.lib.in.us, has one of the best genealogical collections in the country. Start with the page www.acpl.lib.in.us/genealogy/index.html, which gives you an overview of this wonderful genealogist's treasure house. More than 50,000 volumes of compiled genealogies, microfilms of primary sources, and specialized collections, such as African American and Native American, make this library one you must see. But like the Family History Library in Salt Lake City, you must first plan your visit, or you will be overwhelmed. Search the catalog online for the names you need to see if they have something for you!

Anne Arundel County Public Library (Maryland) has the Gold Star Collection, which contains about 700 titles dealing with Maryland, including some Anne Arundel County genealogy. In their special collections are several Maryland family histories and local histories. The library catalog is located online at www.aacpl.net.

The New York Public Library (New York) contains a genealogy section called The Milstein Division. This department collects materials documenting American history on the national, state, and local levels, as well as genealogy, heraldry, personal and family names, and flags. The page, located at www.nypl.org/research/chss/lhg/genea.html (see Figure 10-2), has good general information. The card catalog of the research library (called CATNYP) is found at http://catnyp.nypl.org; the at-large catalog is at http://www.nypl.org/research/chss/lhg/genea.html.

The College of William and Mary Library (Virginia) is one of the oldest universities in one of the oldest states, and the collection is astounding. The special collections include Virginia tax lists for the 1780s; census microfilms for Virginia (1810–1920), North Carolina (1790–1850), and other states (1790–1820); and compilations of

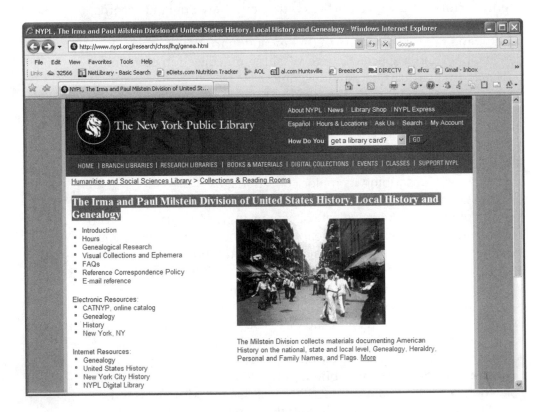

FIGURE 10-2.   *The Irma and Paul Milstein Division of United States History, Local History, and Genealogy ("the Milstein Division") has its own catalog.*

Virginia county, marriage, land, probate, church, military, emigration, and immigration records. The library's catalog is located at http://lion .wm.edu/uhtbin/webcat. Manuscript collections are listed in the online library catalog. In addition, the Reference Department will do limited research in response to phone, fax, or e-mail questions. They will check to see if the library has materials on a certain subject, and they will consult an indexed book or collection for a specific name (see http:// swem.wm.edu/resources/genealogy/research.cfm). Finally, this site has excellent guides to researching genealogy in Virginia and to this collection. Look at http://swem.wm.edu/resources/genealogy/key-guides.cfm and http://swem.wm.edu/resources/genealogy/index.cfm.

The Library of Virginia (Virginia) is home to a set of powerful online card catalogs, located at www.lva.lib.va.us/whatwehave/ index.htm. This site has scanned images of Civil War records, family bible records, letters, and other material, all indexed and searchable by name. I ran a test with "genealogy and Powell" as the search terms. The results can be seen in Figure 10-3. If I want to refine my search further, I could also use Boolean terms, such as AND, NOT, and so on. Overall, the Library of Virginia's card catalog is easy to understand and read—and, I might add, a pleasure to work with.

California University and State Libraries MELVYL (California) is a searchable catalog of library materials from the ten UC campuses, the California State Library, the California Academy of Sciences, the California Historical Society, the Center for Research Libraries, the Giannini Foundation of Agricultural Economics Library, the Graduate Theological Union, the Hastings College of the Law Library, and the Lawrence Berkeley National Laboratory Library. And every single one of those institutions has a history/genealogy section. The California State Library, for example, has books, maps, manuscripts, diaries, newspapers, and photographs pertaining to California history and genealogy. See the collection guide at www.lib.state.ca.us. In the California Information File, you will find an index to almost 1.5 million items, including newspapers, periodicals, and books about California persons, places, and events. The collection also has federal census records (1850–1930) and Soundex listings through 1920 for California, a transcription of the 1852 state census of California (separate from the national one), California cemetery transcriptions made by the Daughters of the American Revolution (DAR) and DAR indexes to early California vital records and wills, and more.

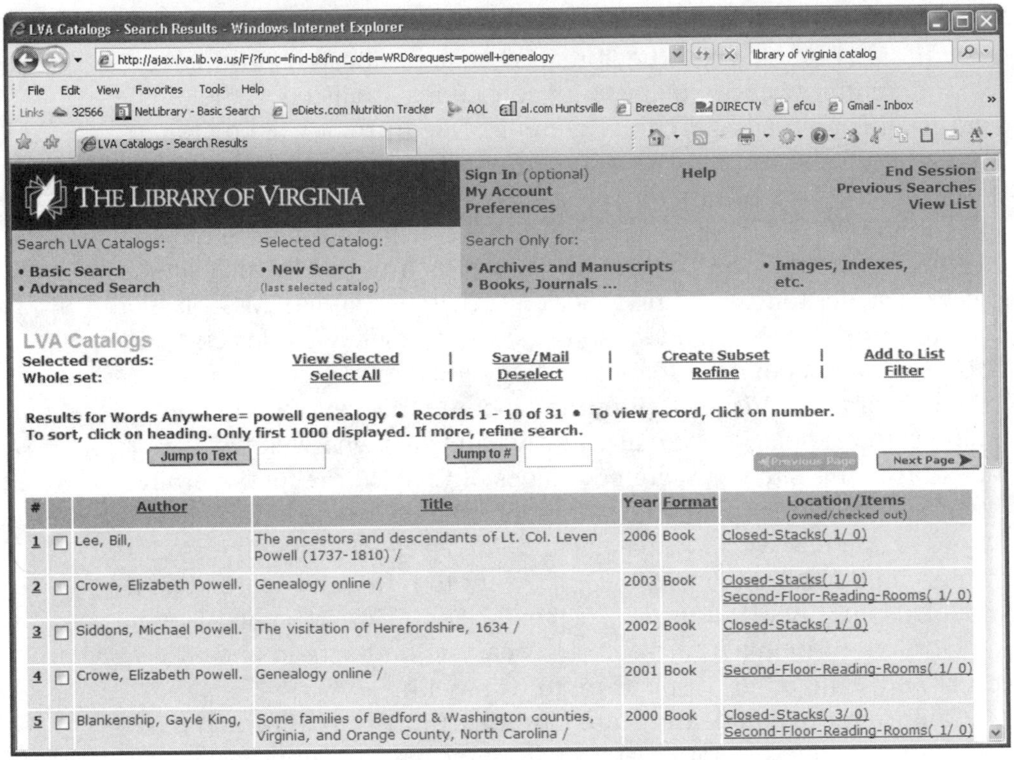

FIGURE 10-3. *The Library of Virginia's catalogs can search "the stacks" (circulating material) and special collections.*

Connecticut State Library (Connecticut) has not only genealogy and local history of Connecticut, but also of the rest of New England. Their special collections include Connecticut town vital records to about 1900. The state library's catalog can be accessed through the state library home page at www.cslib.org or through CONSULS, the Catalog of Connecticut State University and the State Library at http://csulib.ctstateu.edu. To limit your searching to state library holdings, choose the last option, Change Library Catalog on the first menu screen. Then choose Search The State Library Only.

Note

Don't forget the Library of Congress catalog online at http://catalog.loc.gov.

The Frederick Porter Griffin Center for Local History and Genealogy (Indiana) is located directly behind the Harrison County Public Library at 117 W. Beaver Street in Corydon, Indiana. The center is home to thousands of invaluable materials, including historical documents, a wall of bound family histories compiled by individuals, an extensive collection of photographs, and genealogical and historical files. Search the catalog at http://catalog.hcpl.lib.in.us/web/guest/welcome.

The Filson Historical Society (Kentucky), located at www .filsonhistorical.org (see Figure 10-4), exists to collect, preserve, and tell

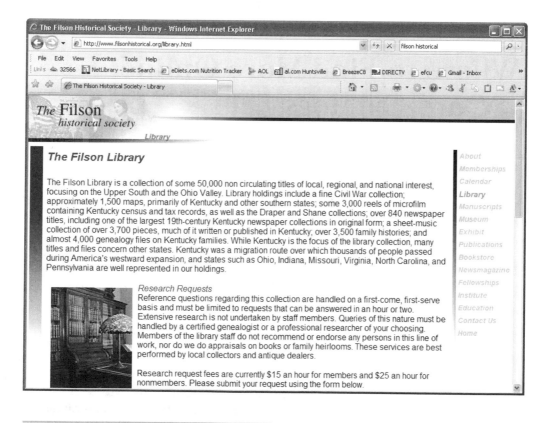

FIGURE 10-4. *The Filson Historical Society library has material on the history of the entire Ohio Valley, especially Kentucky.*

the significant stories of Kentucky and the Ohio Valley history and culture. If you have any genealogy in that area, a personal visit to the Filson is something you will never forget. The library has 50,000 titles, a 1.5-million-item manuscript collection, a collection of 50,000 photographs and prints, and a museum with 10,000 items. The library has such items as original manuscripts, portraits, landscapes, photographs and prints, genealogical materials, printed family histories, local business records, and other primary historical materials with nationally recognized strength in the history of Kentucky, the Ohio Valley, and the Upper South. Search the catalog of the Filson at http://filson.ipac.dynixasp .com/ipac20/ipac.jsp?profile = #focus.

The Ohio Historical Society (Ohio), located at www.ohiohistory.org, has newspapers, federal census records, county histories, and family histories. Government records holdings include the archives for the state of Ohio and local government records from counties of central Ohio, as well as statewide death certificates (909–1953). The library catalog is located at www.ohiohistory.org/occ.

Where to Find More Online Card Catalogs

Once you explore the online card catalogs shown in this chapter, you'll probably want to find some more. Of course, first you'll want to use a search engine (see Chapter 6) and search for the term "library" and the town, province, or county you are interested in. Also search for the name of a state and "public library" because many states have a network of their libraries.

♦ Gateway to Library Catalogs (http://www.loc.gov/z3950) is a page by the Library of Congress. In addition to links to the LOC catalog, you will find an alphabetical list of catalogs around the world.

♦ Libdex (http://www.libdex.com) is a worldwide directory of over 18,000 library home pages, Web-based Online Public Access Catalog (OPACs), Friends of the Library pages, and library e-commerce affiliate links.

♦ National Union Catalog of Manuscript Collections (NUCMC) can point you not only to library card catalogs, but also to archives and repositories with websites. You can find it at http://www .loc.gov/coll/nucmc.

♦ Repositories of Primary Sources (http://www.uidaho.edu/special-collections/Other.repositories.html), maintained by Terry Abraham of the University of Idaho, lists over 5,000 sites worldwide, arranged by region. It includes many of the major genealogical libraries with primary source documents.

♦ The Library of Michigan website has a database with the locations of over 3,700 Michigan cemeteries and lists sources at the library where a researcher can find the names of those buried in each cemetery. The database can be found at http://michigancemeteries.libraryofmichigan.org.

♦ When you visit USGenWeb (www.usgenweb.com), look under the state and then the county you're researching to see if the library catalog is linked.

♦ The WWW Library Directory (http://travelinlibrarian.info/libdir) is a list of library websites sorted by geography, not topic. However, it's useful and international in scope.

♦ The Research Libraries Information Network (RLIN) is a not-for-profit membership corporation of over 160 universities, national libraries, archives, historical societies, and other institutions that gather and distribute the RLIN to make many resources available around the world. Libraries join the RLIN and offer a connection to transfer RLIN records to their local systems for processing. You may find local libraries with an RLIN interface, allowing you to search the holdings of many different libraries.

Wrapping Up

Going to the library in your pajamas is fun!

♦ You can search the card catalogs of many libraries across the world from the Internet.

♦ Some libraries have begun scanning images and actual text of their genealogical holdings.

♦ Some libraries participate in interlibrary loans of books and microfilms. You can search for such libraries at several sites across the Internet.

♦ State libraries and provincial libraries are excellent online resources.

Chapter 11

Genealogy
Database Sites

GEDCOM files are to genealogists what trading cards are to kids. They can be uploaded to databases with lineage indexing and links. Think of a GEDCOM database as all of your pedigree charts connected electronically. You'll see them called GEDCOM files, GEDCOM databases, or just GEDCOMs.

GEDCOM files can be shared with others in an e-mail attachment or on a disk. They can be converted for use in genealogy companion software programs and utilities that will create specialty charts, books, scrapbooks, and websites. GEDCOM files can be uploaded to genealogy sites for searching and swapping. GEDCOM databases are available on CD-ROM, as downloadable files from the Internet, through a search form via a webpage, or at your local Church of Jesus Christ of Latter-day Saints (LDS) Family History Center. Some GEDCOM sites allow you to search and even download for free, while others require that you buy a copy of the database or pay a subscription fee. When you upload your GEDCOM to a certain sites, note that some of these sites will still require a fee for access, even though you just contributed your own data to help add value to their site. Read all the fine print on a site before you upload or download a GEDCOM.

GEDCOM files can also be adjusted for privacy and copyright concerns (see Chapter 5). You should always remember to remove data on living people, as well as to give proper credit to all your sources in your GEDCOM files.

> **Note**
>
> *When you look at someone's GEDCOM file, remember that this is secondary source material and the data may not have the creator's sources and documentation saved with it. You must contact the GEDCOM file's owner to determine the primary sources used.*

GEDCOMs 101

GEDCOM is a generic, database format designed to allow users to share family history database files among different genealogy software programs and platforms. In other words, with a GEDCOM, you can take your genealogy information from Family Tree on a Mac and share it with your cousin's Brother's Keeper on a PC.

The name is an abbreviation of "GEnealogical Data COMmunication." GEDCOM is a defined, specific structure for a file of genealogy data. The file format is a standard ASCII text file, so it can be read by or written to virtually any computer and/or any genealogy program. The GEDCOM standard was written by the Family History Department of the Church of Jesus Christ of Latter-day Saints (also known as the Mormon Church) back in the mid-1980s to have a standard for sharing genealogical information electronically. It has been through several versions, with 5.5 being the latest as of this writing. As this version was issued in 1995, it seems that it is almost etched in stone now.

Note

When you export a GEDCOM, be sure to turn on any privacy features your genealogy software may have to protect data on living people.

To create a GEDCOM file (in most programs), choose File | Export To GEDCOM, and then create a new file with a .ged file extension after the name. To read another person's GEDCOM file (in most programs), Choose File | Import From GEDCOM, and create a new database file that can be opened in your genealogy software program. This will not merge with your existing database file unless you indicate that you wish for the two files to be merged.

Note

A program called GEDmark allows you to mark each entry in your GEDCOM file with your name as the source for that information. That way, if someone merges your GEDCOM file with theirs, you remain the source of the information on each record.

It's not perfect, of course. The GEDCOM standard is complicated, and programmers sometimes do not take the time to read it in detail and understand all the features. It has been said that no program on the market correctly implements every aspect of the standard—even Personal Ancestral File (PAF), the program from the LDS church for which it was developed! Some deviations are minor and merely are a nuisance.

Others are major problems, resulting in loss of data or even computer system crashes when a file is imported into a different program. The size of the problem depends both on the source and destination programs. Some do better than others. If you need a really geeky insight into the standard and how it works, check out the FamilySearch.com FAQ on GEDCOMs at http://www.familysearch.org/Eng/Home/FAQ/frameset_faq .asp?FAQ = faq_gedcom.asp (see Figure 11-1).

One genealogy program, The Master Genealogist (www.whollygenes .com), has a different way of translating data from one program to another called GenBridge, and it reads GEDCOMs as well. As of yet, the Wholly Genes technology has not replaced GEDCOMs. If you are going to examine someone else's data in your genealogy program, or if you are going to search a database someone has uploaded to the Internet, you will most likely be dealing with their program's version of GEDCOM.

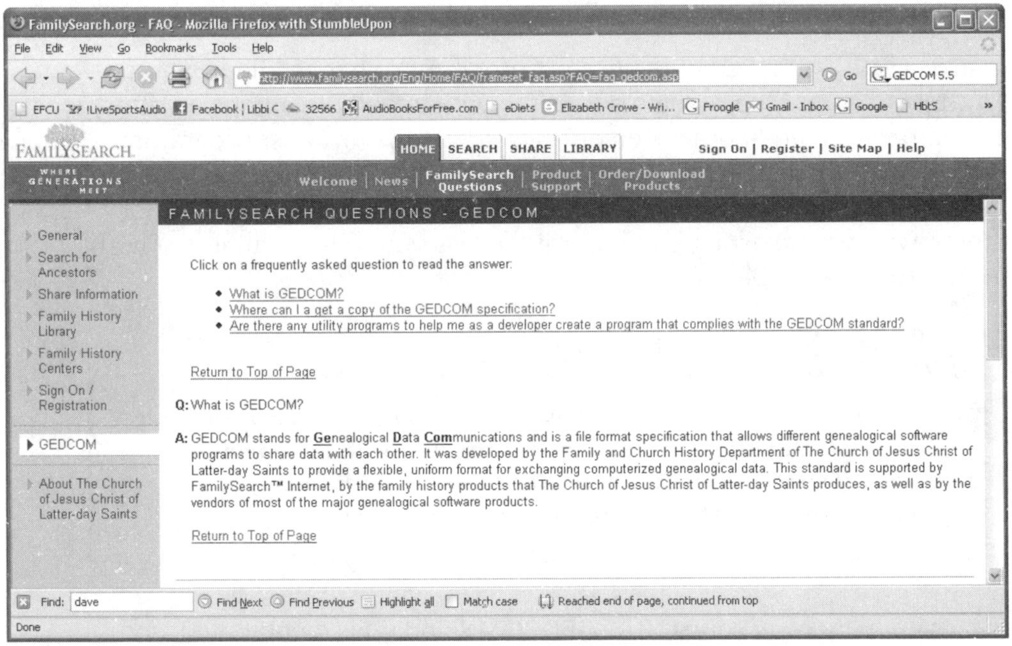

FIGURE 11-1. *The GEDCOM page in the Family Search FAQ explains the standard.*

Because sometimes a GEDCOM is in the eye of the beholder, so to speak, when you get a file from someone, always import it to a *new database* in your genealogy program. Do not merge it to your current genealogy database until you have determined whether it has the data you need and performs well enough with your software to work. Even then, before you merge, make a backup of your original database.

Caution

Never merge a new GEDCOM to your current program's database before you have made a backup. Have you backed up today? This week? This month?

Database Ins and Outs

Once you get the hang of creating, swapping, and collecting GEDCOMs, you can have some real fun! Sites where you can search, download, and upload GEDCOMs abound. Check Cyndi's List Databases – Lineage-Linked at www.cyndislist.com/lin-linked.htm often for new and updated sites. Ancestry.com and FamilySearch are two major sites with GEDCOM searches that are so big, they get their own chapters (Chapter 14 for Family Search and Chapter 17 for Ancestry.com). GenServ, one of the first database exchanges, was covered in Chapter 6, because it exists *only* to search GEDCOM databases. Other sites that may not be so easy to find will be covered here.

Note

Most of these sites require you to remove birth and location data on living people before you upload. This is to prevent identity theft and fraud.

Genes Reunited

Genes Reunited is part of a UK site for a general online community. The genealogy part is located at www.genesreunited.co.uk/ genesreunited.asp (see Figure 11-2).

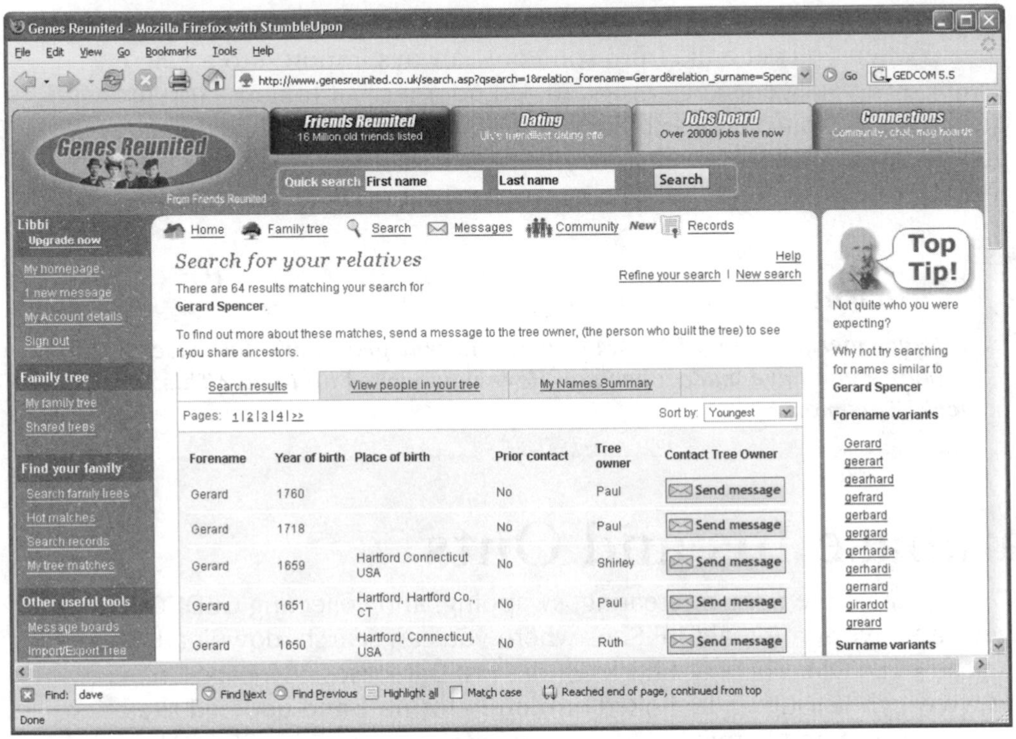

FIGURE 11-2. *Genes Reunited is a UK site for uploading and searching GEDCOM files. This figure shows results for "Gerard Spencer."*

Like many sites, Genes Reunited has some free areas and some for-fee areas. Basic registration is free. You can build your family tree, use the search facilities to find possible matches to your family name, add notes about relationships in your tree, and exchange e-mails with other members. Also, if you already have experience in researching your family history, you can import your GEDCOM file to your Genes Reunited family tree.

Full membership costs $14.49 for six months, which gives you the ability to contact other members from your search results, link up to view other members' trees when they invite you to do so, post photos on your family tree, and add messages to the message boards. In other words, a social network. Like Ancestry.com, Genes Reunited has some primary source material (from the UK, of course) in searchable databases. However the fees for that social networking are separate from the fees for downloading records from the databases. The records downloads are purchased separately. You do not have to be upgraded to the social network buy credits for the records, however.

When you upload your database (or type it into their forms), the My Tree Matches page is divided into three sections:

♦ **Search**   You can search for any surname in the uploaded GEDCOMs up to 50 years on either side of the birth year. You can also search through the newest names, using a drop-down box to select the number of days you wish to view. As spelling was not exactly standardized in past centuries, the site will offer suggested alternative spellings in the column on the right next to your results.

♦ **View People In Your Tree**   This section lists all the names in your uploaded database, showing their first name, surname, birth year, and place of birth. The default view of the names is chronologically, with the youngest first. You can change this view by selecting a different view from the Sort By drop-down box. For larger trees, you might find the Quick Search feature at the top more useful.

Quick search links from this page can search the site for any matches or just matches to the 1851 census, the 1901 census, and also births, marriages, and deaths from 1837 to 2002. It costs £5.00 for 50 credits to view the data in the records section.

♦ **My Names Summary**   This is where you will see a full summary of all the surnames in your uploaded GEDCOM displayed as a family tree. You can also search through the database for all the entries using the same surname. It works much like the Search page. Your results on this page will be displayed in three columns, showing the number of messages added to the History, General, and Trying To Find message boards for that name. Click the number in the column for the message board you are trying to view.

You can view details that match any of the surnames in your tree across the whole Genes Reunited database by name, place of birth, or year of birth. Click Matches In Other Family Trees next to the surname you are interested in to view these results. You will see the details of the relationships and then a Send Message box where you can contact the tree owner for more details. You can also add to one of three message boards that are specific to a particular surname. Note that any entries you make in the Trying To Find board will also be displayed on the main Trying To Find board, enabling any member to see a request even if they do not have a particular surname existing in their tree.

GenCircles

This site, located at www.gencircles.com, is the invention of Cliff Shaw, who also created GenForum. Two things I like about this site are the privacy controls and the fact that your data will not be burned onto a CDROM for someone else to profit from.

Registration is free, as are the searches and the message boards. You upload your GEDCOM file to the Global Tree, removing data on living people first, and a page is created. The displays include family group sheets and pedigree charts. The home page, along with the search input box, is shown in Figure 11-3.

The site uses a proprietary search engine called SmartMatching that compares the individuals in your file against all the individuals in the rest of the Global Tree. The matches are displayed on your page on the site within hours of your upload.

When a search finds a match in GenCircles, you e-mail the submitter directly by clicking his or her name. A drawback is that not all users remember to keep their e-mail address information current.

You can upload as many GEDCOM files as you like using the same user name and password. The system automatically assigns a number to each one of your files and creates a page for it. When you are logged on, you can go to www.gencircles.com/my to change the contact information or to delete old GEDCOMs. Visitors can view your published file by going to www.gencircles.com/users/ <YOUR USER NAME>. To make changes to your GEDCOM file, change it in your genealogy program and then upload the changed GEDCOM.

On the My GenCircles page, you can suppress or display your notes and sources in your GEDCOM file, change the title of the page, and

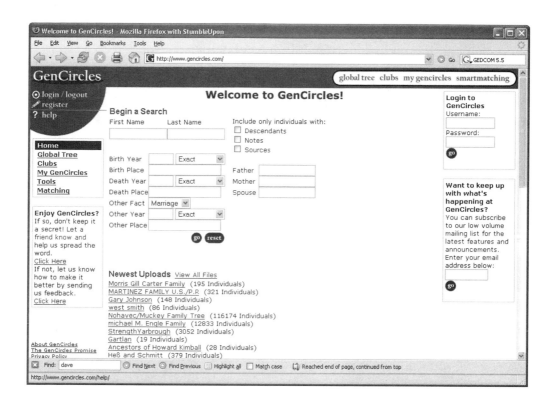

FIGURE 11-3. *GenCircles is a U.S.-based GEDCOM exchange site.*

control other aspects. You can also control the amount of privacy on this page. Indeed, privacy is built in to an extent: If another user has chosen in their file preferences to share their data with other researchers, you still only have the option to download small fragments of their GEDCOM file. You can never download a complete GEDCOM; you have to contact the uploader to exchange information.

ROOTSWEB WorldConnect

ROOTSWEB will be covered extensively in Chapter 17, but we'll explore this little corner here. WorldConnect is a cooperative GEDCOM exchange. It's all free and supported by advertising, but your name and data will not be sold for profit. It is also completely unedited. If there are mistakes, only the submitter can delete the error and upload a corrected GEDOM. Some of these databases were uploaded in the late 1980s, some just last week. I don't mean this pejoratively, but it's not unlike the secondhand stores every town has. Some things were once useful, some are useful now, and some things are real finds and worth a lot.

From www.rootsweb.com, click Family Trees in the navigation bar, or just go to http://worldconnect.rootsweb.com. WorldConnect's global search form can be used for both basic searches and advanced searches. You must enter search criteria in at least one field; you decide how many fields you wish to specify. Of course, the more specific you are, the fewer hits, but the more likely that what comes up will be useful.

What's nice about this site is that along the sides of every page, the genealogy jargon is explained, in case you come to the site unaware of what a GEDCOM is, what "to download" means, and so on.

A search result will give you a chart of the name, birth date and place, death date and place, the name of the database (GEDCOM), and other matches from Ancestry.com. The spouse's information, if available, will also appear in the chart.

If you click the name of the database (GEDCOM), you see the first page of a set of linked pages. The uploader's contact information is presented as a picture file to prevent spammers from harvesting e-mail addresses. Then you will see the alphabet plus No Surname as links. This is how you search that specific database for the name you want. Once you select an individual, you can see ancestor and descendant views of the data. An example of finding Spencers in one database is shown in Figure 11-4.

In this figure, you can see that we could look at an individual's family group sheet, at a pedigree chart, at this view of descendants, at a "register" outline form, or at an ahnentafel, or we could return to the index of each individual name sorted alphabetically. Unlike GenCircles, you can download an entire GEDCOM. However, each individual submitter decides how much to include in the way of notes, sources, and privacy.

The good side of WorldConnect is the sheer volume of data you can search here. In fact, I make it a habit to look at several different GEDCOM files that list the same individual to compare data from one researcher to another. That's hard to do at most other sites.

The downside is that you cannot just accept what you find here. Often, the uploads are works in progress, and the submitters are upfront about

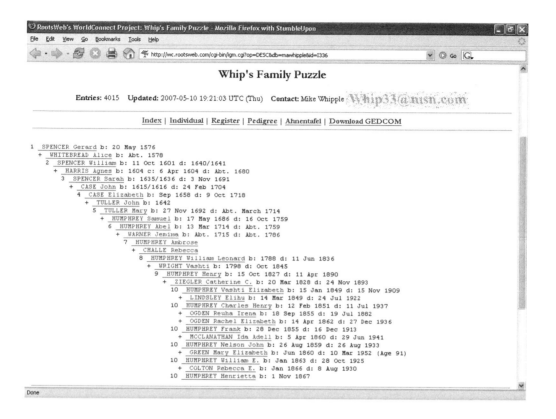

FIGURE 11-4. *A descendant view of Gerard Spencer from a WorldConnect GEDCOM. Each name is a link and can be viewed in several ways.*

wanting to know if there are errors in what they have so far. Look at the data carefully, contact the submitter to compare notes and exchange data, and use WorldConnect as a platform to launch your exploration.

Other Sites

If you use a good search engine site (see Chapter 6) and input "GEDCOM" as a search term along with the surname or full name you're looking for, you will probably come up with some personal genealogy sites with published ancestries, as shown in Figure 11-5.

This should be a weekly habit, in case a new page appears or you want to twiddle with your search terms to see if you get different results.

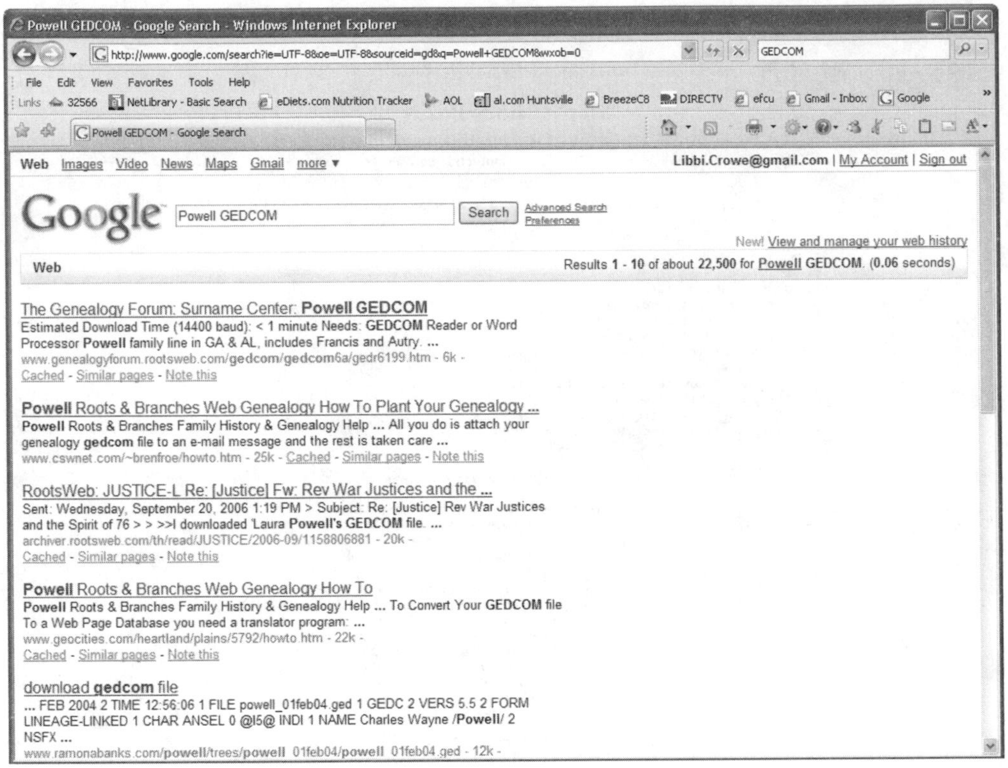

FIGURE 11-5. *Use search sites to find specific GEDCOM files uploaded to webpages.*

Wrapping Up

- ♦ GEDCOM files can be swapped like baseball cards, with precautions.

- ♦ Don't post or export a GEDCOM file with data of living people in it.

- ♦ Don't merge a GEDCOM file to your existing genealogy database without checking it out with your program first.

- ♦ Some sites collect GEDCOM files for searching.

- ♦ Some personal genealogy sites contain GEDCOMs you can search or read as family trees.

- ♦ Some GEDCOM sites are free, and some charge fees.

Part IV

The Genealogy World

Chapter 12

International Genealogy Resources

Sooner or later, you'll get "back to the boat"—that is, you'll find your original immigrant in a certain family line. The first immigrant in your family might have arrived just a generation ago or centuries ago. Either way, that doesn't have to mean your genealogy is "done."

When you find that first immigrant, finding the boat can be just as important. Although finding where he or she boarded won't tell you a birthplace, it is a start. Here are some places for you to start:

- An excellent step-by-step guide to searching for immigrants is at Immigration & Ships Passenger Lists Research Guide (http://home .att.net/~arnielang/shipgide.html).

- Check out Cyndi's List for links to ships' passenger lists projects at www.cyndislist.com/ships.htm.

- Search the Ellis Island site (see Chapter 15).

- Investigate the Immigrant Ships Transcribers' Guild at http://www .immigrantships.net.

- The Ships List, (http://www.theshipslist.com/) which not only has passenger lists, but also newspaper reports, shipwreck information, and information on shipping lines.

- Search the National Archives and Records Administration (NARA) microfilm catalog for immigration records for arrivals to the United States from foreign ports between approximately 1820 and 1982. See http://www.archives.gov/genealogy/immigration for details on how to order microfilms that match.

- Search other indexes at http://home.att.net/~wee-monster/ passengers.html, "Finding Passenger Lists" by Joe Beine.

- Look at naturalization records at NARA, state archives, and county and state courts.

Note

Remember to give back to the Internet by getting involved in a project such as the Immigrant Ships Transcribers' Guild project.

Of course, the next step is to start researching in "the old country," outside the United States. Can you do this online? Well, that depends on the country. Some countries do, indeed, have online records for you to search, especially those countries where English is spoken. But some countries only have sites with the most general information, and you'll be lucky to find the address of the civil records offices. You'll probably wind up doing a combination of online and postal mail research and possibly some in-person research, too.

> **Note**
>
> Immigrate *means to come into and settle in a country or region to which one is not native;* emigrate *means to leave one country or region to settle in another.*

Beyond the Boat

In many of the places covered in previous chapters, you can find links to sites for genealogy beyond the United States. For online links, I recommend starting at Cyndi's List at www.cyndislist.com and ROOTSWEB at www.rootsweb.org. Other good places to look are:

♦ **National archives**   A country's national archives might have a webpage describing genealogy how-tos for that country. For example, I recently searched for `Poland National Archives` in Google. Quickly, I found the English version of the archives' website, www.archiwa.gov.pl/?CIDA = 43. This site has pages that explain how to start a genealogy search (see Figure 12-1), what to ask for, and where to look for records.

> **Note**
>
> Be sure to look at FamilySearch *for research guides to the country you need.*

♦ **Genealogical societies**   Search in any major search site (Yahoo!, Google, Excite, and so on) for the country of origin for your immigrant and "genealogy." Often, at the top of the list will be a genealogical society devoted to that particular nationality.

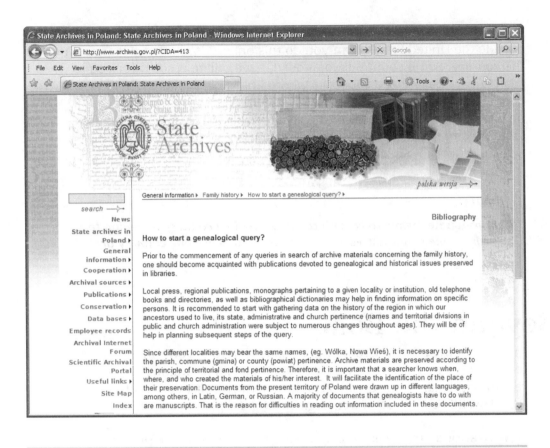

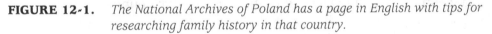

FIGURE 12-1. *The National Archives of Poland has a page in English with tips for researching family history in that country.*

You need to learn how to research in those countries. Each place has its own method of recording vital statistics, history, and other information.

♦ **LDS Research Guides** Before you start looking for records, you need to know what those records are called and who keeps them. The Church of Jesus Christ of Latter-day Saints (LDS) has developed pamphlets on researching immigrants and ancestors around the world. These Research Guides are indispensable for these tasks. You can order them for a nominal fee from any Family History Center. Look in the Yellow Pages or in the White Pages for The Church of Jesus Christ of Latter-day Saints for a Family History Center near you.

The first one to read is the guide "Tracing Immigrant Origins," a 49-page outline of tips, procedures, and strategies found online at http://www.familysearch.org/Eng/Search/RG/guide/tracing_immigrant_origins.asp or available in hard copy from a Family History Center for a small fee.(see Figure 12-2).

Other Research Guides give you step-by-step pointers on the best way to pursue historical records in a particular state, province, or country. The letter-writing guides tell you what you need to know before you write the letter, where to write, how to address the envelope, how to enclose return postage, and include a sample letter in the appropriate language.

Arm yourself with the research outlines and, if available, a letter-writing guide for the appropriate country before you begin. Also, look at the LDS

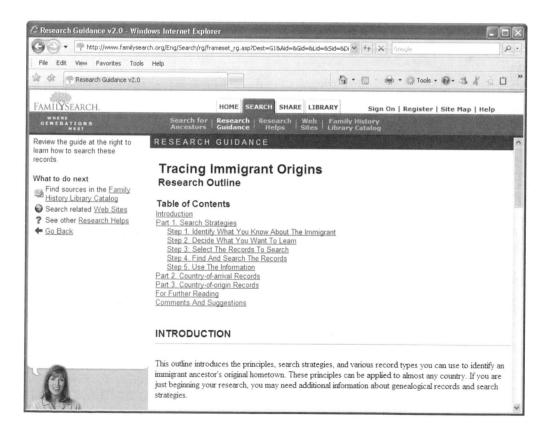

FIGURE 12-2. *"Tracing Immigrant Origins," located online at Family Search or available in printed copies at Family History Centers, can help you plan your search.*

"word lists" for various languages; this can help you recognize the words for "birth," "marriage," "death," and so on in the records, even if you can't read the language.

WorldGenWeb

The WorldGenWeb Project was created in 1996 by Dale Schneider to help folks researching in countries around the world. The goal is to have every country in the world represented by a website and hosted by researchers who either live in that country or are familiar with that country's resources. The site is www.worldgenweb.org (see Figure 12-3).

FIGURE 12-3. *WorldGenWeb can help you find genealogy sites in your country of interest.*

When the WorldGenWeb Project launched on the Internet in October 1996, volunteers were recruited to host country websites. By coordinating with the USGenWeb Project, soon the major countries in the world had websites. Throughout the next year, WorldGenWeb continued to grow. On September 13, 1997, the WorldGenWeb Project decided to move to ROOTSWEB. The support of the ROOTSWEB staff helped WorldGenWeb expand to its present size.

Divided into 11 regions (Africa, Asia, British Isles, Central Europe, Caribbean, Eastern Europe, Mediterranean, Middle East, North America, Pacific, and South America), WorldGenWeb gives links to local sites with local resource addresses of county/country public records offices, cemetery locations, maps, library addresses, archive addresses, association addresses (including Family History Centers or other genealogical or historical societies), and some history and culture of the region. Other resources may include query pages or message boards, mailing lists, historical data (including census records), cemetery records, biographies, bibliographies, and family/surname registration websites.

Between ROOTSWEB and WorldGenWeb, you should be able to find something about the country you need to search.

Other Good Starting Places

In addition to the places mentioned so far, there are many good starting places for an international search. Some are general and provide all sorts of international research, and some are for specific locations. The following sections describe some to get you started.

International Internet Genealogical Society

This all-volunteer effort aims to collect international genealogical material in one site, promote ethics in international genealogy, and promote cooperation among genealogists all over the world. The main features of the site include:

- ◆ A list of volunteers involved in the Global Village Representatives page

- ◆ The many Internet Relay Chat (IRC) chats held on a regular basis

- ◆ A library of links to resources all over the world

- Free online courses on how to conduct international genealogy

- Translation pages

- A series of online lessons on research in countries such as Germany, South Africa, Canada, Australia, and New Zealand

Sites that can provide a translation of a webpage into English include the following:

- Alta Vista Babel Fish http://babelfish.altavista.digital.com/translate.dyn

- Google Language Tools http://www.google.com/language_tools?hl = en

Asian Genealogical Sites

The Singapore Genealogy Forum, at http://genforum.genealogy.com/singapore, allows Singaporeans of all races to look for their relatives and ancestors.

- AsianGenNet, at www.rootsweb.org/ ~ asiagw, is part of WorldGenWeb and has some sites, but needs hosts for many more.

Chinese Surnames (www.yutopian.com/names) is a fascinating page with the most common Chinese surnames and their history.

European Genealogical Sites

There are many sites where you can research your European roots. I recommend you start with the following:

- **Benelux (Belgium, Netherlands, Luxembourg):** Digital Resources Netherlands and Belgium (http://geneaknowhow.net/digi/resources.html) is one place you can find resources from the Netherlands and Belgium, including over 350 Internet links to online resources (with more than 150 passenger lists), nearly 900 online resources on Dutch and Belgian bulletin board systems, and hundreds of digital resources.

- **Family Explorer Benelux**, at http://freepages.genealogy.rootsweb.com/ ~ jberteloot, is a list of links to databases, mailing lists, and other Benelux resources.

♦ **The Federation of East European Family History Societies (FEEFHS)**, at http://www.feefhs.org, was organized in 1992 to foster family research in Eastern and Central Europe without any ethnic, religious, or social distinctions (see Figure 12-4). You'll find a forum for individuals and organizations focused on a single country or group of people to exchange information and be updated on developments in the field. While it primarily serves the interests of North Americans in tracing their lineages back to a European homeland, it welcomes members from all countries. The site has historical maps, information on conferences and workshops offline, information on organizing tours to Europe for hands-on research, and a quarterly e-mail newsletter.

FIGURE 12-4. *FEEHS can help you with Eastern European research.*

- **The Ukrainian Roots** genealogy webring begins at http://ukrcommunities.8k.com/ukrroots.html. The webring is community of webpages on Ukrainian genealogy research. The pages are personal home pages of people who want to share information that they have accumulated on their family history and Ukrainian heritage. You'll also find pointers to sources of information that would be of help to others doing research into their Ukrainian family history.

- **Eastern Slovakia, Slovak, and Carpatho-Rusyn Genealogy Research**, at http://www.iarelative.com/slovakia.htm, has articles, links, message boards, and transcribed records.

France

French genealogy online is growing rapidly. This short list will get you started.

- Besides the usual sites, such as Cyndi's List and WorldGenWeb, check out **FrancoGene** at www.francogene.com. In addition to a dictionary of Quebec's pioneers and resources in Europe, you'll find links to genealogy sites in former French colonies around the world, such as Quebec and Haiti, as well as to genealogy societies and institutions.

- Much like Ancestry.com in the United States, **Genealogy.tm.fr** (http://www.genealogy.tm.fr) is a for-fee site that allows you to search documents and records in French. This was started in 1994, when Laurent Fondant began his own genealogy and found a need to transcribe, index, and scan documents. You pay a subscription for a period of time to access the documents you find in searching indexes. You can search for the geographic distribution of your surname in France (based on censuses from 1891 to 1990) at http://www.geopatronyme.com.

- **France-genealogie.fr** is a search portal of French genealogy databases. Only two years old, it already has links to the archives of France, the French Federation of Genealogy, and a link to Nomina.

- **Nomina**, http://nomina.france-genealogie.fr/nomina, is a meta-search of 13 million names in genealogy databases (GEDCOMs), marriages records, and military records. You can search them all at once, or narrow it down to one of four categories.

- **Genealogie.com** is much like Genealogy.com in the United States. People upload their data for searching and exchanging information.

Germany

The Germans keep wonderful records, but wars and other disasters sometimes left holes in the lexicon. Still, using these sites may be helpful.

- **Genealogy.net**, at www.genealogienetz.de/genealogy.html, is a treasure trove of information. From the home page, you can find the monthly newsletter in German, information on genealogical research in local regions, links to 35 different German genealogical societies, 60 mailing lists, a FAQ on German genealogy, a GEDCOM database, a gazetteer, a list of heritage books, and much more. Most of it is in German, so remember the translations sites mentioned earlier! You can search many of these databases with just one query in the meta-search engine.

- **GermanRoots**, at www.germanroots.com, offers tips, links, and research hints. It has lists such as "The Best German Resources," "The Best General Resources" "History, Language, and Culture," and a basic guide for research in German genealogy by Joe Beine.

- The telephone book for Germany can be found at http://www .dastelefonbuch.de/.

Italy

Italians love genealogy! Again, this is a short list to get you started.

- The Italian Genealogy Homepage, at www.italgen.com, is the place to start when researching your genealogy in Italy (see Figure 12-5). This page includes links to how-to articles, discussion groups, and history.

FIGURE 12-5. *The Italian Genealogy Homepage is a portal with articles, discussion groups, and more.*

- Visit **D'addezio**, or The Italian Heritage and Genealogy page, at www.daddezio.com/italgen.html. It has links to atlases, cemeteries, genealogy articles, genealogy newsletters, genealogy software reviews, genealogy supplies, helpful organizations, history and culture resources, information on coats of arms, local (Italian) societies, maps, military records, passenger lists, research services, surname studies, vital records, and more.

- The **Italy World Club** has a page with links to archives in Italy by region at www.italyworldclub.com/genealogy/state_archives.htm.

Spain

The Spanish Empire in the New World as well as Europe left many records that family historians can use. Here are some examples.

- The place to start is the **Society of Hispanic Historical and Ancestral Research** at http://members.aol.com/shhar. This 20-year-old organization is non-profit and all-volunteer, and is dedicated to family history. Besides good pointers for beginners and a message board, this is the only site I've seen with information on African-Hispanic families. The books and journals are worthwhile, too. Don't miss the monthly online magazine at http://www .somosprimos.com.

- A personal site, **Spanish Genealogy** at Spain Genealogy Links (http://www.genealogylinks.net/europe/spain/index.html) has tips, data, and links about Spain and more. Another one, called Researching Your Spanish Roots, is at http://members.aol.com/ balboanet/spain. Both have good tips and links.

- A site called **EuroDocs** from Brigham Young University has a page on Spanish history at http://eudocs.lib.byu.edu/index.php/ History_of_Spain:_Primary_Documents. This has transcribed Spanish documents from the Visigothic Code to wills of individuals.

- A list of mailing address for archives and libraries in Spain is on the Genealogy Forum at http://www.genealogyforum.rootsweb .com/gfaol/resource/Hispanic/SpainNA.htm.

Portugal

Portuguese ancestry is almost as widespread as Spanish. Online resources are not as prevalent, however.

- Doug da Rocha Holmes has a page at www.dholmes.com/ rocha1.html dedicated to Portuguese genealogy, where you can get started.

- **LusaWeb** is a site dedicated to Portuguese ancestry at www.lusaweb.com/genealogy. This is an organization with dues, like many genealogy societies.

- The **Portuguese-American Historical & Research Foundation** has a page for genealogy questions and answers at www.portuguesefoundation.org/genealogy.htm.

- The **National Library of Portugal** is online at www.bn.pt, in Portuguese, of course.

> **Note**
>
> *Most European national libraries are searchable from The European Library webpage at www.theeuropeanlibrary.org/portal/index.html.*

Scandinavia

Census records of Norway are being transcribed and posted by volunteers at these pages, which also have good information on research in Norway:

- The **Digital Archives** is a public service from the National Archives of Norway. Here you can search transcribed source material for free at http://digitalarkivet.uib.no/index-eng.htm.

- **Norwegian Research Sources** (www.rootsweb.com/~wgnorway/NorLinks.htm) is an excellent starting place. It has links to articles on the Ancestors from Norway site and "Basics of Norwegian Research," among other things.

- **Ancestors from Norway** (http://homepages.rootsweb.com/~norway/index.html) was created in 1996 to document and inform Norwegian ancestry. It now has excellent articles on research, links to over 100 sites with information and records, and even recipes!

- The **Norwegian Emigration and Genealogy Center** offers information in Norwegian for descendants at www.emigrationcenter.com.

> **Note**
>
> *Are you finding lots of good information? Have you backed up this week? This month? This year?*

♦ **Martin's Norwegian Genealogy Dictionary**, at www.geocities.com/
Heartland/Estates/5536/eidhalist.html, can help you decipher
words for relationships, occupations, and so on.

♦ **Genealogy Research Denmark**, at www.ida.net/users, really is a
personal page of one woman's collected research, with links to
other resources.

♦ **Swedish Genealogical Society of Minnesota,** at www.rootsweb
.com/~mnsgsm, has queries, data, a few transcriptions of
records translated into English, and meeting dates of the society.

United Kingdom

Genealogy is as popular in the UK as it is in the US. Here are some good
starting places for online information.

♦ **The United Kingdom (UK) and Ireland Genealogy site**, at
www.genuki.org.uk, is the best starting point. This site has
transcribed data, such as parish records, plus links to individuals'
pages where genealogy research (secondary material) is posted.
Look at the index page (http://www.genuki.org.uk/mindex.html)
for specific counties, surnames, and so forth.

♦ **The Free BMD (Free Birth, Marriage, and Death Records)
Project**, at http://freebmd.rootsweb.com, provides free Internet
access to the Civil Registration Index information for England and
Wales from 1837. The transcriptions are ongoing, and the
updates are posted once or twice a month. You can volunteer to
help!

Note

*Remember to search library and archive sites for each county in
the UK!*

♦ **AncestorSuperSearch**, at http://www.ancestorsupersearch.com,
has 1.46 million English birth, marriage, and census events (from
1355–1891) that are searchable online.

- **The National Archives of Ireland** has a genealogy how-to page at http://www.nationalarchives.ie/genealogy/beginning.html. From the site, you can search the indexes of 1901 or 1911 census returns 1840s, 1850s, and 1860s Primary Valuation (also known as Griffith's Valuation); and 1820s or 1830s Tithe Applotment Books. There are also some marriage records, although a certain number of records were destroyed in "The Troubles."

- **The UK National Digital Archive of Datasets**, at http://www .ndad .nationalarchives.gov.uk, has archived digital data from UK government departments and agencies. The system has been available since March 1998 and provides open access to the catalogs of all of its holdings, as well as free access to certain datasets when you register online.

- **The National Archives of Scotland** has records from the 12th century. The family history page at http://www.nas.gov.uk/familyHistory/, has good how-to information. You can download PDF files of fact sheets on adoption, deeds, wills, and other topics.

Australia and New Zealand

Australia is rich with genealogy websites.

- Start with **Cyndi's List** at http://www.cyndislist.com/austnz.htm.

- The **Society of Australian Genealogists**, at http://www.sag.org.au, offers materials, meetings, and special interest groups. The library catalog is online as well.

- The **Dead Person's Society**, a site for genealogy in Melbourne, Australia, has a graphic of dancing skeletons at http://home.vicnet .net.au/ ~ dpsoc (see Figure 12-6). It has guides to searching Australian provinces, databases of cemeteries, census and other records, and general articles on Australian genealogy.

- **Convicts to Australia**, a guide to researching ancestry during the time when Australia was used as a large prison, can be found at http://www.convictcentral.com/index.html. The site has some how-to guides, many census and ships' passenger lists, and more. However, the site cannot handle individual questions or requests for research help.

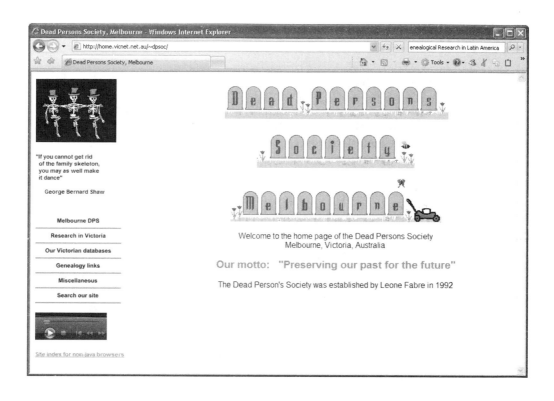

FIGURE 12-6.   *Researching Melbourne and Victoria, Australia, is fun at The Dead Person's Society.*

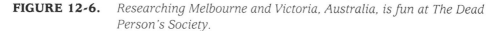

◆ The **KiwiGen Genealogy** webring has links to New Zealand genealogy at http://g.webring.com/hub?ring = kiwigen. With 42 sites ranging from single-family genealogies to geographically based ones, it is a useful site for amateur and professional genealogists alike.

◆ **The National Archives of Australia**, at http://www.naa.gov.au, has an entire section on family history and what records to look for.

Africa

- **Conrod Mercer's** page, at http://home.global.co.za/ ~ mercon, is a personal collection of tips on doing South African (white) genealogy.

- **The African Atlantic Genealogy Society**, at http://www.africantic .com, has newsletters, queries, and census data to help you get started.

You may want to check out Cyndi's List (search for the African nation of interest) and WorldGenWeb first.

North America

The following sites are good places to start to search for information on ancestors from Canada and Mexico.

Canada

Canadian history is as long and varied as the US. Here are some good starting places.

- **Canadian Genealogy and History Links (CGHL)**, at http://www .islandnet.com/ ~ jveinot/cghl/cghl.html, lists online sites for vital records, genealogies, and general history, sorted by province. The CGHL search engine will look for your search term in the descriptions or titles of pages listed on the site. For example, if you are looking for "Powell," you'll find one match to a personal genealogy page with Powells on it.

- **Immigrants to Canada**, at http://ist.uwaterloo.ca/ ~ marj/ genealogy/thevoyage.html, offers information extracted from various government records, as well as from shipping records. You can read and search such documents as ships' lists, immigration reports, and first-person accounts. It also has links to other genealogy sites.

♦   **The Canadian Genealogy Centre**, at www.collectionscanada
.ca/genealogy/index-e.html, is a page from the National Archives
and Library of Canada. You can read a PDF file of the free booklet,
"Tracing Your Ancestors in Canada," which describes the major
genealogical sources available at the National Archives and other
Canadian repositories. You also want to read "Sources by Topic,"
at http://www.collectionscanada.ca/genealogy/022-900-e.html,
which is updated more often than the brochure and describes in
detail what can be accomplished online.

Mexico

Mexican records are fairly detailed when it comes to church matters
(births, baptisms, marriages, burials and so on). Some states in Mexico
have less information on civil matters, however.

♦   **Archivo General de la Nation**, at http://www.agn.gob.mx/inicio.php,
is the National Archives of Mexico site. It's as rich and deep as the
NARA site in the United States. Note that the site is in Spanish.

♦   **Archivo Historico de Arzobispo**, at http://aham.arquidiocesismexico
.org.mx/ubicacion.htm, has the archives of the Archbishop of
Mexico, a treasure trove of Church records. This site is also in
Spanish.

♦   **Local Catholic Church History and Ancestors**, at http://home.att
.net/ ~ Local_Catholic/Catholic-Mexico.htm, has addresses to write
for parish records in Mexico.

♦   **The Texas General Land Office** has a page at http://www.glo
.state.tx.us/archives/archives.html for their archives. This state
office has records dating back to Spanish times. The page tells
you how to write for these records, including the proper
addresses and what is available.

♦   **The Genealogy of Mexico**, at http://members.tripod.com/
~ GaryFelix/index1.htm, is one genealogist's compilation of
starting places. He covers the conquistadores, coats of arms,
a DNA surname project, and more.

♦ **The Hispanic Genealogical Society of New York**, at http://www
.hispanicgenealogy.com, includes Mexico, Puerto Rico, and
other North American Hispanic genealogy. You can learn about
their regular meetings and publications, as well as find links
to resources.

A Success Story: German Ancestry Discovered

Denzil J. Klippel had quite a bit of success in his international genealogy
search, but it didn't happen overnight. Denzil started with what he
knew, researched back to the boat, and finally found his family's village
of origin. How he did this is fascinating.

Denzil only knew his parents, his grandmother on his mother's side,
and her brother and sister.

"In the beginning, I didn't take advantage of the resources on the
Net like DearMYRTLE and so forth, and ask questions. But I soon
learned everyone in the online genealogy community is willing to help
answer questions. We don't need to reinvent the wheel—just ask if
anyone has done this or that," Denzil says. So he did eventually ask
DearMYRTLE, who pointed him to research at a local Family History
Center (FHC).

Denzil visited a local FHC in New York City. There he found his
grandmother's family, but not his grandmother, on one of the microfilms.
Requesting the name and address of the submitter, he contacted him with
a query, including his e-mail address. Soon, another researcher contacted
him by e-mail, and everything began to fall together.

Note

*Denzil could have searched the Family History Library Catalog at
FamilySearch.com before going to the FHC.*

Denzil sent for his father's death certificate (New York) and found
his place and date of birth (California) and his father's place of birth
(upstate New York), as well as his mother's maiden name (Settle) and
place of birth (California). He was able to order some of these records
online through various vital records sites maintained by these states.

> ### Note
>
> *You can find where to write for many vital records at The National Center for Health Statistics page (www.cdc.gov/nchs/howto/w2w/ w2welcom.htm).*

"After going back to my great-grandfather and finding he came from Germany, I hit a brick wall. Not knowing what to do, I went to one of the search engines—Yahoo!—and put in the name Klippel. It gave me 6,000 places where the name appeared on the Net, most of them regarding an illness discovered by a Klippel. I captured all of the Klippel e-mail addresses and sent them a message saying I was researching the Klippel family name and, if they were interested in working with me, perhaps we could find some common ancestors or at least discover where the Klippels originated."

Denzil says he does *not* recommend this approach, however. "This shotgun approach never works," he said. What did work, though, was searching for the surname on Google and looking for the genealogy sites. After e-mailing people with Klippel genealogy sites, as opposed to every Klippel he could find online, Denzil heard from people who had been searching the line. Several were cousins he didn't know he had, and since that time, he now calls all Klippels he comes in contact with "cousin."

"One of these cousins had the name of the town in Germany where my Klippel line came from (Ober-Hilbersheim). I found this village had a website (see Figure 12-7) and sent a letter to the mayor. He responded via e-mail and said he knew of my line and told me there were still Klippels living in the village," Denzil said.

"In the meantime, other Klippels in Europe contacted me, and before I knew it, I was planning a trip to visit some of them and Ober-Hilbersheim. When they heard I was going to visit, they all said I had to stay with them. I bought my airline tickets online via Priceline.com and my train pass online."

Now Denzil was really into the in-person, offline mode! Through electronic and regular mail, he made appointments at all the archives he planned to visit in Germany. When he arrived, they were ready for

FIGURE 12-7. *Ober-Hilbersheim's website helped Denzil contact the mayor.*

him and, in most cases, they'd already done all the lookups. As Denzil gathered the research material, he mailed it home to himself. This was important insurance against losing or misplacing any of the papers during his sojourn.

"My trip started in Ober-Hilbersheim, and I stayed with the mayor. He took me to all the archives and helped me get all the Klippel family history back to 1650! My distant cousins in the village welcomed me with open arms. I then went to the Netherlands and stayed with the Klippels there, and they took me to the Island of Tholen, where the first Klippel came from in the 1400s. Then on to Hamburg to visit Helmut Klippel and the archive there," Denzil said.

Site Name	URL
DearMYRTLE	http://www.dearmyrtle.com
Cyndi's List	http://www.cyndislist.com (search for the country of interest)
The International Internet Genealogical Society (IIGS)	http://www.iigs.org/index.htm.en
International Genealogy Meetup	http://genealogy.meetup.com
GeneaSearch International	http://www.geneasearch.com/intl/internat.htm
Babel Fish Translation	http://babel.altavista.com/tr
Tracing Your Immigrant Ancestors	http://www.nysl.nysed.gov/genealogy/tracimmi.htm
	http://www.familysearch.org/eng/Home/News/Press/Free_Online_Records.pdf

TABLE 12-1.   *Helpful Links When Searching for Immigrant Ancestors*

"And last, but not least, on to Sweden to stay with Alf Klippel, who had given me a wealth of information about the origins of the Klippel name via e-mail and did most of the translating of the old German documents I had been receiving over the Net."

It took some footwork and perseverance, but after seven years, Denzil feels he accomplished a lot in his international search, and the online resources made it possible (see Table 12-1 for some good sites to start your international search).

Wrapping Up

- ◆ Once you find your immigrant ancestor, you can use archives and ships' passenger lists to identify their home town.

- ◆ Many national archives have webpages describing research techniques for that country.

- ◆ At FamilySearch, you can download and print research guides for immigrant origins and for specific countries, as well as word lists of genealogical terms in non-English languages.

- ◆ There are specific sites for genealogy of many nationalities.

Chapter 13

Ethnic Genealogy Resources

The international sources cited in Chapter 12 can also help you with ethnic research within the United States and Canada for well-documented ancestry. For some groups, however, the search is a little more complex.

Special Challenges

As I described in the Introduction, sometimes you need to search unexpected resources based on other genealogies, history, and, yes, the infamous "family legend." None of these things alone will solve your special challenges of ethnic research, but taken together, they might lead to that one document, vital record, or online resource that solves the puzzle. It worked for Bill Ammons, the success story in the Introduction, and it might work for you, too.

For example, African-American genealogy often presents special challenges. When researching the genealogy of a former slave, it's necessary to know as much about the slave owner's family as you do about the slave. Wills, deeds, and tax rolls hold clues to ancestry, as do legal agreements to rent slaves. Tracking down all these items can be difficult. You need to know the history of the region and the repositories of the records, and you need to consider family legends to be clues, not answers.

As another example, Native American genealogies are also difficult, because in many cases, very little was written down in the 18th and 19th centuries. A genealogist must contact the tribe involved and look at many different kinds of records. Mixed ethnic heritages, such as Melungeon, are problematic to research because these mixed groups suffered from stigma for many years. If you are researching a Melungeon family line, the true genealogy may have been suppressed or even forgotten by your ancestors. These special cases have led to many online resources.

The sites mentioned in this chapter provide good information on how to begin to search for specific genealogy information, as well as the history and culture of different groups. The challenges you will face can be discussed in the forums and mailing lists; you will often find tips on which records to seek and how to get them. Don't forget, however, that new pages are being added to the Web all the time. Search for "genealogy" plus the name of whatever ethnic group you're seeking on your favorite search engine about once a month to see if new information has become available.

And stay on the mailing lists and newsgroups for the ethnic groups; when you hit a brick wall, perhaps someone on the list can help!

African-American Genealogy

African-American genealogy presents some special challenges, but online genealogists are working hard to conquer them. Search for "African-American genealogy" in any search engine and you'll find many good resources. Also try these sites as starting places.

Note

You will find many African-American resources in the "Caribbean" section later in the chapter, and you'll find plenty of Caribbean information among the African-American genealogy pages listed in this section.

To begin, the **African-American Research Area** (http://www .archives.gov/research/african-americans/) on the National Archives and Records Administration (NARA) site provides a list of articles and other resources not to be missed.

AfriGeneas (see Figure 13-1), at www.afrigeneas.com, is the second-best starting place for African-American research. Transcribed records, discussion groups, monthly articles, and more will help you get started.

The site has a searchable database of surnames (in addition to slave data) from descendants of slaveholding families, as well as from other sources, both public and private. Tips and topics to help people in their search for family history are distributed through mailing lists, chats, newsletters, and the Internet. Volunteers do all of this; they extract, compile, and publish all related public records with any genealogical value. The site also maintains an impressive set of links to other Internet resources to help African Americans in their research.

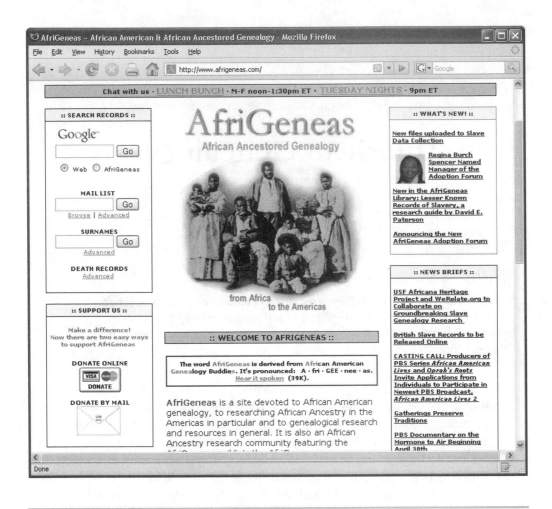

FIGURE 13-1. *AfriGeneas has databases, forums, chats, and more.*

The sections of this site are an important body of work. They include:

♦ **E-mail**   AfriGeneas has a way for you to create a Google e-mail account at the site so that your address is < yourname > @afrigeneas.com. The advantage: You can use this address only for genealogy and not for other correspondence. That way, you don't have so much worry about spam coming in with the stuff you really want to read.

♦ **Search**   The search page lets you search the mailing list, surnames, death records, and the entire site for your surnames or places of interest.

♦ **Resources**   Under this heading on the navigation bar, you can find a site map, with every page on the site and a What's New link. It also can take you to the Beginner's Guide, a slideshow-like presentation that steps you through online genealogy. It's a no-nonsense approach, showing what can and can't be done online. It also includes some success stories. The Resources tab also has links to state resources, a clickable map with links to each state in the United States with history, links to state resources, and queries. The World Resources link does the same for other countries, such as the Bahamas. Volunteers are actively being sought for other countries. From the Resources tab, you also get to some important databases:

   ♦ **Surnames**   This is a set of queries with names, dates, and places of known ancestors. You can search the ones there, as well as post your own.

   ♦ **Slave Data**   This area will help you find the last owned slave in your family. Records kept by the slave owner are frequently the only clue to African-American ancestors, particularly during the period 1619–1869. The site is also designed to help descendants of slaveholders and other researchers. Users share information they find containing any references to slaves, including wills, deeds, and other documents. This site also houses a search engine and a form for submitting any data you might have. To use the database, click the first letter of the surname you're interested in. This takes you to a list of text files with surnames beginning with that letter. Now click a particular file name. The text file may be transcribed from a deed book, a will, or some other document. The name and e-mail address of the submitter will be included, so you can write to that person for more information, if necessary.

   ♦ **Census Records**   These are transcribed census records. As a file is submitted, it's listed at the top of the What's New list on this page. Not all states have volunteers transcribing right now, so you can only click those states that show up as a live link.

   ♦ **Library**   This contains guides, articles, chat transcripts, and images for you to look at online or download to your computer. Among the titles are "Researching in Southwest Louisiana" and "Cherokee Freedmen in Indian Territory."

◆ **Forums**   This area includes not only the original discussion list that gave rise to the site, but also forums on geographic areas, DNA research, and more. You'll find the rules and the archives, plus information about how to subscribe and unsubscribe to the mailing lists.

◆ **Chats**   Discussion on specific topics meet on a scheduled basis, and open discussions are usually available 24 hours a day. The forum is a Web-based list of messages sorted by date, with the most recent at the top.

◆ **AfriGeneas Links**   This page offers hundreds of fascinating links, sorted by topic, from good starting points, such as Christine's Genealogy website (discussed later), WPA Slave Narratives, and Canadian Black History.

Extras include humor, maps, poetry, news, and more. AfriGeneas has come a long way from its beginnings as a mailing list, and it keeps getting better and better.

◆ **Africana Heritage**   A project at the University of South Florida (USF), is at www.africanaheritage.com (see Figure 13-2). The USF Africana Heritage Project is an all-volunteer research project and website sponsored by the Africana Studies department at the University of South Florida. The volunteers concentrate on recovering records that document the names and lives of slaves, freed persons, and their descendants and then share those records on the free site Volunteers search the University of South Florida's library holdings, other library holdings, academic archives, plantation journals, public records, Freedman's Bureau records, early church records, oral histories, family bible records, Internet research, and information contributed by genealogy researchers, historians, and community members. In 2007, USF announced a collaboration with WeRelate.org on historical research sponsored by the Magnolia Plantation Foundation of Charleston, South Carolina. Magnolia Plantation is funding genealogical research in the plantation journals of the Drayton family of Charleston. The USF Africana Heritage Project will reconstruct the lineages of enslaved communities on Drayton family plantations and build family files that anyone can access for free on the Internet.

FIGURE 13-2. *University of South Florida Africana Heritage Project has details on the lives of African Americans from slave times to today.*

Readers are invited to share documents with the site, and material is there from readers, scholars, archives, universities, and historical societies For more information, contact: Toni Carrier, Founding Director, USF Africana Heritage Project, 4202 E. Fowler Avenue, FAO 270, Tampa, FL 33620, e-mail: info@africanaheritage.com.

More Good Resources

Other good African-American sites are in this list.

◆ **African American Genealogy on the Web**   From Princeton University at www.princeton.lib.nj.us/robeson/genealogylinks .html, has links to several good sites, as well as information on singer/actor Paul Robeson.

◆ **The Afro-American Historical and Genealogical Society (AAHGS)**   Is a group for the preservation of the history, genealogy, and culture of those with African heritage. The society's main emphasis is in recording research (as in transcribing sources and so on) and sharing completed genealogies. You'll find AAHGS at www.aahgs.org. They have an annual conference, local chapters, a journal, and newsletter.

◆ **Slaves and the Courts**   (http://lcweb2.loc.gov/ammem/sthtml) is an online collection of pamphlets and books at the Library of Congress about the experiences of African and African-American slaves in the United States and American colonies (see Figure 13-3). It includes trial arguments, examinations of cases and decisions, and other materials concerning slavery and the slave trade. You can locate information by using the collection's subject index, author index, or title index, or you can conduct your own search by keyword. You can look at the items as transcriptions or as images of the original pages. Knowing this sort of history can often give you a clue as to where to look for other records.

◆ **Cases from America and Great Britain**   Are included with arguments by many well-known abolitionists, presidents, politicians, slave owners, fugitive and free-territory slaves, lawyers and judges, and justices of the U.S. Supreme Court. Significant names include John Q. Adams, Roger B. Taney, John C. Calhoun, Salmon P. Chase, Dred Scott, William H. Seward, Theodore Parker, Jonathan Walker, Daniel Drayton, Castner Hanway, Francis Scott Key, William L. Garrison, Wendell Phillips, Denmark Vesey, and John Brown.

◆ **The African-American Genealogy Ring**   Is a cooperative of sites linking different resources. Start at www.afamgenealogy .ourfamily.com.

FIGURE 13-3. *Slaves and the Courts contains about 100 publications on this important topic.*

♦ **U.S. African-American Griots** At www.rootsweb.com/~afamer, discusses the storytellers, or griots. Their roles are hereditary, and their surnames identify them as griots, and they sing and tell the histories of their tribes.

♦ **The Freedman's Bureau Online** At www.freedmensbureau.com, allows you to search many records. The Freedman's Bureau took care of education, food, shelter, clothing, and medicine for refugees and freedmen. When Confederate land or property was confiscated, the Freedman's Bureau took custody. Records include personnel records and reports from various states on programs and conditions.

- **The African-American Genealogical Society of Northern California** Is a local group, but its website has monthly articles, online genealogy charts, discussion groups, and more. It is worth a visit. Find it at www.aagsnc.org.

- **AAGENE-L** Is a moderated mailing list for African-American genealogy and history researchers. Subscribe to the list by sending a message to aagene-l@upeople.com with SUBSCRIBE in the subject line. Details can be found at http://ftp.cac.psu.edu/~saw/aagene-faq.html.

Here are two sites with no online resources but that are important nonetheless:

- **The National African-American Archives Museum** Located in Mobile, Alabama, is dedicated to preserving the rich history contributed by African Americans, particularly those born in greater Mobile. You can read details about the museum's holdings, events, and exhibits at www.800alabama.com/things-to-do/alabama-attractions/details.cfm?id = 1296. From the slave ship *Clotilde* to baseball great Hank Aaron and U.S. Labor Secretary Alexis Herman, you can trace the history of famous African Americans from Mobile. Admission is free to the public.

- **The Alabama A&M State Black Archives, Research Center, and Museum** Located in Huntsville, Alabama, holds public programs and events on African-American family history. Details about upcoming exhibits, lectures, tours, and workshops are available at www.aamu.edu and by clicking the Archives link. The organization is open to visitors Monday through Friday, 9:00 A.M. to 4:30 P.M. For information about exhibits, resources, programs, the museum, and tours, call (256) 372-5846 or fax (256) 372-5338, or you can write to the State Black Archives Research Center and Museum, P.O. Box 595, Normal, AL, 35762.

Arab Genealogy

Genealogy.com has a discussion group for United Arab Emirates genealogy at www.genforum.genealogy.com/uae. Cyndi's List and RootsWeb are both good places to search for mailing lists and discussion forums as well.

Australian Aborigines

The **Aboriginal Studies WWW Virtual Library**, at www.ciolek.com/
WWWVL-Aboriginal.html, has links to resources and articles concerning
Australian aborigines.

The **Genealogy in Australia and New Zealand** page has a link to the
mailing list for Australian/New Zealand genealogy at www.rootsweb
.com/ ~ billingh.

The **National Library of Australia** has a page on genealogy, located
at www.nla.gov.au/oz/genelist.html, that includes links to many specific
ethnic and family sites.

The **Australian Institute of Aboriginal and Torres Strait Islander
Studies (AIATSIS)** has a page just for family historians, located at
www.aiatsis.gov.au/library/family_history_tracing (see Figure 13-4).

FIGURE 13-4.   *A special unit of the AIATSIS helps with family history.*

Caribbean Genealogy

Caribbean Genealogy Resources, located at www.candoo.com/genresources, lists links to archives, museums, universities, and libraries with historical and genealogical information for countries in the Caribbean. Another page from this site is www.candoo.com/surnames, which is a list of Caribbean surnames. The text files list surnames, places, and dates, as well as e-mail contact information for researchers looking for them.

WorldGenWeb has a Caribbean page at www.rootsweb.com/~caribgw. Search RootsWeb for mailing lists for related queries and discussions.

The AOL Hispanic Genealogy Special Interest Group has many Caribbean links. The main page is at http://users.aol.com/mrosado007.

BVI Genealogy

The British Virgin Islands are in the process of indexing their official archives. The indexing program has been progressing in steps. According to Chief Records Management Officer and co-coordinator of the Archives Project Verna Penn Moll, in 2006, the staff worked on it for five months; then they resumed in June 2007 for six weeks. The plan is to finish in the first quarter of 2008. The indexing is being carried out by two professionals from Caribbean Regional Branch of the International Council on Archives (CARBICA) and three trained local officers.

"[The indexing project was] included in my action plan as one of the activities essential to organize the archives as a functional institution," Mrs. Moll told me. "We are creating databases and also hope to launch a website by January/February 2008. We have started with the earliest records. The organizing and indexing come first. The older records will be microfilmed. We hope to outsource some records for digitization. Many government records are now created electronically."

Mrs. Moll said many records have been lost to the ravages of time and weather, although "[s]ome reconstruction is possible, but it is a costly business," she said. "We hope to fill in gaps by obtaining microfilm materials from metropolitan archive repositories. I do not actually get much time with the older archives themselves, as much as I would like to," she added. "The records are a great source of administrative, cultural, social, and historical information. I also have to direct the management of the active, intermediate, and archival records across the government service: draft policies, push for legislation, accommodation, and staff."

Until the project is done in 2008, you'll have to rely on these online sources:

♦ **British Virgin Islands Caribbean GenWeb** At http://www .britishislesgenweb.org/ ~ bvi, has general resources, online records, query boards, and a mailing list.

♦ **Caribbean Genealogy-Resources-Microfilm Indexes** At http://www.candoo.com/genresources/microfilms.htm, is a list of surnames in the Caribbean listed by surname and researcher.

♦ **Genforum.Genealogy.Com** At http://genforum.genealogy.com, features a forum finder, and you can search by surnames. It also offers information on general genealogy topics, such as immigration, emigration, migration, religions, and wars.

♦ **World-Wide Web Resources: Genealogy** At http://www.uky .edu/Libraries/guide.php?sub_id = 67, presents a directory of websites related to genealogy and is provided by the University of Kentucky in Lexington. It offers access to databases, societies, and records offices. It also provides access to discussion lists and research resources. Links to the Social Security Death Index, online publications, heraldry resources, and other directories are provided as well.

The following offices hold BVI records that are relevant to family research. Although they do not all have adequate space and staff to accommodate public searches, if you make an appointment, the appropriate officer would likely find a way to assist you with your search:

♦ **The General Civil Registry Office** Holds records of births, marriages, deaths, and wills from 1859 to present. The Anglican and Methodist churches hold records of baptisms, marriages and deaths as follows: Anglican Church: baptisms (1825–1861), marriages (1833–1946), and burials (1819–1867); Methodist Church: baptisms (1815–1895 and 1889), marriages (1877–1934), and burials (1845–1896).

♦ **The Inland Revenue Office** Records ownership of houses, land, and other property.

- ◆ **Tax lists**   Containing pertinent information are published annually.

- ◆ **The Land Registry**   Holds property identifiers, including indexes and maps from 1972, public library information (newspapers from 1959 and various name indexes), BVI history books, and, from the Survey Department, ordinance 1953 maps and boundary maps from 1975. You can write to them at: The Archives Unit, Deputy Governor's Office, Burhym Building, 49 deCasro Street, Road Town, Tortola. (284) 468-2365 (phone) and (284) 468-2582 (fax).

Creole/Cajun Genealogy

The Acadians/Cajuns were the French settlers ejected from Nova Scotia by the British in the mid-18th century. Some went to Quebec, and some to Louisiana.

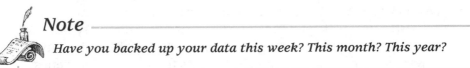

Note

Have you backed up your data this week? This month? This year?

You may be aware that "Creole" means different things in different places. In Latin America, a Creole is someone of pure Spanish blood. In the Caribbean, it means a descendant of Europeans; in the Guineas, it means someone descended from slaves, whether African or native to the islands. In the southern United States, the term refers to aristocratic landowners and slaveholders before the Civil War, part of the overall French/Cajun culture of the Gulf Coast. For almost all Creole research, parish records are your best bet—those and mailing list discussions!

Acadian-Cajun Genealogy and History, at www.acadian-cajun.com, publishes records, how-to articles, history, mailing lists, maps, genealogies, and more.

The Encyclopedia of Cajun Culture, at www.cajunculture.com, will give you good background information.

Vive La Cajun (www.vivelacajun.com) has information on how to research Cajun genealogy.

The Cajun and Zydeco Radio Guide also has a list of family histories that have been posted to the Web at www.cajunradio.org/genealogy.html.

Canada GenWeb has a section on Acadian genealogy in Canada at www.geocities.com/Heartland/Acres/2162.

The Louisiana Creole Heritage Center (see Figure 13-5) is located on the campus of Northwestern State University in Natchitoches, Louisiana, and on the Web at www.nsula.edu/creole.

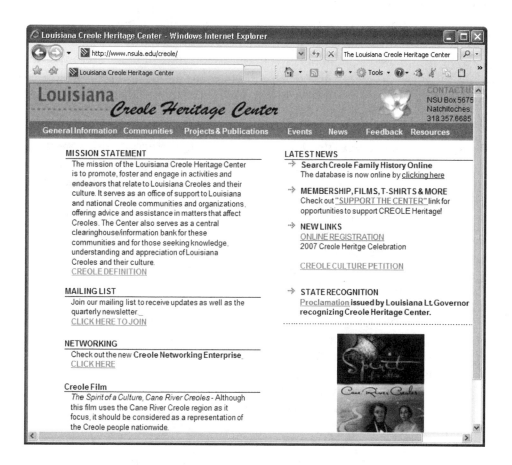

FIGURE 13-5.   *The Louisiana Creole Heritage Center has an online family history database.*

The **Confederation of Associations of Families Acadian**, at www.cafa.org, promotes the culture and genealogy of Acadian families in America.

Search **RootsWeb's** list of mailing lists; there are several for Acadian/Cajun research and data in Louisiana and Canada.

Cuban Genealogy

Good pointers, tips, and exchanges on Cuban genealogy can be found at the **Cuban GenWeb** (www.cubagenweb.org).

Even as you read this, University of Florida researchers are working to preserve and copy about 10 million records in the Cuban National Archives. These records cover Cuban life, business, and shipping from 1578 to 1900, but they were sealed with the revolution of 1959. These records were collected by the Notaries of Cuba and stored by the government. Called The Notary Protocols, these records document births, deaths, property, and slave ownership transactions—basically, data on everything and everybody who passed through Havana from Spain to America and back. Once they're made public, these records will enable slave descendants to trace their genealogy to the time their ancestors were first brought to the Americas.

This resource won't become available overnight, of course. The researchers still need to secure funding. Once they begin, the first stages of the project will take 12 to 18 months. Realistically, it will probably be 2008 or later before you can look at the indexes. The University of Florida will post a guide to the materials, and you will then be able to obtain copies of individual documents on CD-ROM. Read about it at http://www.uflib.ufl.edu/news2/Current_News.html. Click the Back Issues of Chapter One link, then the Spring 2001 link. The article is a PDF file, so you will need Acrobat Reader to view it.

Meanwhile, the **National Archives of Columbia and Cuba**, with the help of United Nations Educational, Scientific and Cultural Organization (UNESCO), has posted documentation on the slave trade in this hemisphere's history at http://www.arnac.cu/trataindex.php (see Figure 13-6). The pages are in Spanish, but remember that Alta Vista's Babel Fish can translate for you.

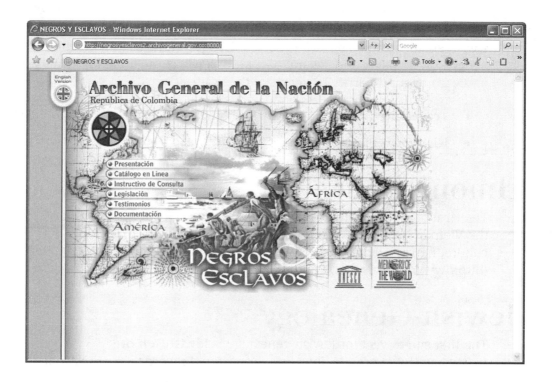

FIGURE 13-6. *Thousands of documents related to the history of the slave trade in Latin America held by the National Archives of Columbia and Cuba are now online.*

Doukhobors Genealogy

The history of this small sect of Russian pacifist dissenters is outlined in **"Who are the Doukhobors?"** at www.castlegar.com/tourism/doukhobor/who.html. Genealogy is covered at **Doukhobors Saskatchewan Genealogy Roots** at www.rootsweb.com/ ~ cansk/Saskatchewan/ethnic/doukhobor-saskatchewan.html. The RootsWeb message boards at Ancestry.com have several topics on this group as well.

Gypsy, Romani, Romany, and Travellers Genealogy

The Gypsy Lore Society maintains a list of links on Gypsy lore, genealogy, and images at http://sca.lib.liv.ac.uk/collections/gypsy/links.htm.

Romani culture and history are covered at **Patrin**, located at www.geocities.com/~patrin. Type "genealogy" in the search box at the bottom of the page, and several past articles will come up in the results.

Learn about the Irish Travellers at these sites:

♦ **Travellers' Heritage**   www.travellerheritage.ie/asp

♦ **Irish Traveller Movement**   www.itmtrav.com/index.html

Hmong Genealogy

The Hmong people came to the United States from Laos at the end of the Vietnam War. **The Hmong** home page, at www.hmongnet.org, has culture, news, events, and general information. **The Hmong Village** (http://www.forums.hmongvillage.com/) has information as well.

Jewish Genealogy

The first site to visit for Jewish genealogy is **JewishGen.org** (www.jewishgen.org). Mailing lists, transcribed records, GEDCOMs, and more are at the site. You can also find links to special interest groups, such as geographic emphasis or genetics. Your next stop should be **The Israel GenWeb Project** website, at www.israelgenealogy.com, which serves as a resource to those researching their family history in Israel.

Sephardic Genealogy, at www.SephardicGen.com, has links to articles and historical documents, as does **Sephardim.org**, at www.sephardim.org, which has an article on Jamaican-Jewish history.

Canadian-Jewish genealogists should begin at the **Jewish Genealogical Society of Montreal**, at www.jgs-montreal.org, which contains a history of the first Jewish settlers there.

Native American Genealogy

Indians/Native Americans on NARA is a reference page with links to various government records resources. It can be found at www.archives.gov/research/alic/reference/native-americans.html. A good source on culture/heritage is a search engine called **Native Languages of America**, located at www.nativelanguages.org.

The Congress of Aboriginal Peoples is a site that presents categorized links to Canadian aboriginal, Native American, and international indigenous sites on the Web. The genealogy page is at www.abo-peoples.org/.

The African-Native American History & Genealogy web page, at www.african-nativeamerican.com, is mostly concerned with the history of Oklahoma and surrounding areas.

Access Genealogy's Native American Genealogy page, located at www.accessgenealogy.com/native, has transcribed records and a state-by-state list of online sites.

All Things Cherokee is a site about many aspects of Cherokee culture, genealogy included (see Figure 13-7). The genealogy page is at www.allthingscherokee.com/genealogy.html.

The Potowami has a site at www.potawatomi.org, with a history of the tribe.

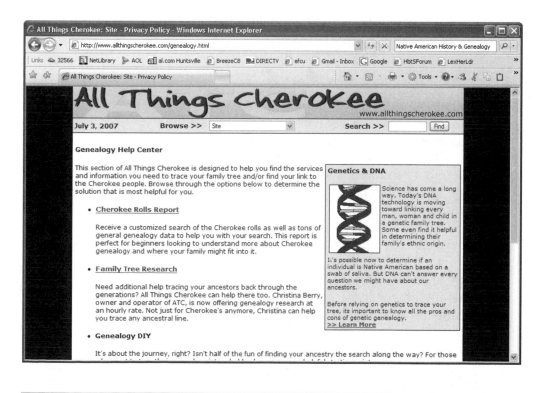

FIGURE 13-7.   *All Things Cherokee started out as The Cherokee Genealogy Page and expanded, but genealogy is still a major emphasis.*

The Cheyenne Ancestors, at www.cheyenneancestors.com, is a site containing a database of some ancestors, a bibliography for further study, and Montana links.

Many other tribes also have sites. Simply use any search engine for the tribe name, plus the word "genealogy," and you'll likely get a hit.

Metis Genealogy

Metis is a name for those of Native American heritage, but mixed tribes. **Other Metis**, at www.othermetis.net/AboGene/genelink.html, has links to resources and records.

Melungeon Genealogy

The origins of the people and even the name are controversial, but the Appalachian ethnic group called Melungeon seems to be of European, African, Mediterranean, and Native American descent. One legend is that Sir Francis Drake marooned Portuguese, Turkish, and Moorish prisoners on the North Carolina shore in the 1560s. Melungeons are documented as far back as 18th century in the Appalachian wilderness. They are found in the Cumberland Plateau area of Virginia, Kentucky, North Carolina, West Virginia, Tennessee, and, some argue, North Alabama.

Melungeon genealogy took on new and exciting relevance with the publication of *The Melungeons: The Resurrection of a Proud People* by Dr. N. Brent Kennedy (Mercer University Press, 1997). One interesting theory in the book is that Abraham Lincoln bears the Melugeon characteristics of his mother, Nancy Hanks. (see also "The Legend of a Mountain Girl and Her Baby" at http://melungeons.com/articles/mar2005.htm).

Melungeons and Other Mestee Groups (http://multiracial.com/site/content/view/310/27) by Mike Nassau is an online book on the subject that you can download.

One of the best places to start besides those listed here is the **Melungeon Heritage Association**, at www.melungeon.org.

An informational page called "Avoiding Pitfalls in Melungeon Research" is at www.continuitypress.com/pitfals.html. This is the text of a talk presented by Pat Spurlock Elder at "Second Union, a Melungeon Gathering" held in Wise, Virginia, in July 1998.

The Melungeon Resource page includes a FAQ file, located at (http://homepages.rootsweb.com/ ~ mtnties/melungeon.html). **The Appalachian Mountain Families** page includes information on Melungeons and is located at http://freepages.genealogy.rootsweb .com/ ~ appalachian.

Some rare diseases are characteristic of Melungeons. **The Melungeon Health Education and Support Network**, at www.melungeonhealth.org, describes some of these diseases and has links to resources about them.

A Melungeon mailing list exists for people conducting Melungeon and/or Appalachian research, including Native American, Portuguese, Turkish, Black Dutch, and other unverifiable mixed statements of ancestry or unexplained rumors, with ancestors in Tennessee, Kentucky, Virginia, North Carolina, South Carolina, Georgia, Alabama, West Virginia, and possibly other places. Details at can be found at http://homepages.rootsweb.com/ ~ mtnties/list.html

Wrapping Up

♦ Many ethnic groups have started mailing lists, newsgroups, and history sites.

♦ Once a month, use your favorite search engine to find new sites.

♦ Stay on mailing lists to discuss your ethnic "brick walls."

Chapter 14

The Church of Jesus Christ of Latter-day Saints

The genealogy research work of the members of the Church of Jesus Christ of Latter-day Saints (LDS) is unsurpassed in scope and size. Every genealogist needs to know how to use this wonderful resource. There are offline and online portions, but it is all helpful.

All these databases are submitted by LDS church members as well as others around the world. About ten years ago, all data was accepted, but this led to duplicates and misinformation being included. Now, submitters must include documentation for their data (original records, interview date and time, and so forth). So the newer uploads are more reliable than the earlier ones.

FamilySearch Internet

The FamilySearch Internet Genealogy Service (www.FamilySearch.org) is a site sponsored by LDS to help people find and share family history information. Launched in May 1999, it is a genealogy database, a catalog to the Family History Library in Salt Lake City, a place to get a free website for your own genealogy, and an education center, with publications and lessons online to help you learn what you need to do next in your family history research. It is designed to encourage all people to find their ancestors and preserve their family histories. To help you do this, the LDS has been actively gathering and preserving genealogical records worldwide for over 100 years.

The databases contain more than 400 million names of people who have died. These names are mostly from the United States, Canada, and the British Isles, and have taken decades to compile. In addition, years have been spent developing, engineering, and improving core internal systems to provide this resource. Using the site (the opening page is shown in Figure 14-1) is free, although you can order some products, such as databases on CD-ROM and research guides.

Here's a short list of the main resources on the site:

♦ **Censuses**, the 1880 United States, 1881 British Isles, and the 1881 Canadian censuses

♦ **The International Genealogical Index**, or IGI (explained later in the chapter)

♦ **The Pedigree Resource File**, or PRF, which is the collection of genealogical information uploaded to FamilySearch since its launch in 1999 (explained later in the chapter)

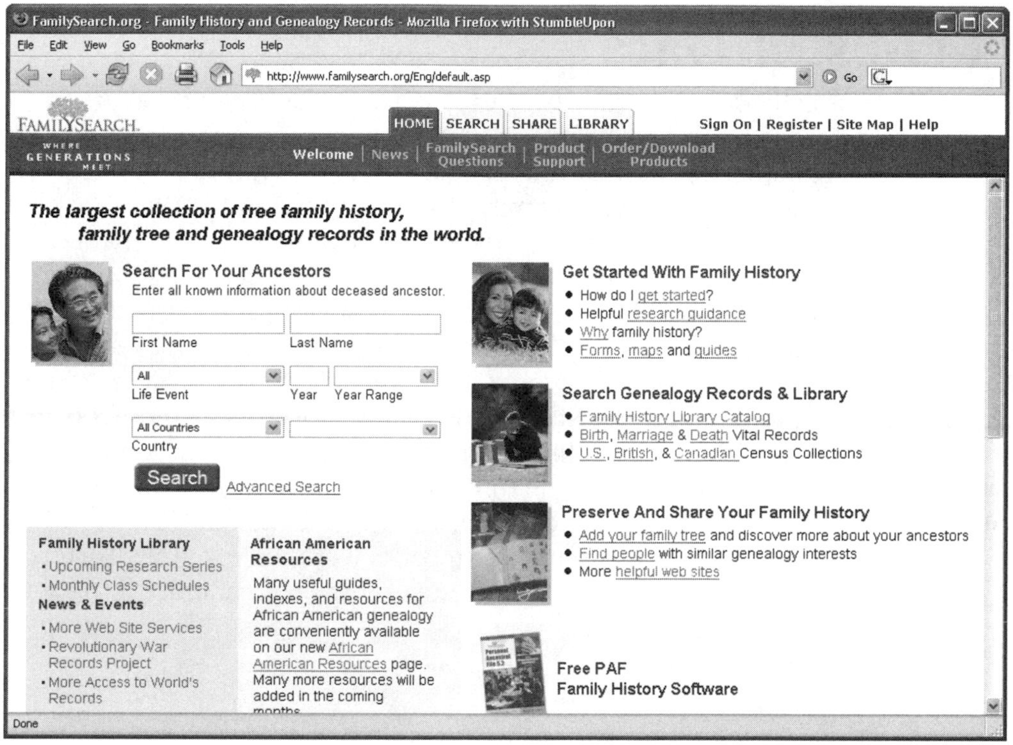

FIGURE 14-1. *The FamilySearch site is one of the most important online genealogy resources.*

♦ **The Ancestral File**, or AF, (explained later in the chapter), which is a collection of genealogies submitted by members and non-members of the LDS

♦ **The U.S. Social Security Death Index**, or SSDI

♦ **The Vital Records Index** for Mexico and Scandinavia

♦ **Family history websites** uploaded by users of the site

Note

You'll find that genealogists online often refer to these databases by their initials: SSDI, AF, IGI, PRF, and so on, in e-mails and forum posts.

Types of Data

The FamilySearch site protects privacy in two ways: The data on the site is already publicly available at other locations, though not always available online. Secondly, living people are not identified.

Records contained in the Family History Library and in the FamilySearch databases have been collected from a wide variety of sources. Individuals, families, and genealogical societies donate records to the Family History Library, for example. The library also purchases other records, such as the U.S. Social Security Death Index, census records, and published family or county histories. Most of the microfilm collection has been produced by the Family History Department's own international effort to microfilm original sources. An index to many of these records is available online through the Family History Library Catalog, on the site, and at local Family History Centers (FHCs). In cooperation with legal custodians of records worldwide, Family History Department employees are currently supervising microfilming projects in 47 countries.

Note

Both www.familysearch.org and www.familysearch.com work as URLs for the site.

Often, what you get in a search is a reference to a document on microfilm that you can rent or buy or view at a local FHC. You can also search the Vital Records Index for Mexico and Scandinavia.

Note

Here's how popular the site is with cybergenealogists: When the 1880 U.S. and 1881 Canadian censuses went online at the LDS site, new visitor traffic surged immediately to more than 500 percent and remained six to ten times above normal the following week.

FamilySearch Internet Genealogy Service is designed to be a first step in searching for family history information. When you're searching

LDS proprietary sources, the first screen doesn't give you the information itself. The search results simply tell you if the information you need is available, with links to the website, Family History Library Catalog citation, IGI, AF reference, or citation in one of the CD-ROMs the LDS has for sale.

This is more helpful than it sounds, however. Just finding a match in the Family History Library Catalog can save you hours of research. Some FHCs are so busy, patrons are only allowed one hour a week at the computer! Searching the catalog before you go can make your trip much more productive. Finding a reference in the CD-ROMs might tell you whether it's worth the price for you to order it. Finding a reference in the IGI or AF can tell you if someone else has already found the primary record or source you're looking for, and sometimes how to contact the person who found it. In short, this can save you a lot of time and travel.

Only rarely, though, can you use this resource to get to primary (original record) sources. Most of the records in the FamilySearch Internet Genealogy Service are abstracts. If you find a reference to a record you want in the LDS sources, you usually can get a complete copy of it from an FHC. FHCs are located throughout the world and have many of the records found in the FamilySearch Internet Genealogy Service. You learn more about FHCs later in the chapter in the section called "A Visit to a Family History Center."

Another big advantage to this site is that it has more international data than most online sources. Although the greatest part of the data is from English-speaking countries, you can find some information from every continent. Asian sources are the most limited, whereas North American and European sources are the most abundant.

Some Background

Mormons consider it a religious duty to research their family history. The Church teaches that families are eternal, and for more than a century and a half, members have been encouraged to identify their deceased ancestors. A detailed explanation can be found at the LDS website, www.lds.org.

One of the LDS Church's objectives is to build its copyrighted databases and to continually improve their accuracy and the software used to search them. The result is a huge database of names with births, christenings, and marriages with their dates. The data is archived at the church's headquarters in Salt Lake City, Utah, and distributed in microfilm, microfiche, and CD-ROM to their many Family History Centers throughout the world. The Family History Department maintains a climate-controlled underground storage facility to safeguard master copies of all its microfilm records. The storage facility, built literally into a mountainside, is located about 25 miles from downtown Salt Lake City.

> ### Note
>
> *The AF offers pedigrees, but the IGI doesn't. The PRF is all secondary material submitted by volunteers.*

International Genealogical Index

The International Genealogical Index (IGI) lists the dates and places of births, christenings, and marriages for more than 285 million deceased people and makes otherwise difficult-to-access information searchable online. Its best use is to find an individual in your family tree and a living person's contact information to exchange data with. The index includes people who lived at any time after the early 1500s up through the early 1900s. These names have been researched and extracted from thousands of original records, mostly compiled from public-domain sources.

The IGI contains two basic kinds of entries: submissions by individual LDS members of data on their ancestors (older submissions may not be as accurate as newer ones) and submissions from the extraction program, which is a systematic, well-controlled volunteer program of the Church. Members all over the world extract birth or christening dates, as well as marriage dates and locations from microfilms of original parish and civil records. The source of the data from information provided for each entry is on the CD-ROM version of the IGI. But, always remember, the IGI is only an index. You should go to the source document to verify the information.

A typical search will turn up lots of hits, so it is best to limit your search for a name with a date and an event (birth, marriage, or death, for example) and, if possible, the most narrow geography. You must specify a country at least; narrowing by state helps even more. FamilySearch will not search for middle names unless you select the

Use Exact Spelling check box, but if you use that search, you cannot also search by any other parameter. You may not get the results you want if you list parents' names and a spouse's name in the same search. Most records from the IGI contain either parents' names or a spouse's name, but not both. Often, the immediate family group (husband, wife, children) is what you find. A typical individual's entry is shown in Figure 14-2.

You will find some duplicate records in the IGI; in most cases, the duplication is caused by multiple people submitting the same name with slight variations in the data. If you decide to contribute data to IGI, contact other family members who are working on the same family lines to help keep these duplications to a minimum.

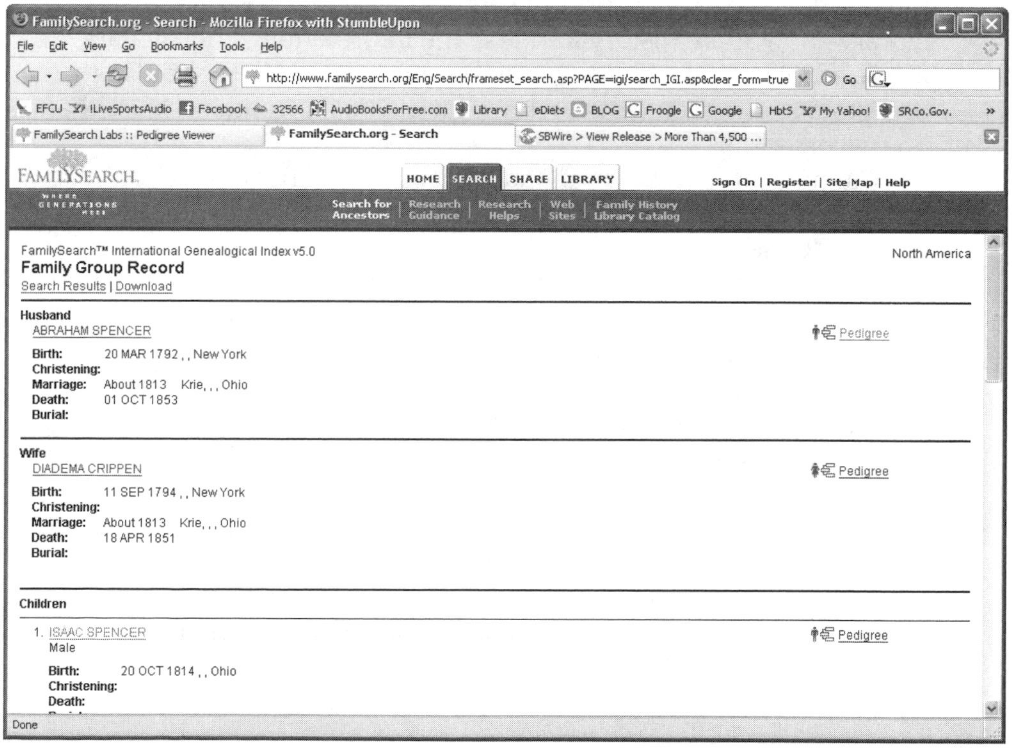

FIGURE 14-2. *A family group record may show spouse and children in the IGI.*

The IGI on CD-ROMs that you view at the local Family History Center and the Internet version have the same data, but the Internet and Family History Center versions display that data differently: The Internet version displays all events and relationships. The CD-ROM version displays only one event per entry. The Internet version also is updated more frequently and contains more information. With both, if you want to look at the documents in microfilm, you order by film number or find it at your local FHC.

Ancestral File

The Ancestral File contains a compilation of genealogies of families from around the world and records that have been contributed by thousands of people, including users of the Church's Family History Library and Family History Centers. The information—mostly data about people who have died—is linked into pedigrees to show both ancestors and descendants of individuals. The file contains more than 35 million names.

You must at least enter an individual's last name (unless you search for children of the same parents or search by Ancestral File number). Like the IGI search, middle names don't count, unless you specify exact spelling, and then you cannot use other parameters. You may search for any combination of first and last names for the individual, parents, and spouse. You may also search for just a last name. For common surnames, fill in additional fields to improve your search results. You will get better results if you enter an individual's first name and last name. Last names are standardized so that spelling variations are retrieved in the results.

The results will have family and spouse information, as well as the submitter's information. This is usually a mailing address, sometimes with phone and fax numbers as well. You would use this to write a query letter, offering what information you have in exchange for the details on the source of the material submitted.

Pedigree Resource File

The Pedigree Resource File (PRF) is a searchable database of submissions from FamilySearch Internet users. The PRF grows at the rate of 1.2 million names per month. Forty percent of the database is from outside North America and the British Isles. You can search it online or at a local FHC on CD-ROMs that are updated every six months.

The PRF contains compiled pedigrees submitted by users of FamilySearch or gathered from printed family histories and other sources, including government archives. The PRF is becoming a reservoir of names to help individuals identify and link their ancestors.

It is similar to the Ancestral File, but they do not overlap completely. Unlike the Ancestral File (which simply has the name of the person who submitted data), it contains notes and source documentation, which varies in thoroughness.

Social Security Death Index

The Social Security Death Index (SSDI) can help you find people who died after 1938, as described in Chapter 9. You will find that some sites charge you for this search, but on FamilySearch, it is free.

You can search for just a last name, but for common surnames, it is best to fill in additional fields to improve your search results. You will also get better results if you enter an individual's first name and last name. Last names are standardized so that spelling variations are included in the results.

To search for a woman, use the surname she registered with the Social Security Administration. If the woman was married, search using her married name. Areas under U.S. administration for Social Security number issuance include Canal Zone, Canton Islands, Caroline Islands, Mariana Islands (other than Guam), Marshall Islands, Midway Islands, and Wake Islands.

Where it gets tricky is which event you choose to search by. If a birth is the selected event, you will want to search for where you think the Social Security number was issued (which may not necessarily be the birthplace). If a death is the selected event, FamilySearch Internet Genealogy Service will search for the state or territory of the ZIP code at time of death. If you select all events (birth, marriage, and death), FamilySearch Internet Genealogy Service will search for both location of Social Security number issuance and location at the time of death.

Using These Resources

The IGI, the AF, and the PRF are unrelated because data entered in one file doesn't necessarily show up in the other file. Each has a value of its own, and all files are worth searching. The advantage of the AF is that you can get pedigrees from it. The advantage of the IGI is that it provides more detailed information. The PRF has the work of other genealogists, which makes it one or two times removed from the original sources, but it's useful nonetheless. They all will help you find other people searching your surnames.

It used to be common wisdom that the IGI was a little more reliable than the AF, because although errors turn up in both, the IGI is closer to the original records (data is normally entered into the IGI first), and it had better bits and pieces of information, especially its references to where the information originated. Since about 2003, however, controls on all the databases have improved, and documentation has been added. Although errors do exist, the percentage seems low. Plenty of genealogy books printed in the past 100 years have more errors than these databases.

Treat the PRF, AF, and IGI the same way you treat a printed book about a surname—with informed caution. Used as an excellent source of clues, they can always be crosschecked with primary records. Just remember: Although the computer increases the amount of data you can scan, making your work much easier, it doesn't necessarily improve accuracy. Human beings are still the source of the data.

Success Story: FamilySearch Proves a Family Legend

I had the names of my great-grandfather, his two brothers, and both parents—along with the name of the little town they were born in and raised in Wales. For three years, I searched for evidence of the parents who were presumably named Hugh Jones and Mary Ellen Williams. The information was furnished by their grandson.

In the quest to acquire as much evidence as possible on every person in my line, I ran a query on the LDS site. Some of this information was transcription, and some was by submission of family group sheets (without source citations). I was fortunate to find what could potentially be my great-grandfather's christening record as a transcribed set of bishop's records for the parish. Correct place, correct year, wrong parent names—or so I thought. I was able to run a query using the parents' names only so that I could find all birth records in that county where these two names appeared as mother and father. Sure enough, each of the other two boys and a bonus daughter appeared. The parents were Moses Jones and Elizabeth Jones.

Subsequent research further supports the information. In fact, both died before the grandson informant was even born! Perhaps he mistook an "adopted" set of grandparents as his own ... who knows? Three years of trying blown away by a total of five minutes worth of Internet research.

I use the Internet for a large portion of my research.

—Heather Jones DeGeorge

The LDS apparently wants to make the AF and IGI available to more people. Originally, you had to visit the Family History Library in Salt Lake City, Utah, to use these databases. Today, that library has CD-ROMs on a local area network (LAN) that's connected to the Joseph Smith Memorial Building next door and about 200 access terminals scattered about the buildings.

About 20 years ago, the church set up local FHCs around the world. In 1988, they started selling the databases on microfiche. In 1991, the Church released them on CD-ROM to their local centers, and later to societies and libraries. The New England Historic Genealogical Society has a complete set at their library in Boston, as does the California State Sutro Library in San Francisco.

Right now, programmers at FamilySearch Labs in Salt Lake City are working on a new way to display the family relationships you find in the databases at FamilySearch. At www.familysearchlabs.org, you can give this beta software a test run, and it's really fun.

First, look at the Pedigree Viewer, shown in Figure 14-3. You can use a GEDCOM of your own or use a demonstration GEDCOM on the site. You can zoom in and out; expand each capsule to see more data; pan up, down, right, and left in the tree; and line up an individual with direct ancestors. It is very cool.

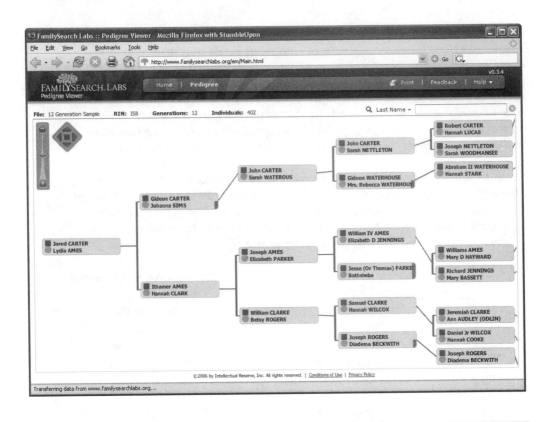

FIGURE 14-3. *Pedigree Viewer is under development to give FamilySearch users more ways to view genealogies.*

Life Browser, in Figure 14-4, is being developed to allow uploading of the details of an ancestor's life, such as occupations and photographs. It's a way to give sources as well.

The pattern here is more and more access via more and more means. The Mormons are cautious, though, and they take small steps, one at a time. The LDS Church is still working on more reliability, more accuracy, and more controls on privacy for living people, and works hard to present a useful, viable program and database for its members and the rest of the world. The main concern of the LDS Church is not to turn out a bad product.

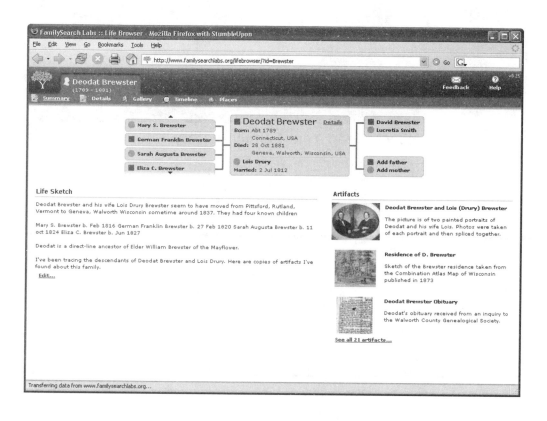

FIGURE 14-4.   *Life Browser will allow multimedia documentation of ancestors.*

A Run-Through

The opening page of the FamilySearch Internet Genealogy Service was shown in Figure 14-1. On the top is a navigation bar to the most-often used features of the site. On the home page are links to information about the Church and the site. It's worth your while to click Why Family History? and How Do I Get Started? (see Figure 14-5) on this page. These take you to basic how-to files.

On every page, you will see four tabs on the navigation bar: Home, Search, Share, and Library.

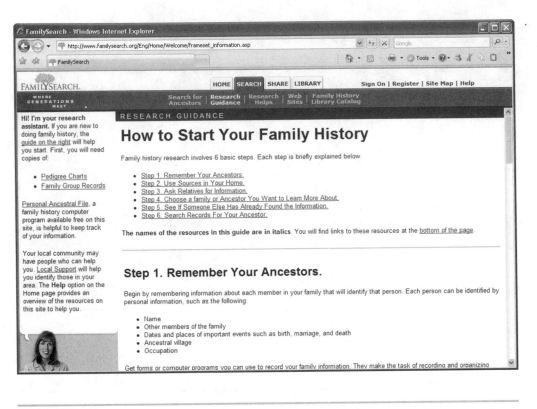

FIGURE 14-5. *The How Do I Get Started? link is a good beginner's guide to genealogy on the FamilySearch site.*

Home Tab

Under the **Home** tab, you find links to the following resources—Search For Ancestors, Share Information, and Family History Library System—under the word "Welcome" in the navigation bar. The **News** link is where you go to find out about new features, updates, and news releases on the site.

Family Search Questions is the link to the FAQ files for the site. There you'll find answers to common questions about everything from GEDCOMs to the LDS Church.

Product Support helps you with frequently asked questions about each product, as well as questions organized by topics, common solutions, information about how to contact people locally who may be able to help you, and instructions on how to use the built-in online support that comes with the many CD-ROMs and other software you can buy from the LDS Church.

Order/Download Products is the link to the online store, which offers books, forms, CD-ROMs, and other items. You can also download the free PAF genealogy program using this option. All you have to do is register.

Search Tab

Click **Search**, and you get the screen shown in Figure 14-6. You can type information about an ancestor and find out whether any of the cataloged websites, resource files, and donated information available through the service may contain additional information about the ancestor. You can search through all resources at once or choose just one from the AF; the 1880 United States, 1881 British Isles, or the 1881 Canadian census; the IGI; the PRF; the U.S. Social Security Death Index; the Index to Vital Records from Mexico and Scandinavia; and the catalog of genealogical websites.

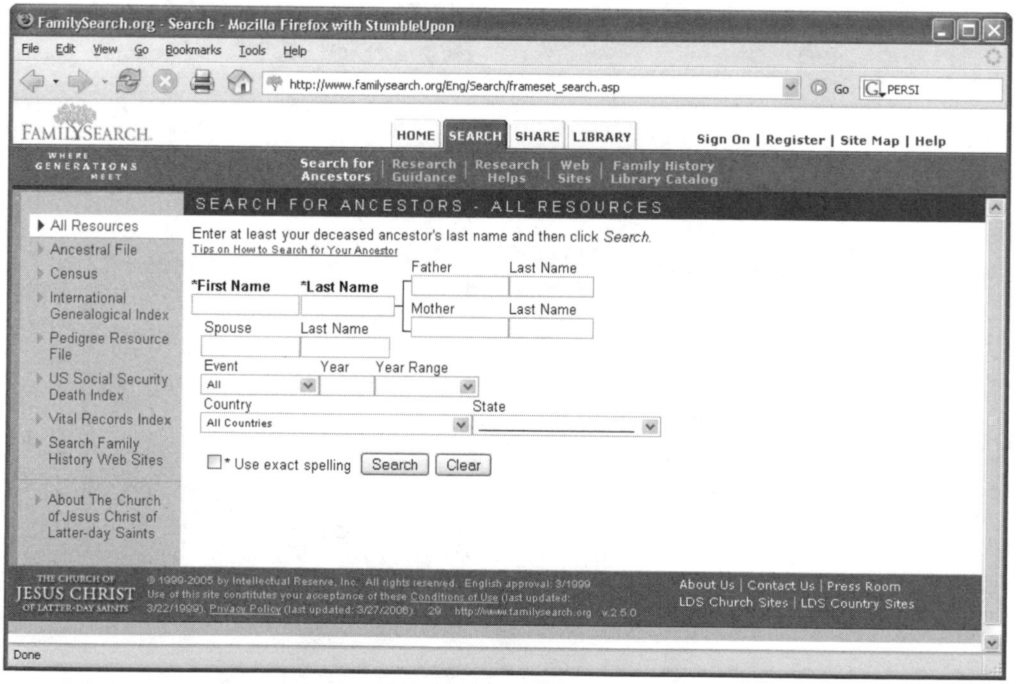

FIGURE 14-6.   *The basic search screen at FamilySearch*

You can get to the same page by clicking the Search For Ancestors link from the Home/Welcome page. The link above the input form— Tips On How To Search For Your Ancestors—is worth exploring. This tells you in plain language what can work and what won't work on the search page and how to narrow your search.

Using a pedigree chart form on this screen, you can input a last name or both first and last names and even the names of a spouse and parents if you know them. Of course, the more information you put in, the fewer matches you get. The less specific you are, the more matches you get.

I searched for my family's ancestor, Abraham Spencer. We know he was born in New York in 1792, so I limited my search to that year and to the United States. The results are shown in Figure 14-7. This illustrates what I said before about duplicates: IGI has six different

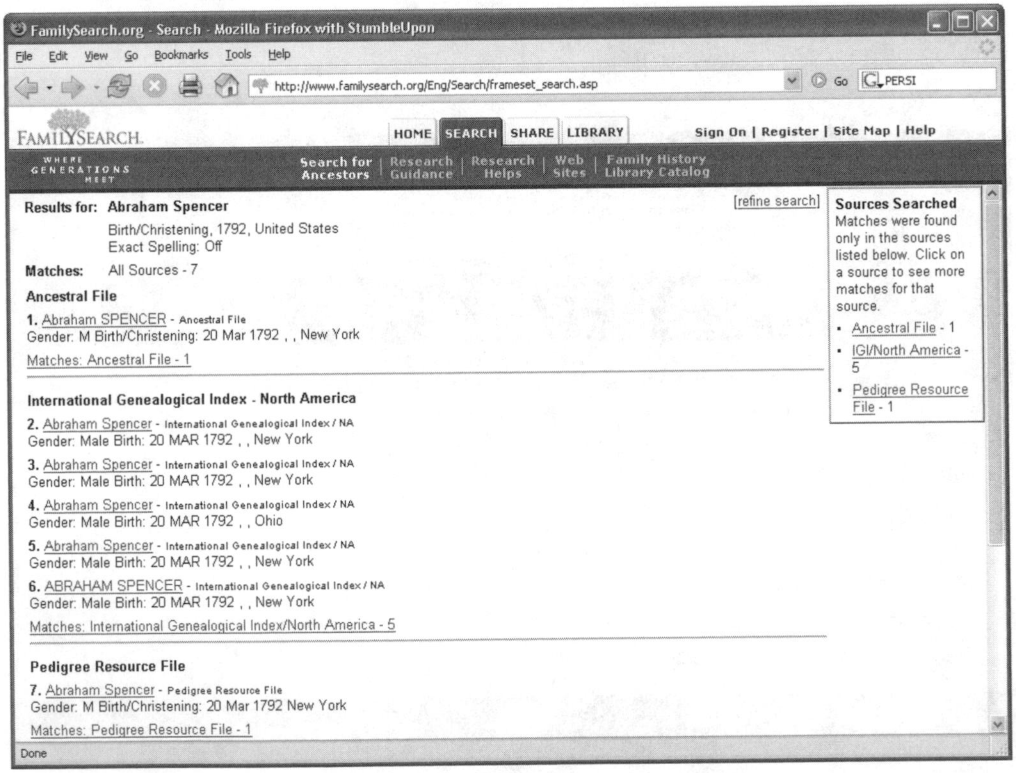

FIGURE 14-7. *Searching several databases at once on FamilySearch gives you a starting place.*

entries for my Abraham from six different submitters. But AF and PRF have only one each.

From here, I clicked the PRF file, and that gives me a page with the name and address of the submitter and a link to the entire upload that has my Abraham in it. I can browse through all that submitter's genealogy, write him a letter about what he knows about Abraham's ancestors and tell him what I know about his descendants, and so on.

The record on FamilySearch gives the known data, with links to download the information, view a pedigree of the individual, and the family group sheet.

The **Research Guidance** link goes to LDS publications. They are all online in PDF and Hypertext Markup Language (HTML) format; there are also links to order hard copies. Research Outlines on genealogy techniques and resources are alphabetized by location.

Research Outlines can help you decide what records to look for next. I can't say enough good things about the LDS Research Outlines. For each topic, they list the best records to use, recommend the order in which to search them, provide step-by-step instructions for finding information in the records, and tell you where the copies of the records may be located. Select a place where your ancestor was born, christened, married, or died, and read the outline for that area to see what I mean. If you aren't sure of the country, click **Determining The Country Where Your Ancestor Lived** for some ways to nail it down. Only places for which research outlines have been created are listed on the page. As more are added, they'll appear. So, for example, you can find outlines for Baden, Germany, but not for Zaire.

Research Helps is another way to access the Research Outlines, as well as many other publications, such as almanacs, gazetteers, and blank charts for organizing your research. These include forms, maps, historical backgrounds, information on how to find such documents from other sources, name variations, and so forth. You can sort the list of links by place, title, subject, or document type. You can sort by document type and choose helps that are forms, government publications, LDS research guides (excellent resources, and they're all available online!), maps, and word lists.

Web Sites links you to the catalog of genealogy sites that have been submitted and reviewed by genealogists. This catalog is organized by category. The site has guidance on the quality and usefulness of other genealogy websites. Hundreds of volunteers review every genealogy-related website linked to the service and classify the sites according to an established cataloging system. The resulting index allows users to make advanced searches by category, place, surname, subject, country or locale, family relationship, and so forth.

Finally, **Family History Library Catalog** takes you to the FHL card catalog, which is discussed in the following section, "Library."

Share Tab

Under the **Share** tab, you find two links: Share My Genealogy and Collaboration E-mail Lists. To use either one, you must fill out the registration information and agree to a standard terms-of-use form (no spamming, no pornography, and so on).

Share My Genealogy allows you to submit personal genealogies in a GEDCOM format to the LDS Church for preservation in the Granite Mountain Records Vault and to be published on CD-ROM in the PRF. Your information stays separate from the others in the PRF. (However, you may also submit the same GEDCOM to AF and IGI.) You have to agree to this use before you can upload. When you submit your data, it will be available for searching through the PRF. When a person uses the Search For Ancestors link, the service searches the entire index. If it finds information that might be relevant, the user gets a reference to which resource (AF, PRF, IGI, and so on) had matches.

The **Collaboration E-mail Lists** link takes you to the sign-up page for mailing lists.

Library

The **Library** tab of the navigation bar leads to information on the Family History Library in Salt Lake City, a search form to find a Family History Center near you, an online version of the card catalog to the Family History Library, and a list of courses and classes on the library and genealogy.

With a custom-built search engine, the Family History Library Catalog describes the library's more than 3 million microfilm, microfiche, and books, letting you pinpoint available resources. Many of the cataloged items can be sent on temporary loan for use at any one of the more than 3,400 Family History Centers worldwide. Usually, the item must stay at the FHC while you use it, and a small fee for shipping and packaging is charged. Still, it's always less expensive than actually going to Salt Lake City for most of us!

Family History Library, the first selection on the Library tab's navigation bar, gives you details of how to find the Salt Lake City facility and some statistics on it.

Family History Centers is a link to a form to search for the FHC nearest you. FHCs are in LDS parishes and are considered branches of the Family History Library, providing access to most of the microfilms and microfiches in the FHL to help you in your research. The general public is welcome to come to the centers and use the Family History Center resources.

Family History Library Catalog is a form for searching the holdings of the Family History Library in Salt Lake City. Click the **Help** link, and you'll find hints on searching each available field: Surname, Place, Film/Fiche, Call Number, and Author. For example, the Help files tell you that a surname search mainly finds family histories. The more of a surname that you type as a search term, the smaller the list of results will be.

The results list will have the title and author of each hit; click the title and you get the complete library record for that work, including its call number. You can use that to have the work, microfilm, or microfiche sent to your local FHC for a short time so that you can copy it or make notes.

Education in the navigation bar of this section will take you to a list of classes on genealogy offered at the Family History Library in Salt Lake City. There are also lists of publications from the library on subjects such as forms and letter-writing guides. You'll find a list of conferences and classes offered by other organization, such as the National Genealogical Society, and a list of university and home-study courses. See Chapter 5 for more discussion on how valuable these can be.

Freedman's Bank Records

You can buy some records collected by the LDS Church on CD-ROM; one such resource is the Freedman's Bank Records CD-ROM. First released in this form in February 2001 by the LDS Church, this database contains biographical information on the roughly 500,000 African Americans who deposited money into Freedman's Bank following the Civil War. It is estimated that 8 to 10 million African Americans living today have ancestors whose records are contained in the Freedman's database. This CD-ROM has records that cover 1864 to 1871 and document the names and family relationships of those who used the bank.

The information contained in these records is rather fragmentary by normal genealogical standards, but they are some of the very few records that document these individuals and are a vital source of information for those with African-American ancestry. There are approximately 480,000 names in the file, which have been entered in a pedigree-linked GEDCOM format. This means that they are indexed for searching; before this CD-ROM, the records were available but unindexed, making them hard to use. It took 11 years to complete the indexing and formatting for the CD-ROM.

The Freedman's Bank Records CD-ROM costs $6.50 as of this writing. It can be ordered over the Internet at www.familysearch.org or by calling Church Distribution Centers at 1 800-537-5971.

A Visit to a Family History Center

Family History Centers are to genealogists what candy stores are to kids. There are big ones and little ones, elaborate setups and simple ones. But they all have something to help your search, and going to one is usually a treat.

Note

Some FHC directors insist that if you use a disk to take home information, you buy one from the FHC. This is to prevent accidentally introducing a virus to the system. Similarly, while Wi-Fi may be available in a certain FHC, if your laptop has a virus, you will be asked to take out your connection card.

The best way to find a Family History Center near you is to look in the White Pages of the phone book for the nearest Church of Jesus Christ of Latter-day Saints. Call them and find out where the nearest FHC is and the hours. Honestly, because the hours vary so much from place to place, the best time to call is Sunday morning around 10:00 A.M. Everyone's at church then! If you call any other time, give the staffers lots of rings to answer the phones, which might be on the other side of the church from the FHC. Another easy way: Use the search box on the

FamilySearch.org main page. Scroll down about halfway on the page, and you'll see a box to input your ZIP code. For a more detailed search, go to www.familysearch.org/Eng/default.asp.

> ### Note
> *The contact information for the main Family History Library is 35 North West Temple Street, Salt Lake City, UT 84150-3400 Phone: (801) 240-2331 or (800) 453-3860 × 22331 Fax: (801) 240-5551 E-mail: fhl@ldschurch.org*

All FHCs are branches of the main LDS Family History Library in Salt Lake City. The typical FHC has a few rooms at the local Mormon Church, with anywhere from one to ten computers; a similar number of microfilm and microfiche readers; and a collection of atlases, manuals, and how-to genealogy books. Figure 14-8 shows the FHC in my neighborhood in Navarre, Florida. Others in bigger towns are larger and more elaborate.

It's a cozy place, open two nights a week, but it's a branch of the library in Salt Lake City just like the big ones in cities such as New York and Los Angeles. Exciting things are happening there.

WorldVitalRecords and Ancestry.com

More than 4,500 FamilySearch Family History Centers throughout the world have free access to WorldVitalRecords.com's genealogical records and resources as a result of an agreement signed between FamilySearch and WorldVitalRecords.com in May 2007.

WorldVitalRecords.com has collections of genealogical materials, including vital, land, immigration, and military records; newspapers; international databases; and a collection of reference material. WorldVitalRecords.com also partnered with Everton Publishers last year to provide the Everton Genealogical Library, containing numerous databases, as well as 60 years of the Everton Genealogical Helper and 150,000 Everton pedigree files and family group sheets. In addition to making all WorldVitalRecords.com content free, each FHC has

FIGURE 14-8.   *My local FHC has four computers; two film readers; one fiche reader; and a small collection of books, CD-ROMs, fiches, and films.*

FamilyLink.com, a new social genealogical website that enables individuals to connect with genealogists from more than 1,600 cities.

WorldVitalRecords.com was founded by Paul Allen, who also founded Ancestry.com, which will be covered in Chapter 17. Ancestry.com is available through all FHCs as well. The full services, as the FHC is the "subscriber," can be searched at any FHC. The results you get will have to be e-mailed, printed, or saved to a disk for you to take home.

Kindred Konnections

This site will be covered in Chapter 18, but a quick mention of the things there: Canadian, U.S., New Zealand, and UK genealogy records; extracted vital records from those countries; and a database of GEDCOM files uploaded by users, as well as information from files indexed from the Internet. It also has a program that will search your GEDCOM and all the ones on the site, looking for matches. From a Family History Center, you have the same access as if you had a subscription.

Godfrey Memorial Library

The Godfrey Memorial Library was founded in Middletown, Connecticut, in 1947 as a genealogy library. It has approximately 200,000 books and periodicals in its collection, including state and local histories, international resources, family histories, biographies, records by religious organizations, church records, funeral records, cemetery records, military records, maps, etc. And you can search it all from an FHC!

Heritage Quest Online

This has been available through most public libraries for a while and now from FHCs as well. As you see in Figure 14-9, you can search census records, the Periodical Source Index, Revolutionary War records, Freedman's Bank, and the full text of several thousand books.

Footnote

Footnote was also mentioned in Chapter 9. It is a site for scanned and indexed documents, maps, and images. It is a way to search original source material not found in other places. And, at a FHC, you can search it for free.

Other Services

Research help from volunteer staff. Staff members will not do research for you, but they can give you an orientation about the center, answer some research questions (research expertise in each center varies), help you use center resources, and order microfilms and microfiche from the Family History Library. Most centers have a small collection of published reference sources that include research helps, genealogies, histories, gazetteers, atlases, and maps. A few centers have large collections of these resources that many a public library would envy!

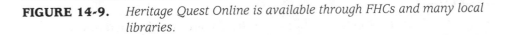

FIGURE 14-9. *Heritage Quest Online is available through FHCs and many local libraries.*

A typical FHC will have a running copy of Personal Ancestral File so that you can give that genealogy program a test drive. Many offer training classes in genealogy and in the use of LDS resources. Some centers offer training on the programs, some insist they train you before you start using the computers, and some only help if you ask. The FHC computers usually run Windows. In the typical FHC setup, you must reserve a computer, and you're given a certain block of time to use it. Printouts of what you find usually cost a nickel a page.

Because the larger, busier FHCs may require you to make a reservation, before you make a trip to the one near you, check out FamilySearch Internet Genealogy Service and determine which resources you need. Make a list of your research chores before you go. This can save lots of time!

Wrapping Up

- The LDS Church is the largest online resource for genealogy.

- The site also includes mailing lists and a catalog of genealogy sites.

- Family History Centers are where you can view microfiches and microfilms of actual records, as well as order copies of records.

- Most FHCs also have Internet access, including access to subscription online databases.

Chapter 15

Ellis Island Online: The American Family Immigration History Center

Are you one of the 40 percent of Americans who can trace an ancestor to the immigration center at Ellis Island? If so, you definitely want to check out Ellis Island Online at www.ellisislandrecords .org (see Figure 15-1). This site is the best thing to happen to online genealogy since the launch of FamilySearch. The interface has improved in the last few years and is easier to navigate. The response to search input is fast, and the results are understandable.

FIGURE 15-1. *Immigration records from 1892 to 1924 are available at EllisIsland.org.*

> **Note**
>
> *Be sure to use the Uniform Resource Locator (URL) www.ellisisland .org. The site www.ellisisland.com has information on the park at Ellis Island concerning tours, hours of operation, and so on.*

The Family History Center is available on this website, as well as on a first-come, first-served basis or by appointment at the Ellis Island Immigration Museum. The Family History Center features an electronic database of immigrants, passengers, and crew members who entered the United States through the Port of New York between 1892 and 1924, the peak years of Ellis Island's processing. The data, taken directly from microfilms of the ships' passenger manifests provided by the National Archives and Records Administration (NARA), has never before been available electronically. It was extracted and transcribed through the phenomenal efforts of 12,000 volunteers from The Church of Jesus Christ of Latter-day Saints (LDS), spending 5.6 million hours on the project. With over 22 million records, the countries with the highest representation in the database are Italy, Austria, Hungary, Russia, Finland, England, Ireland, Scotland, Germany, and Poland.

The Grand Opening

On April 17, 2001, the Statue of Liberty-Ellis Island Foundation (the Foundation), the National Park Service (NPS), Ellis Island immigrants and their families, dignitaries, and other guests gathered at the Ellis Island Immigration Museum to celebrate the opening of the American Family Immigration History Center. The grand opening included appearances by Tom Brokaw, Charles Grodin, and Joel Grey; a search for Irving Berlin's immigration records involving his daughters and great-grandson; an overview of the Family History Center's Family Scrapbook activity; and a presentation by Foundation Founding Chairman Lee A. Iacocca.

It was also the first annual Ellis Island Family History Day, an event that's co-sponsored by the Foundation, the National Genealogical Society, and America's governors. That date was chosen because April 17, 1907 saw the largest number of immigrants ever processed on one day at Ellis Island—11,747 people, more than twice the usual number. This record-breaker will be honored every year.

The American Family Immigration History Center (not to be confused with an LDS Family History Center) provides easy access to information such as an immigrant's given name and surname, ethnicity, last town and country of residence, date of arrival, age, gender, marital status, ship of travel, port of departure, and line number on the manifest. The database is free of charge on the Internet or can be accessed at the Center for an entrance fee of $5, which includes a printout of an immigrant's arrival data. A scanned reproduction of the original ship's manifest, as well as a photo of the ship of passage, will be available in the near future either on CD-ROM or on archival paper for an additional fee. The site also has a Family History Scrapbook, which is discussed later in this chapter. As with previous Ellis Island projects, funding has come from the private sector, with no government funds employed.

The original ships' manifests show the passenger names, ages, and associated passengers, which is useful for clues to relationships. The ship information, often with a picture, gives the history and background of each ship that brought the immigrants (see Figure 15-2).

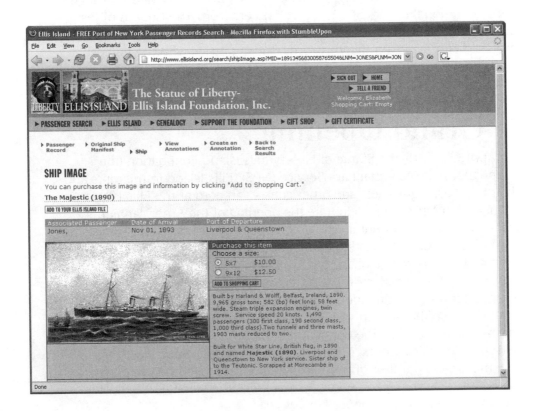

FIGURE 15-2. *In many cases, you can learn the history and see a picture of the ship that brought your ancestor to Ellis Island.*

If you register as a regular user, which is free, you can keep copies of the passenger records, manifests, and ship images in "Your Ellis Island File." This can be opened on the computers at Ellis Island or on this website. You can purchase copies of these documents at the online gift shop (more about this follows) or at the Interpretive Shop on Ellis Island.

If you join as a Foundation member at $45 per year, you can:

♦ Annotate passenger records in the Ellis Island Archives

♦ Create and maintain your Family History Scrapbook

♦ Order one free copy of your initial Scrapbook (printout or CD-ROM)

♦ Receive a ten-percent discount at the online gift shop or at the Center

♦ Possibly get a tax deduction (check with your accountant)

Your membership also helps to support the work of The Statue of Liberty-Ellis Island Foundation to preserve and protect the sites and their records.

A Guided Tour

The site has two parts: free services and services available only to Foundation members. Even without the free registration, however, you have access to several areas. "The Immigrant Experience" is comprised of two sets of articles on the population of the United States. "Family Histories," the first set, gives real-life examples of people whose ancestors passed through Ellis Island. "The Peopling of America" is a companion series of articles showing the timeline of people coming to the United States from all over the world, beginning with those who crossed the Bering Straits 20,000 years ago. You can also look at a history of Ellis Island and a timeline that begins in 1630. All of these would be a great help to a student writing a paper on Ellis Island!

However, to gain access to the free searches, you must register. This involves choosing a logon name and password and giving your name and address, and when you return, cookies on your computer will allow the site to show you saved searches.

Searches

As a registered user (remember, registration is free), you can use the Passenger Search. Simply put in a first and last name from the opening screen, and then click Search Archives. If you want to perform a more targeted search, click Passenger Search at the top of the page, and then click New Search. On that search page, you can input a first and last name, and then choose Male or Female (or don't use gender at all).

The results will be presented to you in a table, as shown in Figure 15-3. If the results list is too long, you can refine the search using the choices in the bar on the left of the screen, filtering for year of arrival, ethnicity,

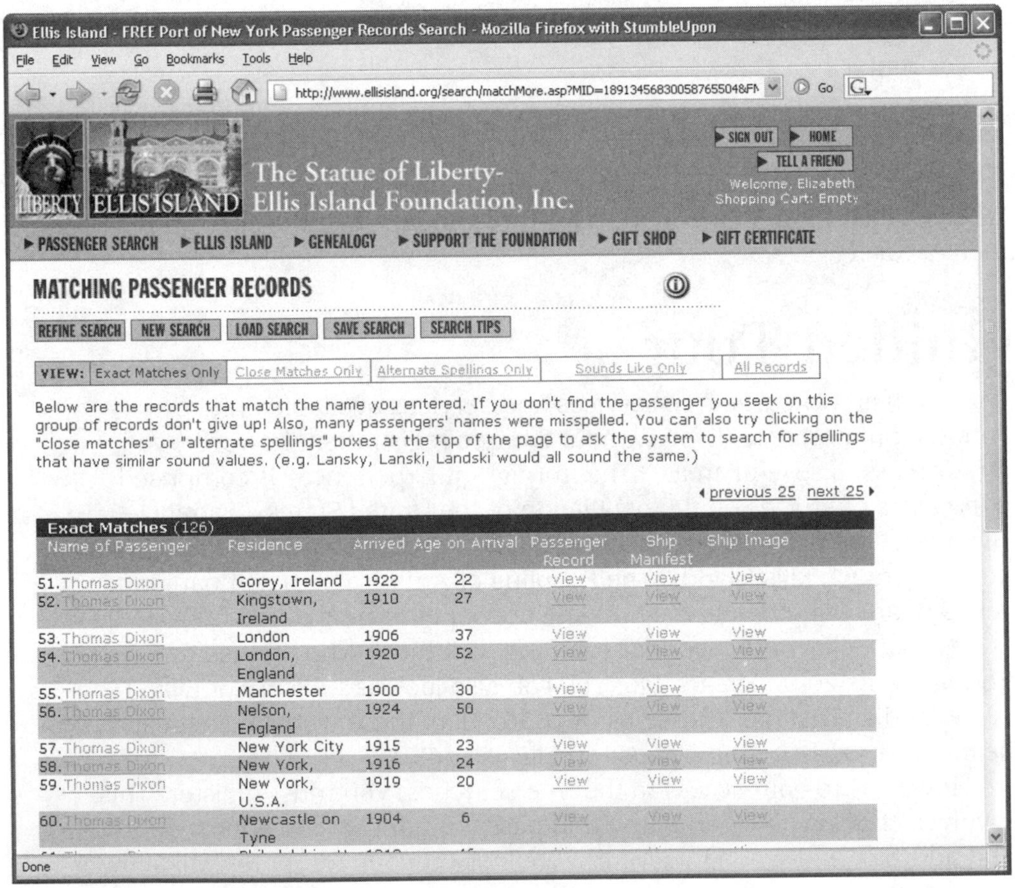

FIGURE 15-3. *In this table, the search was for Thomas Dixon, with no date of birth in the search terms.*

and so on. The information on passenger records comes from passenger lists, called *ship manifests*. Passengers were asked a series of questions; their answers were entered into the manifests. Ellis Island inspectors then used the manifests to examine immigrants. Click the links on the left to view the passenger's ship and the manifest with the passenger's name. On some passenger records, click to read information added to the Community Archive by members of the Foundation. (If you're a Foundation member, you'll be able to add annotations of your own.) To save the passenger record, click Add To Your Ellis Island File. As a registered member, you can access this file at a later logon.

Choosing one of the names gives you a screen like that shown in Figure 15-4, where you can choose to see the original ship's manifest

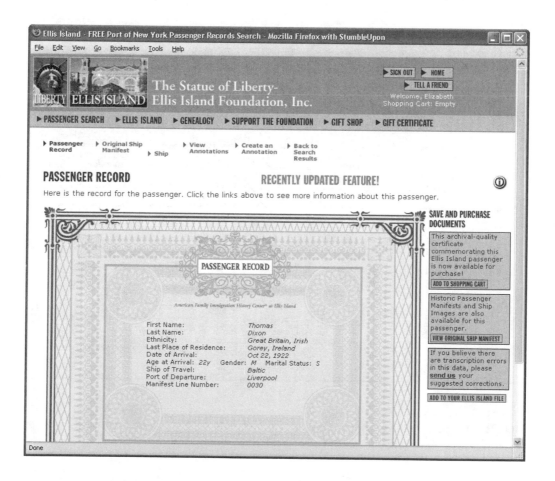

FIGURE 15-4.   *You can order a certificate of the displayed information on a passenger.*

(before about 1900, these were handwritten), and the details of the person as they appear on the manifest are listed. You can look at the transcription of the ship's manifest to see who is recorded near the person (see Figure 15-5). In this example, Figure 15-4 shows that Mr. Dixon's record is Line 30. Figure 15-5 shows the enlarged scanned copy, scrolling down to the information on Line 30. You must look at two images for the complete records, which ran across both pages of the original books.

Click the Ship link to view details about the vessel, as described previously. Registered members can save their searches and results in an online file for later reference and use. All of these images, as well as an official Ellis Island Passenger Record, can be ordered in hard copy.

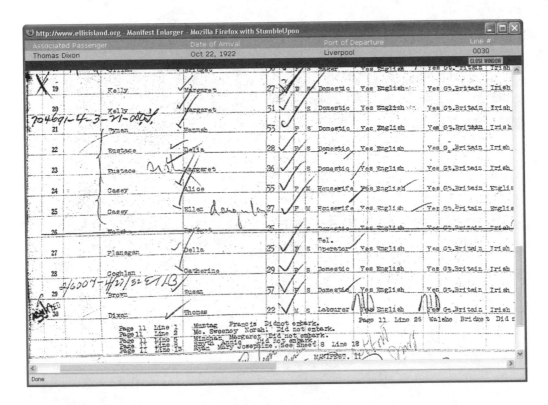

FIGURE 15-5. *You can zoom in on the scanned image of the original manifest.*

The Ellis Island search form lets you enter just the leading characters of the last name. It also allows you to search on ethnicity, ports, and ships. However, the search on the Ellis Island site requires you to first have an exact spelling match, whereas the Morse form (see the following section) does not. For example, suppose you are searching for a Polish immigrant named "Hoffman." To make sure you also get hits for "Hofman" (with a single f), you can do the search by entering only the first three letters—Hof. Then from the Ellis Island search page, you would click Edit-Ethnicity.

Morse's Forms

This search, as described on the Ellis Island site, is better than it was the first summer the site went online, but it still has many steps. Dr. Stephen Morse, with collaborators Michael Tobias, Erik Steinmetz, and Dr. Yves Goulnik, created One-Step Search Tools for the Ellis Island site, which you can also use at the JewishGen site page (www.jewishgen .org/databases/eidb/intro.html).

This project consists of different search forms, but they necessarily overlap somewhat, causing some confusion about which one to use for a certain search. They are:

♦ **Ellis Island Database 1892–1924 (Main Search)**   This is the white form. Use it to search New York passengers from 1892 to 1924 using basic search options. It employs the database and search engine at ellisisland.org, with features not found at the ellisisland.org website.

♦ **Ellis Island Database 1892–1924 (Enhanced Search)**   This is the gold form. Use it to search all New York passengers from 1892 to 1924 using enhanced search options.

♦ **All New York Arrivals 1820–1957**   Use this to search all New York passengers from 1820 to 1957. You can include the Ellis Island years as well as many other years. It uses the database and search engine at Ancestry.com, but has its own search form, which provides features not found on the Ancestry.com website.

The forms on this site can search by town of origin, use "sounds-like" codes, and can search microfilms that are in the index but that are not accessible through the Ellis Island site's algorithms. An extensive FAQ on the site can be found at www.jewishgen.org/databases/eidb/faq.htm, with tips and explanations. You should read the FAQ before you try a search. I'll provide a quick overview here.

White Form

The first form on the site, called the white form (see Figure 15-6), searches all passengers, has a restricted town search, and has a somewhat-restricted "sounds-like" (similar to but not Soundex) search.

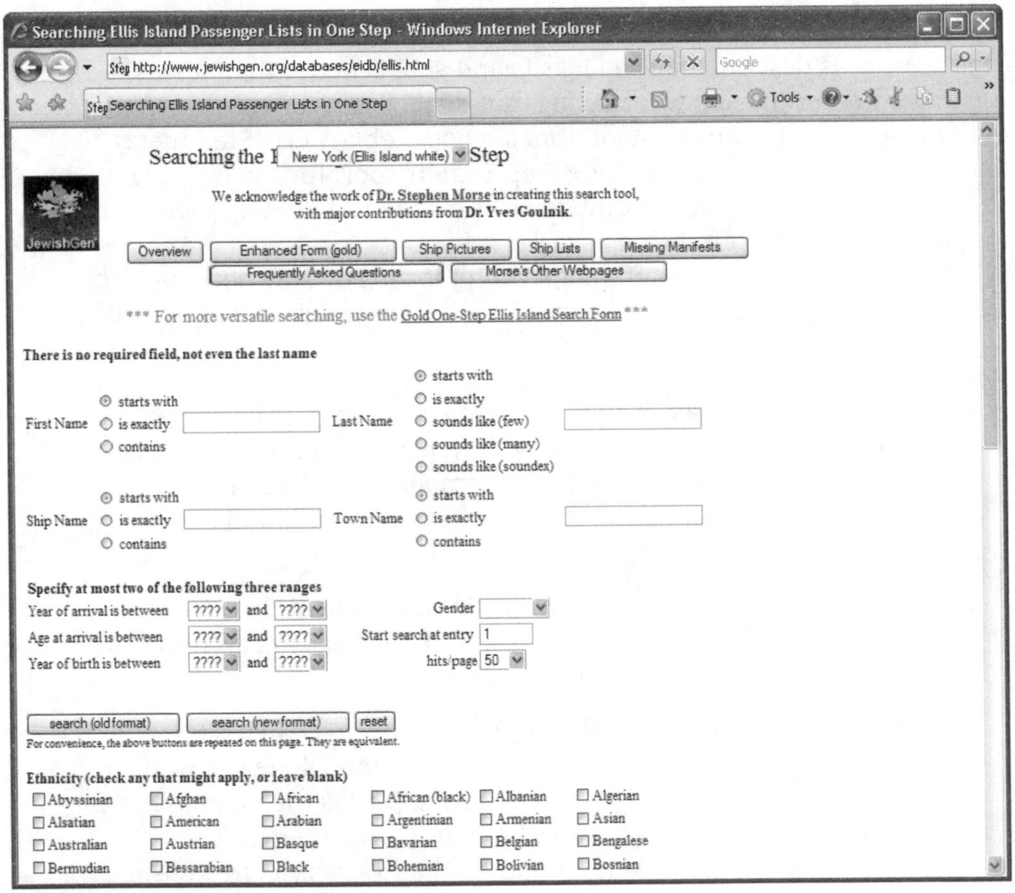

FIGURE 15-6. *The white form can search for names and towns.*

On this form, you must input exact spelling matches for the ports. You can find those spellings in the links at the bottom of the form, which sorts the more than 700 port names by country. You can also enter a town name at the bottom under Advanced Search Features. In this case, you can enter just the starting letters of the town name, but the advanced search has a serious flaw: It doesn't do a real town search, but instead downloads all matches, regardless of town, and filters for your match on your computer.

The white form allows you to perform "sounds-like" searches on the last name only, but it does not use Soundex. Instead, it generates a list of all names that are known to be in the database that sound like the name you are interested in. Then it searches for all passengers with those names. While this looks only for names known to be in the database, it also misses some similar-sounding names, for example Spenser and Spencer.

The town search and name search are mutually exclusive on the white form. You can do one or the other, but not both at the same time.

Gold Form

In the gold form, you can also search for traveling companions, exact dates, marital status, and better control the display of results. Dr. Morse has many more excellent search pages that will be covered in Chapter 18. See Figure 15-7 for an view of the golf form.

Missing Manifests

One of the most useful features of the Morse site is the Missing Manifests feature. Now these manifests are not really "missing" because they have been microfilmed and even indexed. But the search on the Ellis Island database will not find them because, for some strange reason, the Hypertext Markup Language (HTML) links to them are written wrong. Usually, you will use this form if you have found your ancestor and a date, but the image did not appear when you looked at the individual result, or you got a picture of the wrong page of the manifest instead of

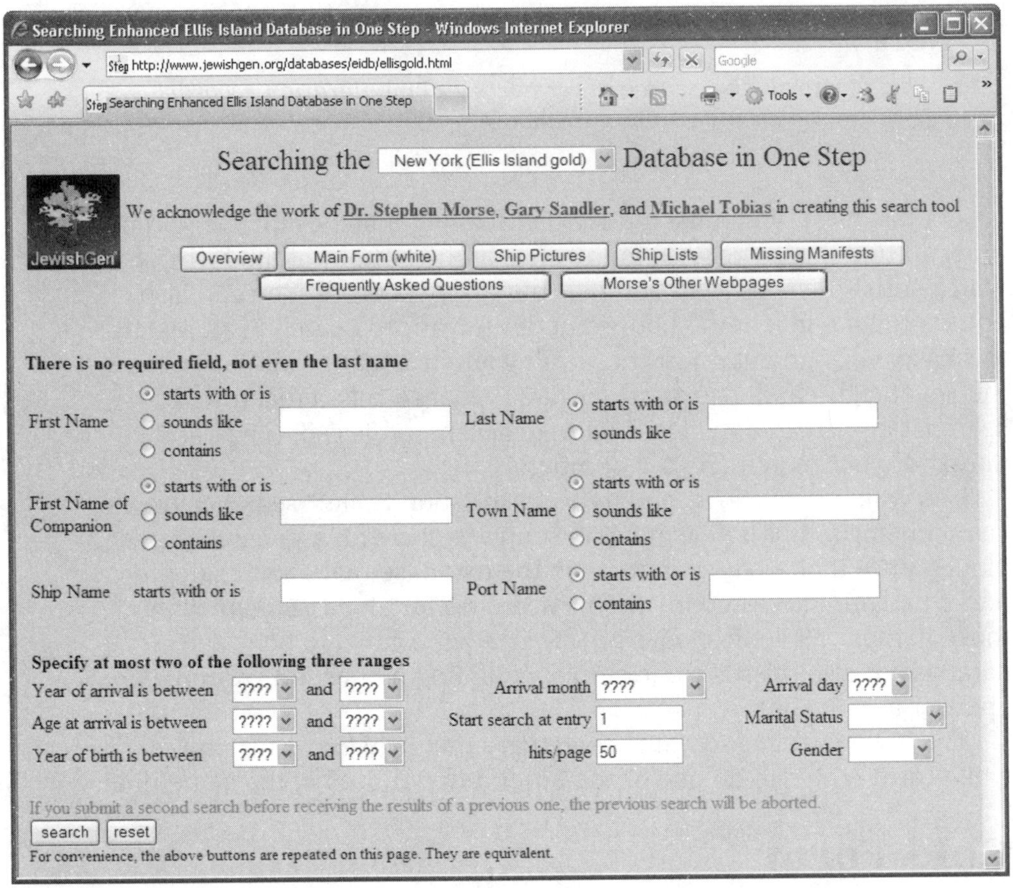

FIGURE 15-7. *Dr. Morse's gold form allows searching the Ellis Island records in more detail.*

what you wanted. But since you have the ship and date, you can use the Direct Access To Manifests form for the particular arrival port and view the manifest.

It's something only a Web wonk would understand, but Alex Calzareth discovered that the images are in the Ellis Island database, even though the links to them aren't, and Michael Tobias figured out a way to catalog these images with bad HTML links, and Yves Goulnik figured out how to find the start and end of each roll of film as represented in the image database. Then Dr. Morse put it all together into this search page.

Now all of that was a lot of technical stuff, but this should deglaze your eyes: What it means is that this page can find images of ships' manifests that the Ellis Island search will not find. You can search for all arrivals of a certain ship, or all ships arriving in a certain date range, or all ships leaving a certain port in a date range. Use of this Missing Manifests page is greatly simplified if you know the roll and frame number for your ship, which may be listed in the Ellis Island results, or you can get them from the gold and blue forms on Morse's site.

Note

As an aside, Dr. Morse's pages are so much better at finding things than the Ellis Island site, I think they should pay him to substitute his code for theirs. However and alas, they haven't asked my opinion.

Community Archives

On the Ellis Island site, only members of the Foundation can create annotations to the records, but all registered users of the website can view them. Annotations supplement information in the record, telling more about the passenger's background and life in the United States. This information has not been verified as accurate and complete—it's simply what the annotating member believes to be the facts.

Click View Annotations on the passenger record (if no View Annotations button exists, the record hasn't yet been annotated). If you're registered with the site, you'll see a list of annotations. If you haven't yet registered, a screen will appear enabling you to do so.

Ellis Island Family History Scrapbooks

If you have paid for a membership to The Statue of Liberty-Ellis Island Foundation, you can contribute Family History Scrapbooks on the website or at the American Family Immigration History Center itself on Ellis Island.

Family Scrapbooks combine member-submitted pictures, images from the Ellis Island archives, written stories and memories, and sound recordings. Members can choose to keep the Scrapbook private or add it to the publicly available Ellis Island Family History Archive. If you visit the Center, you can use a scanner, a camera, and recording equipment.

Scrapbooks

When you begin your Scrapbook, you have 16 pages to work on, including a title page and an author page. Ten of those pages have space for your images, and four have space for an image from the Ellis Island Foundation archives. The site's documentation suggests that you decide on a particular story or theme for your Scrapbook. Begin with a passenger search in the archives to find passenger records, ship images, and ship manifests to save in Your Ellis Island File and add to your Scrapbook, for example.

If you're a paying member, you can click Family Scrapbooks on the main menu and then click Start New Scrapbook (if this is the first time) or Create New Scrapbook (if previous Scrapbooks exist). You get to choose a style and create a title page and an author page. Once you complete those steps, you'll see the Scrapbook's table of contents. From there, you compose the pages.

The Scrapbook pages can accept both pictures and audio recordings. The easiest way to do this is to gather everything you want to upload into one directory to make them easier to find. On a Scrapbook page, under Add An Image, click Your Computer. In the Upload Image window, you can browse the local computer for the file or simply enter the filename. The files are uploaded one at a time, and they can be 180 kilobytes (KB) or smaller. If a file is larger than 210 × 210 pixels, it will be resized proportionally. If a file is smaller, it won't be resized. When Use Selected Image is clicked, the image will appear on the page and the window will close.

Members can also add files from the Ellis Island Library by clicking Our Library on a Scrapbook page under Add An Image. Your Ellis Island File may also contain passenger records, ship images, and ship manifests you saved during a passenger search. Click the left and right arrows to review the images in Our Library or Your Ellis Island File, and then click Use This Image to add an image to the page.

On a Scrapbook page, under Add Audio, click Your Computer, and choose an audio file. You can upload files up to 1.8 megabytes (MB) in size. Then enter a title for the audio file. When you click Use Selected

File, the title assigned to the file appears on the page and the window will close. To remove an audio file, under Remove Audio?, click Delete This Audio File.

At the online gift shop, paid Foundation members can order one free copy of their Scrapbooks, choosing either a high-quality printout or a CD-ROM copy. Additional copies are available for purchase. At the table of contents, click Purchase Scrapbook.

Visiting in Person

You can also take care of these tasks on site at the museum, but you have to make an appointment within 90 days of your arrival. Click Schedule A Visit in the navigation bar at the top of any page on the site. You can simply choose to perform a passenger search ($5 entry fee to the museum) or to work on a Scrapbook (as with the online version, you must be an annual member of the Foundation to work on a Scrapbook).

You select the things you want to accomplish on your visit, list the number of people in your party and whether any will need wheelchair assistance (up to seven people), and then select the date and check-in time. Your appointment time will be assigned at check-in. You'll get a confirmation number at the end of the process to present at check-in. Print a copy to present at the desk. The screen also gives you links to articles on how to research and gather information for either a search session or a Scrapbook session.

Wrapping Up

- Ellis Island Online is a wonderful resource on the Web.

- You can search for immigrants from 1892 through 1924—the peak years of Ellis Island's processing—by name, date, and ship.

- You can upload pictures, sounds, and text to an online scrapbook if you're a member of the Statue of Liberty Foundation (it costs $45 to register) or if you visit the museum itself in New York.

- Steven Morse and several others have created alternative search forms for the Ellis Island database that are faster and, in some cases, more useful.

Chapter 16

The National
Genealogical Society

The National Genealogical Society (NGS) is one of the important genealogical societies in the United States. On its website (www.ngsgenealogy.org), you'll find announcements of NGS seminars, workshops, and programs; information on its home-study course; youth resources; and other NGS activities. This is an excellent site for learning genealogy standards and methods.

Note

It seems intuitive to use www.ngs.org as the Uniform Resource Locator (URL) for this organization, but the National Geographic Society got there first.

NGS was organized in Washington, D.C., in 1903. The preliminary first meeting was held on April 24, and the formal organization was effected on November 11. Now, the NGS has over 17,000 members, including individuals, families, genealogical societies, family associations, libraries, and other related institutions.

National Genealogical Society

The NGS is one of the best umbrella organizations for family history. Its workshops, meetings, and publications are invaluable. You can see its home page in Figure 16-1. On the home page, you'll find links to the newest and most relevant items on the site, including upcoming meetings, trips, courses, and competitions. And on every page of the site, you'll find a navigation bar at the top that leads to the following sections:

- ◆ Home
- ◆ Membership
- ◆ NGS Publications
- ◆ Conference and Activities
- ◆ Learning Center
- ◆ Research Help
- ◆ News and Events

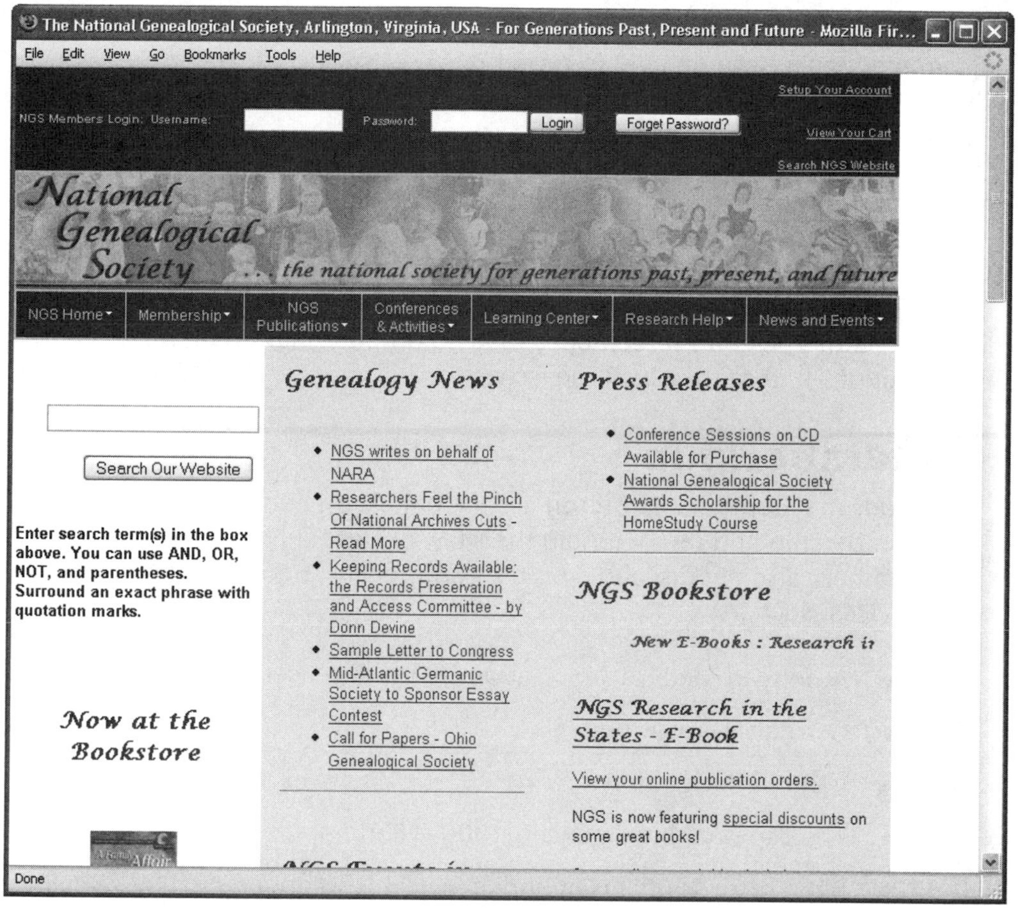

FIGURE 16-1.   *The National Genealogical Society website has searchable data as well as information about the organization.*

Home

Under the Home button on the navigation bar, you'll find information about the Society itself, from how to join to competitions. You'll also find the headquarters' street address, phone numbers, a map to the NGS headquarters, e-mail addresses, and the hours of the library.

Programs include the Consumer Protection Committee, which maintains a page on how to recognize a scam, such as those described in Chapter 2. Another page in this section describes the activities of the Records Preservation and Access Committee of NGS, which is striving to develop a consistent and logical long-term strategy to deal with the preservation of records and access issues at all levels, from local to national. Because state and local governments are so strapped for cash, valuable records are being lost due to lack of funding and space to keep them. (People don't get excited about preservation when the budget gets cut!) The committee hopes to head off potential problems with solutions before they become issues.

Membership

Under the Membership button are the details on benefits of membership and forms to join the NGS. Besides the NGS publications, members also get discounts on the conferences, books, and research services, such as:

- American Medical Association (AMA) deceased physician research

- German immigration

- Italian immigration

- The National Intelligencer (1800–1850)

- Bible records (this is an index available to anyone for free; PDF files of the actual pages are available to members only)

- NGS Family Papers Collection

- NGS Member Ancestry Charts (MACs)

- Discussion forums on genealogical research in several European countries

- A special members-only query section

NGS Publications

The *NGS Quarterly*, published since 1912, is 80 pages of scholarship and practical help in genealogy. The *NGS NewsMagazine* features articles about genealogy as well as news of the society. It is published in January, April,

July, and October. Feature articles include interviews, a spotlight on research facilities and special collections, committee reports, focused genealogical subjects, technology-related articles, and software reviews.

NGS is a free, monthly genealogy newsletter by e-mail, free to members and the general public. The online newsletter will bring you the latest genealogy news, information about upcoming events, and brief articles to help you with your genealogical research. Each issue typically contains NGS announcements, helpful articles, bookmarks from NGS members, news, press releases, and an NGS events calendar.

In this section of the NGS site, you'll find the NGS standards guidelines for your genealogy research. The standards are listed on the page at www.ngsgenealogy.org/comstandards.cfm. You'll also find the standards at the end of this book in Appendix A. These standards give you a good roadmap to valid, ethical genealogical research. NGS has also published several guides to genealogy.

Conferences and Activities

Besides the annual NGS conference and genealogy fair, members have the opportunity to participate in a number of NGS activities, such as:

◆ **NGS GENTECH Advisory Committee** administers GENTECH, a division of the National Genealogical Society. This is the genealogy geek group of the organization. They present national conferences, sponsor programs with other societies, and publish white papers based on analyses of problems of common interest to genealogists and technologists.

◆ The **Awards** programs include recognition of those who have made outstanding contributions to NGS programs or who have performed outstanding work in the fields of genealogy, history, biography, or heraldry.

◆ The **Consumer Protection Committee** keeps an eye out for scams and frauds. The article "Psst! Wanna Buy Your Name?" (www.ngsgenealogy.org/comconsumerpsst.cfm) is a must-read and free for anyone to access.

◆ The **Family Health and Heredity Committee** advances and promotes the research of ancestral medical information in genealogy.

- ◆ The **Family History Writing Contest** recognizes writers of exceptional family histories.

- ◆ The **Filby Prize** recognizes outstanding librarians who serve genealogists.

- ◆ The **Genealogical Standards Committee** develops standards and guidelines in response to needs it perceives and recommendations from Society members.

- ◆ The **Genealogical Writing Competitions** program recognizes excellence, scholarship, and achievements in the field of genealogy.

- ◆ The **National Genealogy Hall of Fame** honors those individuals who have made significant contributions to genealogy.

- ◆ The **Records Preservation and Access Committee** seeks to ensure access to historical records of genealogical value.

- ◆ The **Rubincam Youth Award** encourages the participation of young people in the field of genealogy.

- ◆ The **Youth Resources Committee** gathers genealogical resources for teachers and children ages 5 to 18.

Non-members can benefit from the work of these committees as well by competing for the prizes and reading the results of their work.

Learning Center

The courses offered online, through correspondence, and through conferences, covered in Chapter 3, are listed here. You'll find the current costs, as well as dates and times for in-person educational opportunities.

Research Help

The NGS has a circulating library available to members. Interlibrary loans are available. Reference material, records, and members' ancestral charts are among the holdings available online. Also available is the online card catalog (see Figure 16-2). In addition, you can pay a fee to have research done for you in the Physician Data Base, a listing of AMA records of physicians who died after 1905 and before 1965 and other sources held by the Society. The site also has a list of books by NGS members.

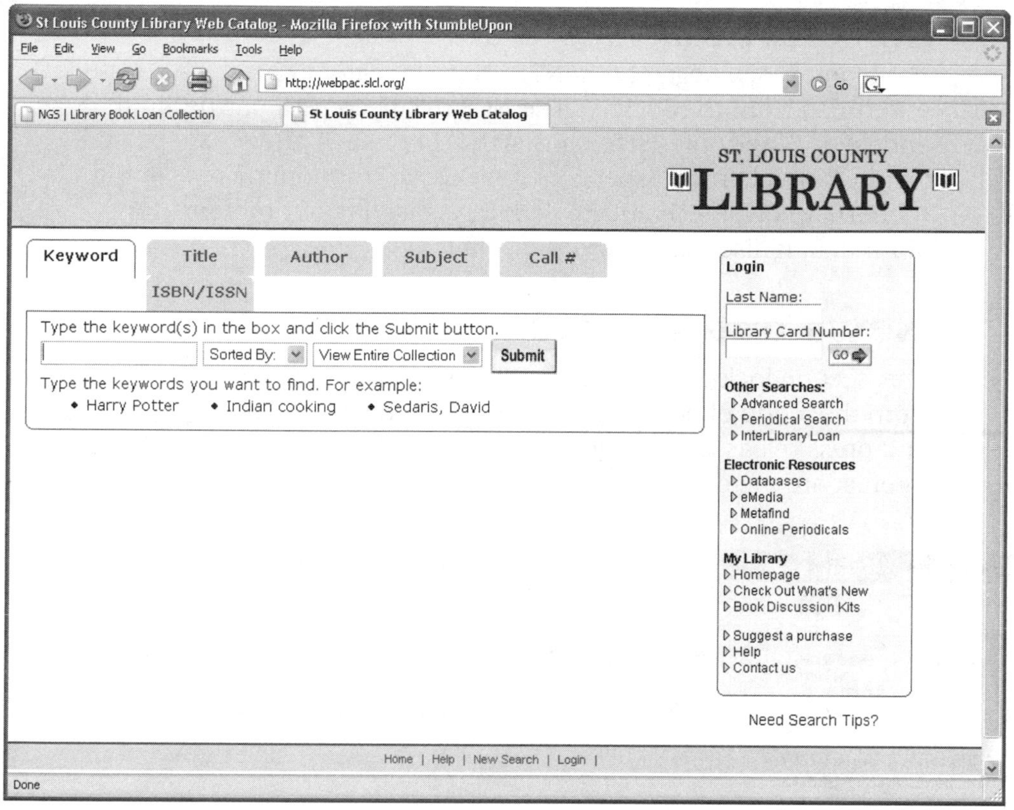

FIGURE 16-2.   *The National Genealogical Society's circulating library is located in St. Louis, Missouri, and the card catalog is online.*

You'll also find information on their research trips, where you learn by doing at locations around the United States and abroad.

Conferences

Here you'll find links to information on the annual conference, regional conferences, research trips, competitions, and the NGS Hall of Fame. The conferences are excellent; experts from all over the world teach all levels of research techniques, from beginner to expert. You can also find many supplies and genealogy-related items from vendors.

NGS GENTECH

This conference began as GENTECH in the early '90s as a separate enterprise from the Society. The NGS has become a partner in the endeavor. The conference consists of three days of workshops and lectures on technical aspects of genealogy, from online research to modern archival techniques, with a special day of programs for librarians. It also has a vendor display.

News and Events

This section includes news about the organization and its members, news from the world of genealogy, articles from recent genealogy conferences, and press releases (see Figure 16-3) from other organizations. Of special interest are the online articles on aspects of genealogy and the queries.

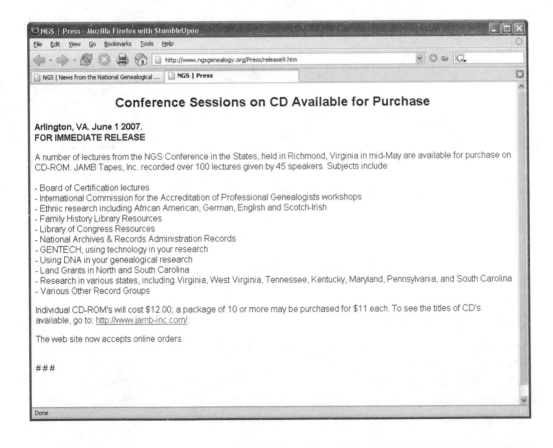

FIGURE 16-3. *Press releases from NGS are on the site.*

Under this button on the navigation bar, you'll also find announcements of genealogy events and family reunions; you can submit your own to be included here and in the *UpFront* newsletter. You will also see genealogy news, such as articles on the budget cuts at NARA and a call for papers for a state genealogical society symposium.

Bookstore

From reference books and archival supplies, such as acid-free paper, to NGS apparel and desk blotters, the NGS bookstore offers a wide variety of items for the genealogist.

Wrapping Up

+ The NGS is an umbrella institution for education and resources in genealogy.

+ You can take online and at-home genealogy courses from NGS, take research trips, and attend NGS conferences to learn about genealogy.

+ Certain databases can be searched online at the site; you can also pay a fee to have NGS staffers research for you.

+ National and regional meetings also offer genealogy courses.

Chapter 17

The Generations Network and RootsWeb

The Generations Network, formerly known as MyFamily.com, and before that known as Ancestry.com, is the largest entity in the online genealogy industry. This chapter is going to look at four parts of it: RootsWeb, the oldest online genealogy community; Ancestry.com; MyFamily.com; and Genealogy.com. Ancestry.com.ca, Ancestry.com.au, Ancestry.de, and Ancestry.it; the divisions in the UK, Canada, Australia, Germany, and Italy, respectively, all work pretty much the same as the one in the United States, and you can get access to each part of the empire individually, or with a mega-membership, the whole enchilada!

Ancestry.com at first had only one site, and then merged with RootsWeb. Then it launched MyFamily.com and renamed itself after that service. Once the company absorbed Genealogy.com and Family Tree Maker genealogy software and expanded worldwide, the name was changed to The Generations Network, Inc. All these Generations Network divisions together receive 10.4 million unique visitors worldwide and over 450 million page views a month. The Generations Network also has a cross-marketing agreement with A&E's The History Channel, giving us the "mini-documentary" style advertisements. You have probably also seen Ancestry.com's banner ads on the Internet any time you used "genealogy" as a term in any search engine.

I want to start this chapter by discussing RootsWeb, the free, volunteer part, because that's where a lot of this got started and where most online genealogists go first.

RootsWeb

How would you like a place where you can search dozens of databases of genealogical materials, look through hundreds of genealogical webpages, and subscribe to thousands of mailing lists? How about a place where you can publish your own page, upload your own data, and create your own mailing list? And all for free!

Note

www.rootsweb.com and www.rootsweb.org take you to the same site.

Welcome to RootsWeb (www.rootsweb.org). Once upon a time, RootsWeb was a site for a group of people working at the research center RAND who dabbled in genealogy on the side and had a club for family history. They had a little mailing list, hosted by the University of Minnesota, and a little database on the RAND server for their club. That was nearly 20 years ago. Today, RootsWeb is the largest all-volunteer genealogy site on the Web.

RootsWeb started and continues as a volunteer effort. But the costs of servers, disk space, and connections got so high that what was once a little club of genealogy enthusiasts that worked together merged with Ancestry.com. This means two things: First, people were no longer asked to contribute $25 a year to RootsWeb to help defray the costs the volunteers were incurring. Ancestry.com now subsidizes the hardware and software to keep RootsWeb up and running. Second, almost all of the secondary information is free, but some of the primary source evidence is on Ancestry's site, and you have to subscribe. It's not a completely black-and-white situation; there are still plenty of transcribing projects that are free to access, such as ship's passenger lists, census transcriptions, and so on. And Ancestry.com hosts some of the free stuff, such as the message boards.

In the months immediately following the merger, many were concerned that RootsWeb's privacy and fair-use policies would change, but so far, they haven't. To date, if you submit data to RootsWeb, it won't be slapped onto a CD-ROM and sold by Ancestry.com. However, if you upload information through Family Tree Maker to any of the Generations Network sites, it will probably be part of some future set of CD-ROMs. Nevertheless, for the RootsWeb user, little has really changed.

Note

Remember, any time you post genealogical data anywhere, you still need to be sure that data on living people isn't included in your submissions because anyone can copy publicly posted data.

The mission of RootsWeb is summed up in the following statement, published on its home page:

"The RootsWeb project has two missions:

To make large volumes of data available to the online genealogical community at minimal cost.

To provide support services to online genealogical activities, such as Usenet newsgroup moderation, mailing list maintenance, surname list generation, and so forth."

A quick guided tour of RootsWeb only scratches the surface of all the helpful and informative services available on this site. The following story gives you an idea of the unique possibilities RootsWeb offers.

Success Story: RootsWeb Leads to a Reunion

About three years ago, I started searching for my Powell ancestors (on my father's side), but about the only thing I knew how to do was search the surname and message boards.

One night, after having done nothing in about two months, I decided to get online and read the [RootsWeb] surname message boards. On a whim, I went into the Hubbard message boards (on my mother's side). The first message I read was about someone searching for descendants of my grandmother's parents.

When my grandmother was about three or four, her mother passed away and she went to live with an aunt and uncle. Eventually, my grandmother lost contact with her brothers. She did see her oldest brother once when she was about 15, but after that she never saw or heard from him again. That night, I found him—a person my grandmother had not seen in over 70 years.

We flew to Washington state and met all kinds of new cousins, aunts, and uncles. Over the next two years, my grandmother spoke with her brother many times. Unfortunately, he had passed away the summer before, but she did see him twice and was able to speak with him on numerous occasions.

We figured out that the message I responded to had been posted for about a minute before I discovered it. The surname message boards are a wonderful tool in searching for the ancestors and relatives you never knew you had, or those you had but didn't know who they were.

—Jennifer Powell Lyons

RootsWeb has more genealogical information than you can shake a stick at. Some of this is secondary source information, such as what genealogies members have submitted. Some of this information is close to primary source information—for example, transcripts of wills, deeds, census forms, and vital records, with citations of where exactly the original information can be found. Some of it is primary information (for example Ancestry.com's Census Images), and you have to pay a subscription fee to Ancestry.com to access that information.

At the top of all RootsWeb pages, you'll see a navigation bar with these categories: Home, Searches, Family Trees, Mailing Lists, Message Boards, Web Sites, Passwords, and Help (see Figure 17-1).

Home and Help are self-explanatory, and the following text explains Searches, Family Trees, Mailing Lists, Message Boards, and Web Sites.

FIGURE 17-1. *The main page serves as an index; all RootsWeb pages have a navigation bar.*

The Passwords link displays a Help page for retrieving lost passwords to mailing lists and websites.

When you look at the RootsWeb home page in your browser, you'll find two search templates to input a surname, first name, or any keywords (see Figure 16-1). One searches RootsWeb's free information; the other searches Ancestry.com, and the results may be in the free area or in the subscription-only area. The search will look in all the RootsWeb pages or Ancestry.com databases and show you the results. It's a great way to get started on your genealogy!

Finding information on RootsWeb can be that simple. However, you can use many different tools on the site to get more targeted results.

Getting Started at RootsWeb

On the Home page index is a section called "Getting Started." The sections there—Getting Started at RootsWeb, Ancestry Tour, RootsWeb's Guide to Tracing Family Trees, RootsWeb Review Archives | Subscribe, and What's New—will give the beginner a good grounding in RootsWeb.

Getting Started at RootsWeb is a short page on how to share, communicate, research, and volunteer with the site. Ancestry Tour is a multimedia overview of what the commercial side offers. RootsWeb's Guide to Tracing Family Trees is really a collection of guides sorted by general genealogy, sources, and countries. What's New lists the newest additions to the pages and databases on the volunteer side, and subscribing to *RootsWeb Review* will bring the same information to your e-mail inbox.

Available Files and Databases

ROOTS-L has tons of files and databases, which you can get access to by e-mailing the appropriate commands to the list server that runs ROOTS-L. You can search the ROOTS-L library for everything from a fabulous collection devoted to obtaining vital records, to useful tips for beginners, to book lists from the Library of Congress, and more. Some of the available files include:

♦ **Surname Helper (http://surhelp.rootsweb.com)**   Looks at the RootsWeb message boards and personal websites.

♦ **U.S. Town/County Database (http://resources.rootsweb.com/ cgi-bin/townco.cgi)**   Looks for locations. It's a sort of online gazetteer.

♦ **The WorldConnect Project (http://worldconnect.rootsweb
.com)** Searches GEDCOMs of family trees submitted by
RootsWeb members, as covered in Chapter 11.

♦ **The USGenWeb Archives Search (http://www.usgenweb
.org)** Looks for pages posted across the United States in the
GenWeb Project.

♦ **WorldGenWeb (http://www.worldgenweb.org)** Searches for
genealogy resources in nations outside the United States.

RootsWeb Surname List

The RootsWeb Surname List (RSL), shown in Figure 17-2 and located at
http://rsl.rootsweb.com, is a registry of who is searching for whom and
in what times and places. The listings include contact information for
each entry. When you find someone looking for the same name, in the
same area, and in about the same time period, you might be able to
help each other. That's the intent of the list. You don't have to pay to
submit your own data or to search for data.

To search the list, you can use the form on the search page or go to the
page http://rsl.rootsweb.com. On the RSL page, you type the surname you
want to search for. You can narrow your search by including a location
where you think the person you are looking for lives or lived, using the
abbreviations you'll find in the link below the location box. Use the options
to choose whether you want to search by surname (names spelled exactly
as you've typed them) or by Soundex or Metaphone (names that sound like
the one you've typed but spelled differently). In future attempts, you can
limit the search to new submissions within the last week, month, or two
months. The list is updated once a month. The Migration field shows you
the path the family took. SC > GA, for example, shows migration from
South Carolina to Georgia.

WorldConnect Project

The WorldConnect Project is one of several GEDCOMs discussed in
Chapter 11. Searching it from the RootsWeb home page, you can only
input first and last names. The results page has another input form at the
bottom, enabling you to fine-tune the search by adding places and dates.

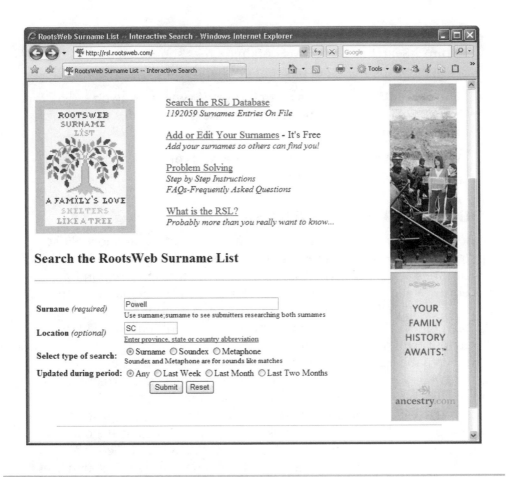

FIGURE 17-2. *At RSL, you input a name, a date, and a place and see who else is looking for the same data.*

If you go to the WorldConnect page at http://worldconnect.rootsweb .com, you can find links to tips and hints for using the site. Remember, all the data here is uploaded by volunteers, so errors might exist!

Social Security Death Index

The Social Security Death Index (SSDI), located at http://ssdi.rootsweb .com, searches the federal records of deaths. Anyone who died before Social Security began in the 1930s won't be in this database.

Searching from the RootsWeb home page, all you can input is the first and last name, but the results page will let you link to the Advanced Search page, where you can narrow the search by location and date. This is an excellent tool for researching 20th-century ancestors.

GenSeeker

GenSeeker looks for your search terms on the thousands of personal genealogy webpages at RootsWeb, plus any other registered documents, such as records transcriptions. You can also perform Boolean searches (see Chapter 6).

Other Search Engines

RootsWeb has several other ways for you to search both the site and the Web at large. Search Thingy (http://sitesearch.rootsweb.com/cgi-bin/search) looks at all the databases and text files, and MetaSearch (http://resources .rootsweb.com/cgi-bin/metasearch) looks for names across RootsWeb. The Surnames search index, United States Counties/States index, and the Countries index all search different subsets of RootsWeb information. All these are worth looking at, and all can be accessed from http://searches .rootsweb.com.

These searches can be helpful in your research, but they assume you're a rank beginner with no more than a name or a place to launch your inquiries. Perhaps you know for sure that you're looking for a land record in Alabama or a cemetery in Iowa. RootsWeb has several searchable resources for items such as these. You'll find the search engines for the RSL and the other databases at http://searches.rootsweb.com (see Figure 17-3).

Research Templates

This collection of links from the home page index will lead you to lists of pages for different subjects. The surname list, for example, leads you first to an alphabetical list, then to all surnames under a certain letter, then to a page for a specific surname. The Spencer Research Template page is shown in Figure 17-4.

Other research templates are for geographic locations, such as states in the United States or a whole country, such as France.

FIGURE 17-3.   *Search engines at RootsWeb can search everything or a subset of the site's thousands of pages.*

Message Boards and Mailing Lists

Among the best resources on RootsWeb are the mailing lists and message boards, now hosted on Ancestry.com. A message board is a place where messages are read, sent, and answered on the Web, using a browser to read them. A mailing list is where messages are e-mailed to and from the members. A mail client is used to read them. Both the

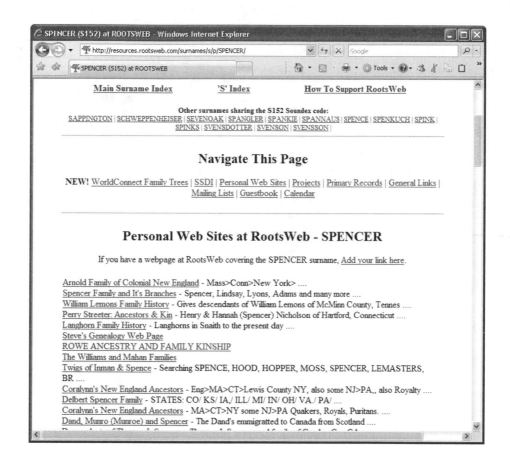

FIGURE 17-4. *The Spencer Research Template leads you to resources on RootsWeb that have Spencer information, from personal genealogy pages to a calendar of Spencer events.*

message boards and the mailing lists are archived and searchable. Figure 17-5 shows a typical message board on RootsWeb since the Ancestry.com merger.

Click the bottom of any message board's page to read the frequently asked questions (FAQs), request a new board, read the rules, or get help.

The mailing lists, located at http://lists.rootsweb.com, cover many topics, such as the RootsWeb newsletters, described later in this chapter. Lists exist for specific surnames, every state in the United States, other countries (from Aruba to Zimbabwe), and topics such as adoption, medical genealogy, prisons, and heraldry. From the Mailing

FIGURE 17-5. *Ancestry.com's message boards are often mirrored to RootsWeb mailing lists.*

Lists page, you can click a link to each one, and you'll get instructions on how to use the list, including subscribing, unsubscribing, sticking to the topic, and so on.

Besides ROOTS-L, which is the grandparent of genealogy mailing lists on the Internet, RootsWeb hosts literally thousands of mailing lists. As mentioned in Chapter 8, you can find lists for surnames and family names, regions, and topics being researched. The index, located at www.rootsweb.com/ ~ maillist, has thousands of lists you can join, along with instructions explaining how to subscribe. It won't include all the mailing lists at RootsWeb, however, because it's a voluntary listing and not all list owners choose to be featured.

A good rule of thumb: Be choosy in joining lists! Take on only a few at a time. Read the lists for a while, sign off if they don't prove useful, and then try some others. Some lists are extremely active—sometimes overwhelmingly so. One RootsWeb user who signed up for every possible mailing list for the United Kingdom had 9,000 e-mails in his inbox within 24 hours! Be careful what you wish for ...

And remember, some lists are archived, so you needn't subscribe to see if that list is talking about subjects of interest to you. Just search the archive for your keywords, and save the important messages.

You might even want to start a mailing list of your own someday, which contributors can do. You can learn more about what's required of a list owner by going to the Help page and clicking the Request a Mailing List link or by going to http://resources.rootsweb.com/adopt.

Gen-Newbie

Gen-Newbie (see Figure 17-6) is a mailing list for people who are new to computers and/or genealogy. It is the place to ask questions, help others, and generally share information, research techniques, brick walls, and computer/genealogy woes. It began on October 31, 1996, as an offshoot of the renowned ROOTS-L. Subscribing is as simple as clicking one of the buttons at the bottom of the page at www.rootsweb.com/ ~ newbie. The Gen-Newbie archives include a six-part course in genealogy by Jean Legreid, a Certified Genealogical Records Specialist.

GENMTD-L

Genealogical methods and resources are the topics for GENMTD-L. This isn't a queries list. Instead, it's a list about the nuts and bolts of genealogy research. You can participate through e-mail or through Usenet news. The discussions are archived, searchable, and retrievable. You can learn more at www.rootsweb.com/ ~ genmtd.

GENMTD-L is a moderated group intended for helpful discussions on the research methods, resources, and problems genealogists have in common, regardless of the different families or different cultural groups they study. The exception is methods relating to computing databases,

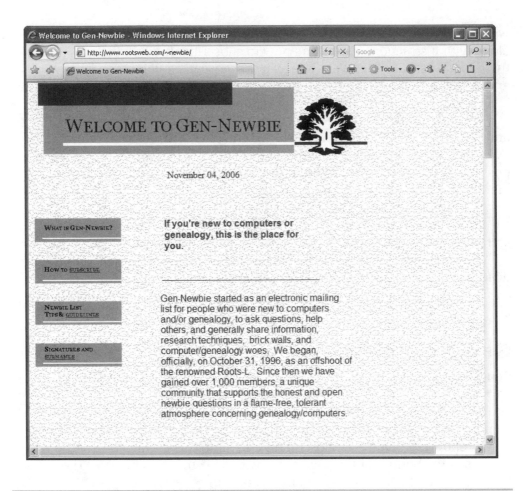

FIGURE 17-6.   *Gen-Newbie is where to go for those questions you were afraid to ask about genealogy research.*

and online research. Often, a problem is presented to the group, which then discusses possible solutions. Also, useful research strategies and resources might be posted. Like most RootsWeb mailing lists, you send a message with SUBSCRIBE in the body to the list's subscribe address. In this case, it's GENMTD-L-request@rootsweb.com for single-message format, GENMTD-D-request@rootsweb.com for digests of messages, and GENMTD-I-request@rootsweb.com for index format.

Newsletters

A newsletter, like a mailing list, comes straight to your e-mail inbox. Unlike the lists discussed previously, however, they are not for discussion; the communication is one-to-many. Like a print magazine, a newsletter will have news, notes, stories, and the occasional (text) advertisement. RootsWeb has several e-mail newsletters, all of which are worth reading. Here are some descriptions of them.

RootsWeb Review

RootsWeb is always growing, and you can't depend on luck to find out about the latest and greatest sites! *RootsWeb Review* is a free weekly newsletter sent to subscribers with the news about RootsWeb. You'll find announcements of programs and services for RootsWeb users, new mailing lists, GenConnect boards, and websites, plus success stories from other online genealogists.

If you're interested in reading through previous issues, you can click on the Archives link (http://rwr.rootsweb.com). You can subscribe by sending an e-mail to RootsWeb-Review-L-request@rootsweb.com with only the word "subscribe" in the subject line and message area.

Webpages at RootsWeb

RootsWeb hosts thousands of genealogy websites. Some, such as the USGenWeb Project's main site at www.usgenweb.com, you've already read about in this book. RootsWeb also hosts the WorldGenWeb Project at www.worldgenweb.org and a majority of the country sites.

RootsWeb-Sponsored Pages

Books We Own (www.rootsweb.com/~bwo), shown in Figure 17-7, is a list of resources owned and accessed by volunteers who are willing to look up genealogical information and then e-mail or snail mail it to others who request it. It works like a worldwide research library, where your shelf of genealogy books is one branch and you're one librarian of thousands. This is a volunteer service, and participants might ask for reimbursement of copies and postage if information is provided via snail mail. The project began in 1996 as a way for members of the ROOTS-L mailing list to share their resources with one another, and now some 1,500 people are involved.

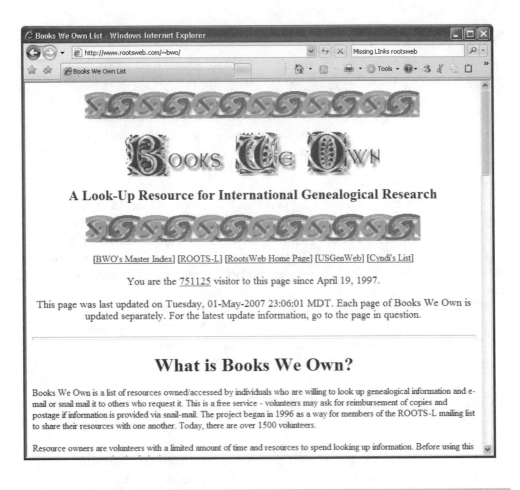

FIGURE 17-7. *Books We Own is a cooperative effort to look up information for each other in reference books owned by the members.*

FreeBMD (England and Wales), at http://freebmd.rootsweb.com, stands for Free Births, Marriages, and Deaths. The FreeBMD Project's objective is to provide free Internet access to the Civil Registration index information for England and Wales. The Civil Registration system for recording births, marriages, and deaths in England and Wales has been in place since 1837. This is one of the most significant single resources for genealogical research back to Victorian times.

Immigrant Ships Transcribers Guild (www.immigrantships.net) is a group of volunteers dedicated to making the search for our ancestors' immigration easier. The aim is to make as many ship's passenger lists as possible available online—and not just for U.S. ports. There are databases for Australia, Canada, Irish passengers to Argentina, and more. This group would also be happy to have your help!

Random Acts of Genealogical Kindness (www.raogk.org) is a cooperative effort. Once a month, the volunteers of this movement agree either to videotape cemeteries or to visit county courthouses in the county (or an area of a country) they live in to transcribe records. The cost to you would be reimbursement of costs incurred in granting your request (videotape, copying fees, and so forth).

State Resource Pages, one of the main areas of RootsWeb, is at www.rootsweb.com/roots-l/usa.html. It offers a wealth of information to those researching in the United States.

Freepages

Freepages are genealogy pages by volunteers. These pages must fit the RootsWeb mission; cannot contain copyrighted, commercial, or multimedia material; and cannot redirect to another site. If you meet these and all the other rules stated on http://accounts.rootsweb.com, you can have free Web space at RootsWeb. The freepages include sites of major RootsWeb projects, such as USGenWeb and WorldGenWeb, as well as genealogical or historical organizations.

You can find kids' pages, lessons and help pages, memorials, and timelines among these pages. If you already have a genealogy-related website and want it linked from RootsWeb, you can register it as well.

The Help Desk

The Help Desk (http://helpdesk.rootsweb.com) maintains a page to help you find a FAQ file about RootsWeb and its services. If you have a question or problem, check here first. If you can't find an answer here, you can follow the links from this site to the message board, where you can post a question for the Help Desk team to answer.

This quick tour is just enough to whet your appetite, but isn't even half of what's there. Spend some time getting to know RootsWeb. Now let's get acquainted with Ancestry.com.

Ancestry.com

With 24,000 searchable databases and titles, Ancestry.com (see Figure 17-8) is a major online source for family history information. Since its launch in 1997, Ancestry.com has been the leading resource for family history and has worked hard at gathering diverse data with many easy-to-use tools and resources. The Ancestry.com part has the only complete online U.S. federal census collection (1790–1930),

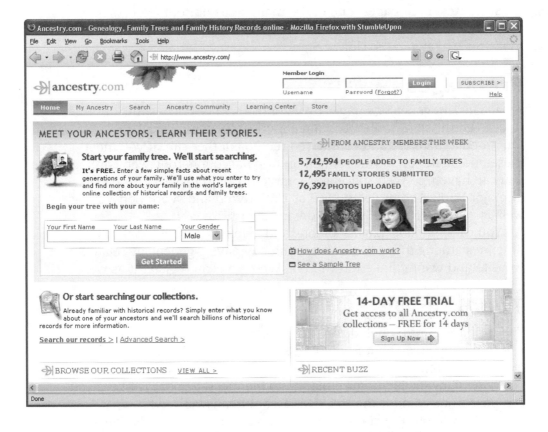

FIGURE 17-8. *Ancestry.com is a major player in the online genealogy industry.*

as well as the world's largest online collection of U.S. ship passenger list records featuring more than 100 million names (1820–1960). Based in Salt Lake City, Utah, it is a wide-ranging collection of genealogy resources. You can do some things for free, but fees apply for certain searches, some levels of disk space, and some other services.

Ancestry.com publishes books, magazines, and other genealogy materials, and has subscription-based research materials on their website, with mostly U.S. material. *Genealogical Computing* magazine covers technology issues and breakthroughs in genealogy; *Ancestry* magazine covers general topics, such as research techniques, success stories, and historical topics. *Ancestry's Red Book: American State, County, and Town Sources* by Alice Eichholz (Ancestry Publishing, 2004), *Finding Answers in U.S. Census Records* by Loretto Dennis Szucs and Matthew Wright (Ancestry Publishing, 2001), and *The Source: A Guidebook of American Genealogy* edited by Loretto Dennis Szucs and Sandra Hargreaves Luebking (Ancestry Publishing, 2006) are just three of the well-respected publications under the Ancestry.com imprint.

Ancestry.com has two parts. The research side has databases of transcribed and secondary material, much of which is accessible for a fee. The exchange side includes uploaded GEDCOMs, messages boards, and original articles on genealogy, all of which are accessible for free. Features include the following:

♦ A large online genealogy library, searchable from the Web. The library includes such records as land, birth, marriage, death, census, and immigration records, as well as the Periodical Source Index (PERSI), Daughters of the American Revolution Lineage Books, the 1790 Census Collection, and the Early American Marriages Collection, to name just a few. Of note is the recent addition of the *London Times* (editions from 1786 to 1833) and the UK Census of 1891, with every name indexed for both.

♦ Name-indexed GEDCOM databases, which are updated frequently, so future searches may turn up what today's search did not.

♦ Regular genealogy columns by writers such as George G. Morgan, Dick Eastman, Kip Sperry, Juliana Smith, Elizabeth Kelley Kerstens, and Drew Smith are available free of charge.

Costs

Ancestry.com's various levels of free and pay areas can be confusing. You can choose from several different levels of subscription to the site:

♦ **Ancestry.com free services**   The free services on Ancestry.com allow you to create an online family tree, upload family photos, create life timelines for each person in your tree, and share the tree with family members. In addition, those you invite to see your family tree on Ancestry.com will have full access to the family history records, photos, and more attached to that tree, much like having friends on MySpace or FaceBook. The free services also provide access to the Ancestry.com message boards (which were RootsWeb message boards before the merger), where members can seek help, swap family stories, and receive answers to questions.

Free membership also includes the Ancestry Learning Center and Library—virtual classrooms where you can learn about using the many resources on Ancestry.com. In fact, if you are new to genealogy, be sure to scroll down to the bottom of the page, where you will find links to beginner's guides on topics such as searching newspapers and periodicals and African-American family history. The guides are easy to understand and point you to specific Ancestry.com databases, saving you time and possibly money.

Members can also sign up for the free weekly and monthly newsletters published by Ancestry.com, a good way to stay informed on the latest additions to the databases.

♦ **Family Trees & Connections Membership**   At $19.95 a year, this membership lets you search all the submitted genealogies (GEDCOMs) on Ancestry.com. At this level, you can communicate privately and anonymously with other members that have similar interests.

♦ **U.S. Deluxe**   At either $29.95 a month or $155.40 a year, this membership adds access to all the U.S. records, which include census records; family and local histories; birth, marriage, and death records; member trees' immigration records; maps and photos; court, land, and probate records; directories; historical newspapers; and military records. You can test drive the U.S. Deluxe package with a 14-day free trial.

♦ **World Deluxe**   At either $39.95 a month or $347.40 a year, this membership offers unlimited access to everything in the U.S. Deluxe Membership and also includes Ancestry.com's entire global collection. Historical documents, records, and newspapers from the United Kingdom, Canada, Ireland, and many other locations around the globe are available.

A Sample Search

When you type a name in the search fields, some of the resulting links will be to the pay areas, as described earlier. For example, inputting my husband's great-grandfather Marvin Crowe, I had several hits in the documents, such as war records and U.S. census records (see Figure 17-9). The Ancestry World Tree had several hits, but none in Ohio County, Kentucky, where I know he lived, and matches came up in the Stories and Publications area (newspapers, magazines, and member-submitted material), but none in Kentucky. The Photos and Maps area had no matches on him.

You also might want to check out the software Ancestry Family Tree. You can load your GEDCOM into it, and it will search all the Ancestry.com databases (GEDCOMs) for matches. Ancestry.com automatically searches for matches within other uploaded genealogies to each name in your database. You can also add names, dates, and places as you find them; add sources and connect specific facts to them; and handle divorces and other records. Other good links in the free area include articles on genealogy techniques, genealogy lessons, phone and address searches, Juliana's Links, a searchable database of websites, and maps and gazetteers. The site also features a chat area, bookstore, and sample articles from *Ancestry* magazine, the print version.

FIGURE 17-9. *This figure shows the results of searching for an ancestor in war records in Ancestry.com*

Success Story: Smashing a Brick Wall

I smashed a brick wall recently using Ancestry.com. I have a basic subscription to Ancestry. There has been a family story in my husband's family for as long as anyone can remember that the name Flynt isn't really the family surname, that it is really Damon. No one knew any more than that. Ancestry.com put an index to Maine court records online. I did a search for the great-great grandfather Daniel Flint/Flynt. I was rewarded with "Daniel Flint (Alias)." I copied down the book and page numbers, and contacted the State of Maine Archives for copies of the court records. The records showed a conviction for bigamy and included marriage records for the first marriage as Delafayette Damon to Esther Damon in Reading, Massachusetts, in 1805 and his second, unlawful marriage as Daniel Flint to Lydia Anne Williams in Farmington, Maine, in 1812. He appealed the conviction on the grounds that the first marriage took place in Massachusetts and Maine didn't have jurisdiction. He was granted a new trial, but the attorney general didn't pursue the matter, and Daniel Flint went home to Abbot, Maine, to raise his second family, from which my husband was descended. With this information, I was able to find his ancestors through his mother back to Thomas Flint, one of the early settlers of Reading, Massachusetts, and his first wife's family, as well as their three children. This has all been from secondary sources and not yet proved, but at least now I know where to look for proof.

—*Alta Flynt*

MyFamily.com

MyFamily.com is a password-protected online community—a sort of MySpace for families. With a MyFamily site, you can post news, create albums and calendars, upload video and sound files, and allow your family members to access it all with a password. The site lets you save addresses and phone numbers in an online address book. Members use MyFamily to stay in contact and to keep track of birthdays, anniversaries, and other important dates in a shared calendar.

One of the most popular uses is to collaboratively work on the family tree with data input and GEDCOM uploads. Plus, you can use the disk space to upload images of your source documentation. In other words, this is a way to back up your work, which you should be doing at least monthly.

At the time of this writing, a new version was in beta and probably is live by the time you read this. The beta site works very much like other online communities. Once you create the site, your MyFamily home page will look similar to the one shown in Figure 17-10.

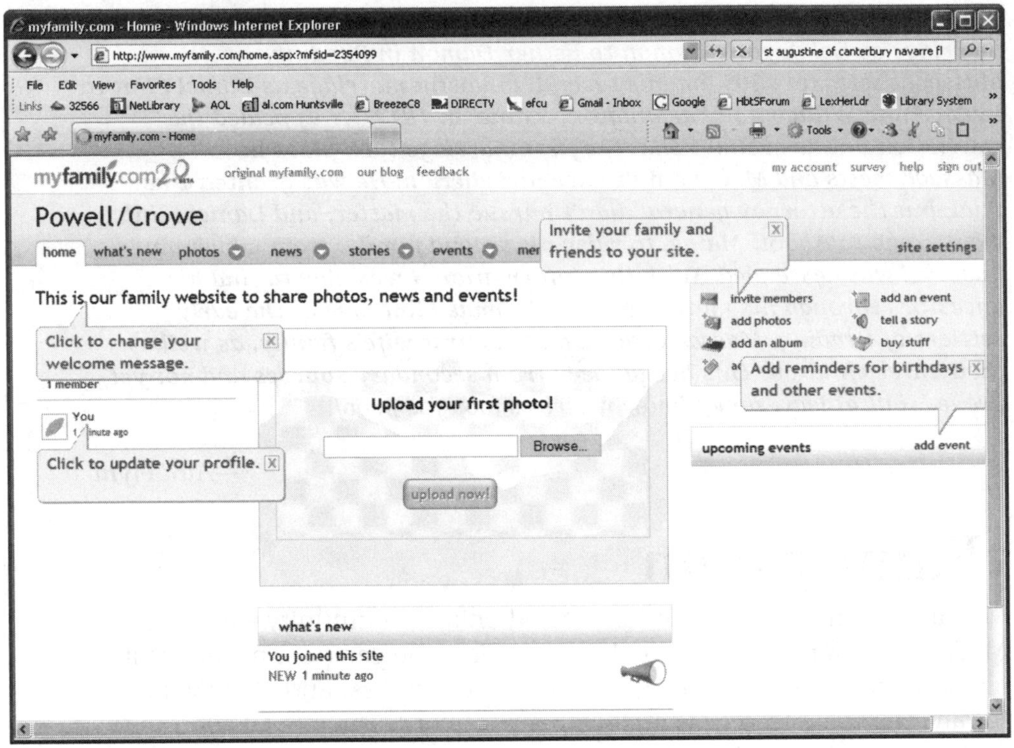

FIGURE 17-10. *Your MyFamily site can be both a social networking site and a genealogy site.*

You can construct a family tree in the Ancestry.com area and link it to the MyFamily.com area. As you fill it out, as shown in Figure 17-11, the site finds matches in all the data on Ancestry.com: census records, other family trees, and so on. The matches are general, not exact: You'll get matches with the same first name but a different or no middle name, for example.

The family tree can be typed in, including sources, or you can upload a GEDCOM. Corrections are as easy as calling up the tree, clicking a name, and editing.

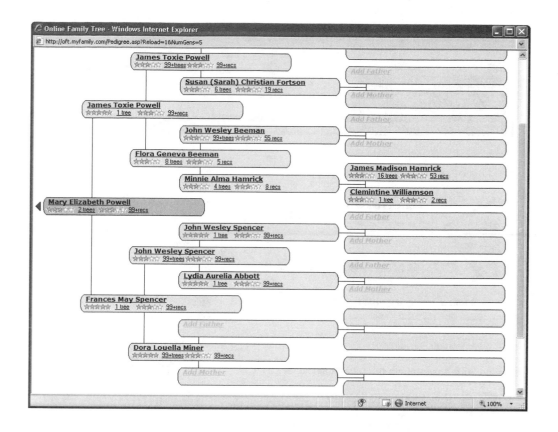

FIGURE 17-11. *You can view, edit, and print genealogies in MyFamily.com.*

Genealogy.com

Genealogy.com (see Figure 17-12) was added to the company around 2002 and has many of the same features and areas. However, the sites differ in specifics. For example, both Ancestry.com and Genealogy.com have marriage index databases in the subscription area, but one might have marriages from Indiana in the 1880s, while the other might have Michigan and Wisconsin from the same time period. Both sites have message boards, and different queries might be posted to one or the other.

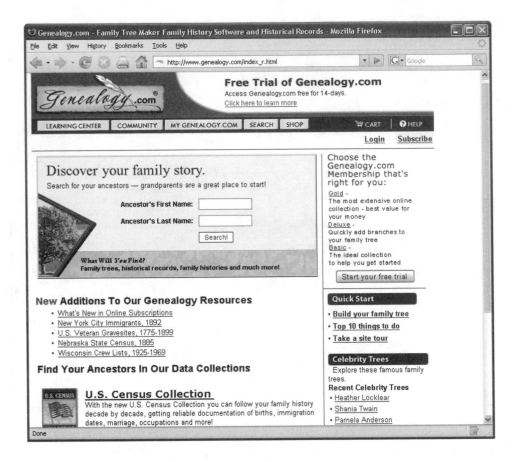

FIGURE 17-12. *Genealogy.com is now part of the Generations Network, but started about the same time as Ancestry.com and has a different set of messages, databases, and genealogies.*

Access to Genealogy.com's library, databases, and uploaded genealogies ranges from $70 to $200 a year. All levels include a downloadable version of Family Tree Maker, a general-purpose genealogy program with a module to upload your database to the site. Family Tree Maker's online search engine can only search the sister site, Ancestry.com. Technical support is provided with Gold Membership.

The cross-promotion agreement with The History Channel began before the merger with the Generations Network, and the site itself has changed very little. Some of the interesting areas of this site are listed below:

♦ **Learning Center** Under the Learning Center link in the navigation bar at the top of every page, you can find articles, self-paced lessons on organization and other topics, as well as references such as a glossary, a relationship chart, and tips on reunions. The beginner can learn a lot from this free information.

♦ **Community** Under the Community link in the navigation bar, you'll find the message boards, where you can post queries, ask and answer questions, and exchange information. The boards are sorted by surname, location, and general topics. Under Community, you can also create a free home page or search through those already there. The pages can be simple, or you can add pictures, links, and other features. You can simply fill out a form with the information you want to appear or upload a page you have created with a Hypertext Markup Language (HTML) editor, such as FrontPage. You can add a family tree by uploading one from Family Tree Maker, by uploading a GEDCOM, or by entering each individual in a JavaScript window on the site.

The Community area also includes celebrity genealogies, from royal families to artists and musicians. Finally, check out the Virtual Cemetery, where volunteers post tombstone pictures and information on where the cemeteries are located. This saves travel and helps create a resource for other genealogists. Contributing to and searching the database are both free.

♦ **MyGenealogy.com** The MyGenealogy.com area includes your home page (mentioned earlier), as well as access to a storage area of about 10 megabytes (MB). This can hold the text, HTML, graphics, and other files you would like to display, and it can serve as a backup point for your genealogy information.

Note

Have you backed up this week? This month? This year? This is one way to do it!

- **Search** The Search page has several forms to use for different searches. The first form lets you input a name, a place, and a date to search all the Genealogy.com data—both the free stuff and the subscription area—for any matches. It also searches a pay-per-view site of UK records called Origins.net. This site has records of vital statistics, as well as apprentice records, wills, and witness depositions. These records cover the years from about 1538 to 1900. The Site Search allows you to type a keyword—for example, "wills" or "Kentucky"—and find pages within the Genealogy.com site that match. I found, however, that it will show links to pages that have been removed or renamed. The last search on the page is the SSDI, a search of the Social Security Death Index. This area has recently gone over to the "subscription" side.

- **Shop** In the Shop area, you'll find books, CD-ROMs of databases (from vital records to GEDCOMs submitted by Family Tree Maker users), videos, and genealogy supplies. The software Family Tree Maker (FTM) is available here, as are paid memberships to the online databases.

Note

Your genealogy information entered into FTM and uploaded to Genealogy.com will appear on some of the CD-ROMs the site sells.

A Virtual Mall of Genealogy

The Generations Network is like shopping in a huge genealogy mall, and it allows you to add your own data to the collections. RootsWeb allows you more creativity in your website design than Genealogy.com and MyFamily, but the latter two sites are more interactive. Either way, all the sites in the company can be useful in continuing and sharing your genealogy research.

Wrapping Up

♦   MyFamily.com has several different sites: RootsWeb, Genealogy.com, and Ancestry.com for research; MyFamily.com for interaction; and the message boards on all of them.

♦   Many Ancestry.com features are free, but the bulk of the data is only available to paying members.

♦   MyFamily.com allows you to create a family site with genealogy data, messages boards, and so on. A small site is free, but over 5MB charges begin.

♦   Genealogy.com has a separate set of data in both the free and pay areas, as well as many similar features to Ancestry.com, MyFamily.com, and RootsWeb.

Chapter 18

A Potpourri of Genealogy

As you've no doubt noticed while reading this book, genealogy websites come in all categories. You will find portals and social networks that aim to be your Web home, with an emphasis on genealogy. You will find sites with images of original documents or transcribed records (perhaps both!) and sites with completed, annotated genealogies. You will find sites where folks have slapped up any data they found, regardless of accuracy or relevancy. You will find primary records, secondary records, family legends, and scams. It's truly an embarrassment of riches out there.

You must remember to judge each source you find critically and carefully. Compare it to what you have proven with your own research. Look for the original records cited in an online genealogy to see if they have been interpreted correctly (remember the lesson about census records in Chapter 1!). Most of all, look for application to *your* genealogy. How helpful is it?

Note

Most online genealogists have at least these five links bookmarked:

- ♦ *Cyndi's List (www.cyndislist.com)*
- ♦ *DearMYRTLE (www.dearmyrtle.com)*
- ♦ *FamilySearch.com (www.familysearch.com)*
- ♦ *NARA (www.archives.gov)*
- ♦ *RootsWeb (www.rootsweb.com)*

Golden Needles in the World Wide Haystack

In the manner of websites everywhere, the sites in this chapter will all lead you to other sites, where (I hope) you'll find the information you need. Note that this isn't even close to an exhaustive list. For that, see Cyndi's List and Chris Gaunt's Genealogy Resources on the Internet at http://www.personal.umich.edu/ ~ cgaunt/gen_int1.html.

I have sorted these sites by topic. This list of websites reflects what I've found to be valuable. Some of these sites are portals and will link you to sites I haven't found or that didn't exist at press time. Other links may be "dead" (as they say in Web parlance) by the time you read this. Don't be discouraged by this. That's part of the fun of online genealogy: There's always something new!

> ***Note***
>
> *Have you backed up your data this week? This month? This year?*

Adoption

The following are places that concentrate on reuniting birth families:

♦ **AdopteeForum.com**   This site offers links to search sites, message boards, and stories about adoptees.

♦ **Bastard Nation (http://www.bastards.org)**   This is an organization dedicated to the recognition of the full human and civil rights of adult adoptees. Bastard Nation states that it is the right of people everywhere to have their official original birth records unaltered and free from falsification, and that the adoptive status of anyone should not prohibit him or her from choosing to exercise that right. They pursue their aims through writing articles, holding rallies, lobbying legislatures for open records laws, and so on.

♦ **RegDay (http://www.regday.org)**   Every November, the Adoption Registration Coalition holds RegDay to increase awareness of adoptee issues. Birth parents and adoptees can register at the site (see Figure 18-1) to find each other.

♦ **Adoption Search and Reunion (http://adoptionsearcher .com)**   This site has a search index for the entire site, information about all 50 states, lists of mailing lists and registries, and over a thousand links to other sites.

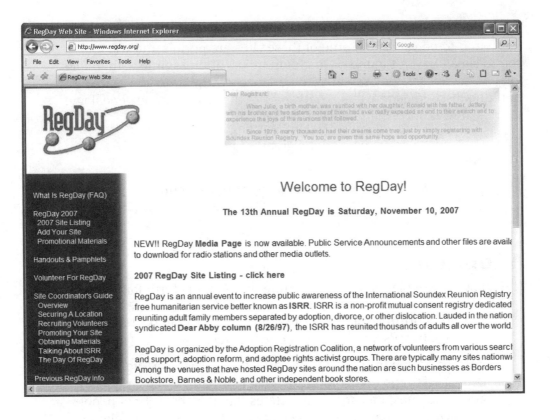

FIGURE 18-1.   *RegDay is a website from the Adoption Registration Coalition to publicize their efforts to reunite adoptees with biological parents.*

- ◆ **PeopleFinder UK Adoption Section (http://www.peoplefinders .co.uk/adoption.html)**   This site explains laws in the United Kingdom concerning finding birth mothers by adoptees.

- ◆ **Reunite.com (http://reunion.adoption.com)**   This site has a birth-family search guide and other free resources.

Beginners' "Classes," How-to Articles, Tips, Etc.

These sites feature articles, lessons, helpful hints, and columnists:

♦ **About.com Genealogy (http://genealogy.about.com/hobbies/ genealogy)**   This site has tips, discussion groups, and weekly articles on genealogy.

♦ **Branching Out Online (http://www.didian.com/branch)**   This is one of many sites that has "Branching Out" in the title, but this site is special. It's a tutorial on learning about online techniques and genealogy sites, and it's great for beginners.

♦ **Family History, How Do I Begin? (http://www.familysearch .org)**   Go to the Family Search site, and then click Search | Research Guidance | How Do I Begin? This is the Church of Jesus Christ of Latter-day Saints' (LDS) basic tutorial.

♦ **Encyclopedia of Genealogy at Eastman's Online Genealogy Newsletter (http://www.eogen.com)**   This site is a cooperative wiki-like clearinghouse of genealogy techniques: where to find records, how to organize the data found, what the terminology means, and how to plan your next research effort (see Figure 18-2). Both contributing to and searching the encyclopedia are free.

♦ **Genealogy Lesson Plan (http://www.teachnet.com/lesson/ misc/familytrees040199.html)**   Located at TeachNet.com, this site has a lesson plan on family history for different curriculum areas.

♦ **Genealogy Today (http://www.genealogytoday.com)**   This site announces and rates genealogy sites, has news updates and links to databases, lets readers vote for their favorite sites, and so forth.

♦ **Internet Tourbus (http://www.tourbus.com)**   This is an e-mail course on how to use every part of the Internet. If you are as new to the Internet as you are to genealogy, take the Internet Tourbus *first*. Get the scoop on computer viruses, search engines, spam, cookies, urban legends, and the most useful sites on the Web. Bob Rankin and Patrick Crispen explain Internet technology in plain English with a dash of humor.

♦ **Kindred Trails (http://www.kindredtrails.com)**   This site has links, lessons, tips, articles, message boards, and more.

♦ **Kinship Calculator (http://www.rootsweb.com/~genepool/ cousins.htm)**   This site has a chart where you can determine your relationship with someone based on your common ancestor.

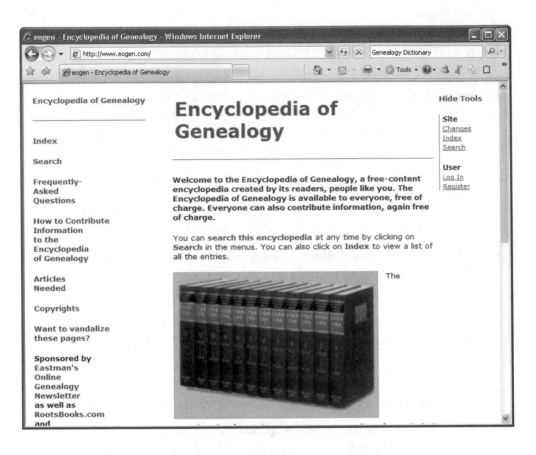

FIGURE 18-2. *Encyclopedia of Genealogy will help you find the meaning of confusing terms such as "yeoman" and "relic."*

+ **Lineages, Inc. (http://www.lineages.com)**   This is the website for a group of professional genealogical researchers who, for a fee, will help you find your roots. Many of them hold professional certification. In addition, their site includes some free information, such as "First Steps for Beginners," a free genealogical queries page, and more.

+ **Personal History Help (http://www.personalhistoryhelp .com)**   This is a step-by-step guide to writing a personal history and keeping your memorabilia organized, and a kit for personal historians just also happens to be for sale.

♦ **StateGenSites (http://www.stategensites.com)** This site has monthly and weekly columns on all aspects of genealogy. Uncle Hiram's weekly column is especially good!

♦ **Treasure Maps, the How-to Genealogy Site (http://www .amberskyline.com/treasuremaps)** This is one of the best sites on the Web for novices. To keep track of the latest news on Treasure Maps, you might want to subscribe to its monthly newsletter. Learn how to decipher old handwriting, turn your genealogy into a published book, get reunion ideas, and more!

Birth, Death, Marriage, and Other Records

Here are just a few of the sites where volunteers are uploading data. Be sure you visit RootsWeb and Cyndi's List often for updates and new pages:

♦ **Cemetery Junction: The Cemetery Trail (http://www.daddezio .com/cemetery/index.html)** This site has transcriptions of tombstones found in cemeteries across the United States, collected and uploaded by volunteers. Through articles, the site also attempts to tell the untold and forgotten stories about the occupants of these cemeteries. Eric Miller is the Cemetery Junction team member with writing responsibilities for the initial series, an accomplished writer focusing on urban issues whose work has appeared in *San Francisco Downtown*, *The Pittsburgh Tribune-Review*, and other publications.

♦ **Census Bureau Home Page (http://www.census.gov)** Lots of interesting facts are at the official census site and, of course, they have a genealogy link on the home page. This site has a list of frequently occurring names in the United States for 1990, a Spanish surname list for 1990, an age search service, and a frequently asked questions (FAQ) file on genealogy.

The Age Search Service costs $65 per person per census to search the confidential records from the federal population censuses of 1910 to 2000 and to issue an official transcript of the results. This information can be released only to the named person, his or her heirs, or legal representatives. Individuals can use these transcripts, which may contain information on a person's age, sex, race, state or country of birth, and relationship to the householder, as evidence to qualify for Social Security and other retirement benefits, in making passport applications, to prove relationship in settling estates, in genealogy research, etc., or to satisfy other situations where a birth or other certificate may be needed but is not available.

♦ **FreeBMD (http://freebmd.rootsweb.com)** FreeBMD stands for Free Births, Marriages, and Deaths. The FreeBMD Project is made up of volunteers transcribing the Civil Registration Index information for England and Wales from the years 1837 to 1898 onto the Internet. Progress is sporadic; volunteer if you can. The home page is shown in Figure 18-3.

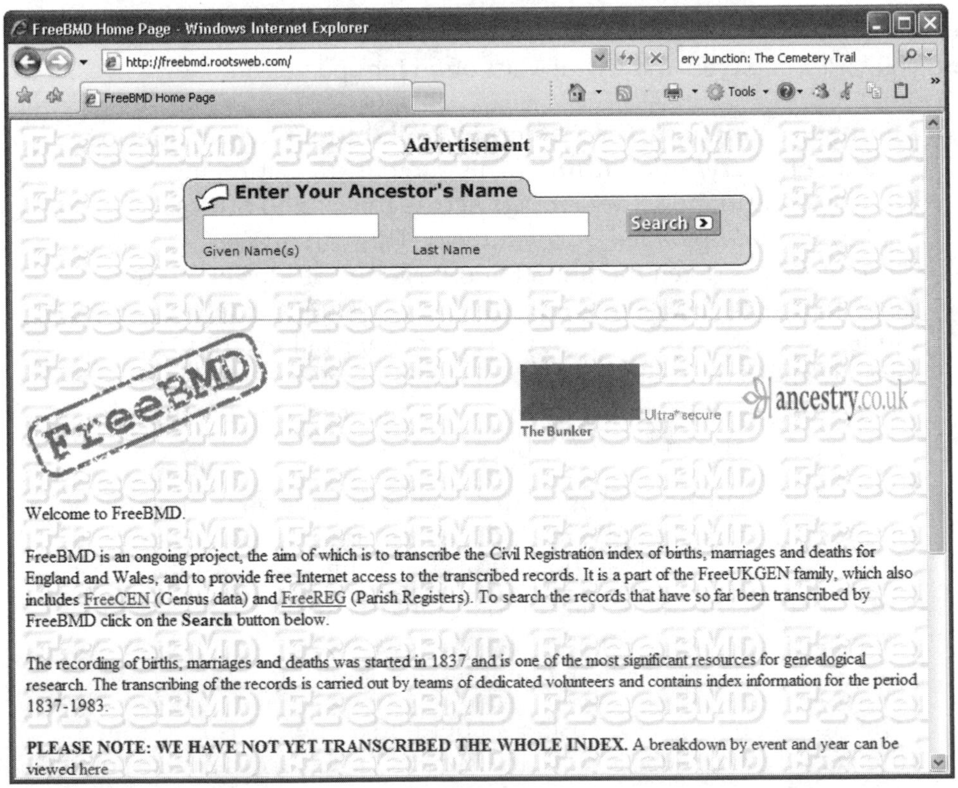

FIGURE 18-3. *FreeBMD is another chance to give back to the world of online genealogy, as this project always needs transcribers.*

DNA

DNA research is becoming part of online genealogy. These are sites you can explore for this topic:

♦ **Chris Pomery's DNA Portal (http://freepages.genealogy.rootsweb .com/ ~ allpoms/genetics.html)**   This is a scholarly article and set of links on the topic.

♦ **Family Tree DNA (http://www.familytreedna.com)**   This is a company you can pay to look for matches with people you suspect are relatives. In searching my mother's genealogy, we had long suspected that our Abraham Spencer was related to a certain Abner Spencer. Using this site, my uncle and another man submitted saliva samples. The other man (who wishes not to be named) was a proven descendant from that Abner. The results showed that he and my uncle have an ancestor in common. Many professional genealogists scoff at such proof (for example, the white descendants of Thomas Jefferson), but we feel this has finally solved our 30-year brick wall on Abraham's parents.

♦ **Genealogy DNA Mail List (http://lists.rootsweb.com/index/ other/DNA/GENEALOGY-DNA.html)**   This is a discussion group about the topic of DNA, hosted by RootsWeb. The searchable archives of messages cover 1970 to the present.

♦ **Oxford Ancestors (http://www.oxfordancestors.com)**   This is a company that does the same thing as Family Tree DNA, but in the UK.

♦ **Sorenson Molecular Genealogy Foundation (http://www .smgf.org)**   Brigham Young University (BYU) has a site explaining its DNA genealogy research. You can learn how this project is progressing and how you can participate in your area at the site. You can also read about how BYU hopes to use the data to further the Mormons' quest to have a family history for all people.

Ethnic/National

Here's a list of some useful ethnic pages:

♦ **Australian National Library (http://www.nla.gov.au/oz/ genelist.html)** The genealogy page has links to national and state archives in Australia, resources, organizations, military service records, and so on, as well as an online card catalog.

♦ **Center for Basque Studies (http://basque.unr.edu)** This site, at the University of Nevada, Reno, covers history, anthropology, and other aspects of Basque culture.

♦ **Center for Jewish History Ackman & Ziff Family Genealogy Institute (http://www.cjh.org/collections/genealogy/ index.php)** Begun by the Center Partners and the Jewish Genealogical Society in 2000, the Ackman & Ziff Family Genealogy Institute helps those looking for their Jewish ancestors (see Figure 18-4). Many seek to understand how the lives of their ancestors relate to the broader context of Jewish history and world history, while others seek to discover the fate of relatives lost during the Holocaust, to explore a Jewish past that was lost due to intermarriage and conversion, or to reconnect with branches of their family separated long ago by migration, war, and the Iron Curtain.

♦ **Byzantines.net (www.byzantines.net/genealogy/INDEX .HTM)** This site is for persons of Ruthenian—Carpatho-Rusyn— ancestry and those of the Byzantine Catholic/Orthodox faiths who came from the former Austro-Hungarian Empire.

♦ **Family History in India (http://members.ozemail.com .au / ~ clday)** This site is for tracing British, European, and Anglo-Indian families, with marriage records, church records, and other databases. It has over 1,340,000 names, including an index to Bengal marriages (1855–1896).

♦ **FamilySearch Jewish Family History Resources (http:// www.familysearch.com; click Jewish Family History Resources)** FamilySearch launched a page of special helps for Jewish genealogy research in August 2007. The new webpage features a Jewish genealogy database called the Knowles

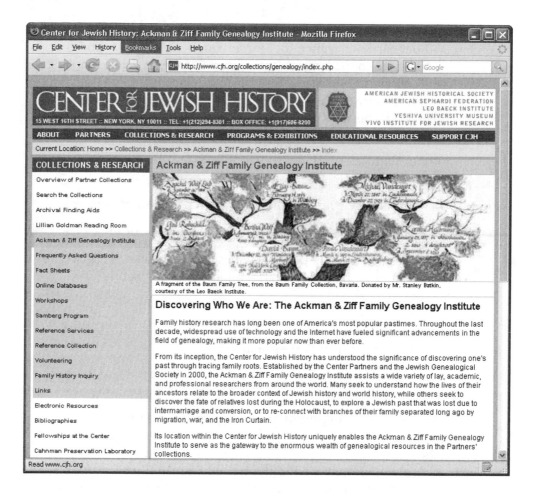

FIGURE 18-4.   *The Ackman & Ziff Family Genealogy Institute explores Jewish family history.*

Collection, as well as a new research guide, "Tracing Your Jewish Ancestors."

The Knowles Collection contains information for thousands of Jews from the British Isles. Building on the work of the late Isobel Mordy, the collection links individuals into family groups, with more names added continuously. The entire work is downloadable as either a GEDCOM or a PAF file.

The "Tracing Your Jewish Ancestors" guide is an excellent, 30-page free reference tool for anyone with a Jewish ancestor who came to the United States from Europe. It gives simple steps to identify an ancestor's birthplace or place of origin—a difficult task for many with Jewish ancestry—and what research tools to use. Both this new guide and the Jewish Genealogy Research Outline can be downloaded in PDF format.

Other FamilySearch Jewish Family History Resources highlights include:

♦ Links to relevant records and searchable databases

♦ Helpful guides and forms to view online or print

♦ Online indexing projects, where individuals can register to volunteer or to see what databases are forthcoming

♦ PAF, a free genealogy database and management program

♦ Directions to receive free personal assistance through a Family History Center near you

Those with Jewish ancestry should bookmark the site. Links to new resources and tools will be added as they become available.

♦ **The National Huguenot Society (http://www.huguenot .netnation.com)**   This site is for the study and preservation of the history of the 16th- and 17th-century Huguenots, especially those who immigrated to the United States. The objectives of The National Huguenot Society, which had its beginning in the 1930s, are patriotic, religious, historical, and educational. The members want to perpetuate the memory, the spirit, and the deeds of the men and women in France known as Huguenots who were persecuted in the 16th and 17th centuries because of their adherence to the basic tenets of the Protestant faith and their devotion to liberty, and who emigrated either directly or through other countries to North America and contributed by their character and ability to the development of the United States.

♦ **Federation of East European Family History Societies (http://www.feefhs.org)**   This site has databases, maps, and directories to help with genealogy in this region. The Federation of East European Family History Societies (FEEFHS) was organized in 1992 as an umbrella organization that promotes family research in Eastern and Central Europe without any ethnic, religious, or social distinctions. It provides a forum for individuals and organizations focused on a single country or group of people to exchange information and be updated on developments in the field. While it primarily serves the interests of North Americans in tracing their lineages back to a European homeland, it welcomes members from all countries.

♦ **Scotland's People (http://www.scotlandspeople.gov.uk)**   This is the official site for Scotland's government vital records. Searches are free, but access to images of and official copies of documents such as wills, censuses, and parish records involves fees. Be sure to read the articles under "Features" for explanations of the records, who collected them, and what they contain.

♦ **Hungarian Genealogy (http://www.rootsweb.com/~wghungar)**   This is a good place to start if your research leads you to Hungary. You'll find maps of Hungary, information on each of the counties, a discussion mailing list or two, and a query database. Suzanne Somodi Jimenez maintains the site.

♦ **JewishGen (http://www.jewishgen.org)**   This is a comprehensive resource for researchers of Jewish genealogy worldwide. Among other things, it includes the JewishGen Family Finder, a database of towns and surnames being researched by Jewish genealogists worldwide, and it can be searched on the Web or via e-mail (you simply e-mail the server commands, and results are e-mailed back to you).

♦ **History and Genealogy of South Texas and Northeast Mexico (http://vsalgs.org/stnemgenealogy)**   This is an interesting source if you're looking for relatives from the South Texas/Northeast Mexico area. The database has over 11,000 names, all linked as lineages.

♦ **Spanish Heritage Home Page (http://members.aol.com/shhar)**   This is an AOL-based site that's the home of the Society of Hispanic Historical and Ancestral Research. It has a free online magazine, *Somos Primos*, and you can be notified by e-mail when the new one is up on the Web.

Historical Background

Certain historical events may have an impact on your genealogy. The following sites can give you some information on these people in history:

♦ **American Civil War Home Page (http://sunsite.utk.edu/ civil-war)** This site has links to fantastic online documents from many sources, including those of two academics who have made the Civil War their career. This page has links to the most useful identified electronic files about the American Civil War (1861–1865). The "American Civil War Homepage" began as a class project for Information Science 560 at the University of Tennessee's School of Information Sciences during the Fall 1994 semester. When the page was first launched in February 1995, it contained slightly more than 30 links to resources about the American Civil War. Now it has hundreds.

♦ **Ancient Faces (http://www.ancientfaces.com)** This site adds a personal touch to genealogy research by including photographs, documents, stories, recipes, and more—all located under individual surnames.

♦ **British Civil Wars, Commonwealth, and Protectorate (http://www.british-civil-wars.co.uk)** This site covers the history of the United Kingdom from 1638 to 1660. It has chronological listings of events during this time; a list of who's who in the civil wars, Commonwealth, and Protectorate; some military history of the civil wars, Commonwealth, and Protectorate; links to websites and online articles relevant to this period; a bibliography; and reviews.

♦ **Heraldica (http://www.heraldica.org)** This site is dedicated to increasing interest in heraldry, genealogy, chivalry, and related topics. It's a no-frills site, but it has in plain language the things you need to know about authentic coats of arms.

♦ **Calendars Through the Ages (http://www.webexhibits.org/ calendars)** Calendars and dates in genealogy can get tricky. This site helps you decipher them. You can use it to explore the fascinating history of how we have tried to organize our lives in accordance with the sun and stars.

♦ **Documenting the American South (http://docsouth.unc.edu/index.html)** Sponsored by the University of North Carolina at Chapel Hill, this site is a digital publishing initiative that provides Internet access to texts, images, and audio files related to Southern history, literature, and culture. It includes ten thematic collections of books, diaries, posters, artifacts, letters, oral history interviews, and songs. You'll even find online versions of several books about antebellum North Carolina history. It's a fascinating site (see Figure 18-5).

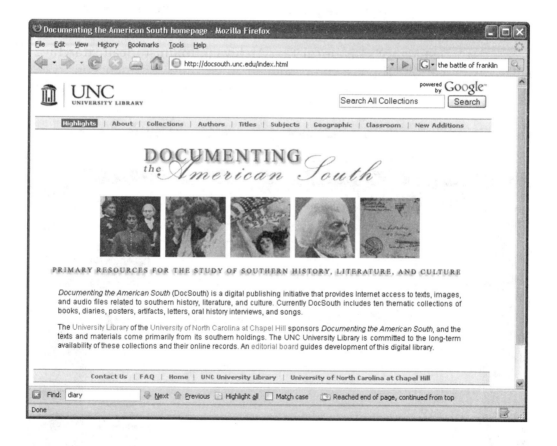

FIGURE 18-5. *Documenting the American South has original documents and articles, as well as online books.*

- **Daughters of the American Revolution (http://www.dar .org)** This is the organization for those who can prove an ancestor fought in the American Revolution. A free lookup in the DAR Patriot Index is just one of the site's many features. Click Genealogy from the home page for manuscripts, abstracts, biographies, histories, and genealogies.

- **Directory of Royal Genealogical Data (http://www3.dcs.hull .ac.uk/genealogy/royal)** This is a database with the genealogy of the British Royal family and many other ruling families of the Western world—they all seem to be interrelated somehow. It contains over 18,000 names.

- **Dan Mabry's Historical Text Archive (http://historicaltextarchive .com)** This is a compilation of articles and documents on various topics (see Figure 18-6). This site is dynamic, with regular

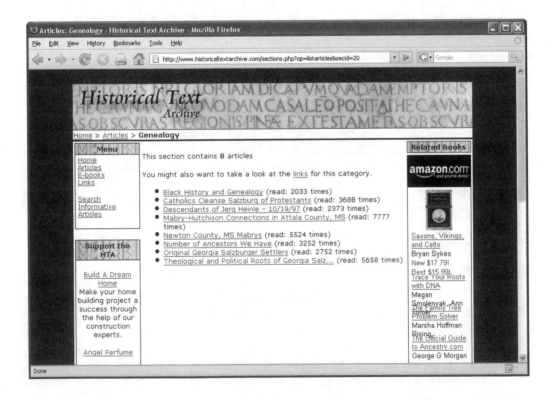

FIGURE 18-6. *Dan Mabry's Historical Text Archive was founded in 1990 in Mississippi and is one of the oldest history-related sites on the Internet.*

additions to its contents and its link collection. Several articles deal specifically with genealogy; many others on some aspect of history that may help you find new records.

♦ **Hauser-Hooser-Hoosier Theory: The Truth About Hoosier (http://www.geocities.com/heartland/flats/7822)**   This site explains how genealogy solved the mystery of "what is a Hoosier?"

♦ **Immigration: The Living Mosaic of People, Culture & Hope (http://library.thinkquest.org/20619)**   This is a student project about immigration in the United States.

♦ **MayflowerHistory.com (http://www.mayflowerhistory.com)** These pages contain the passenger lists of the *Mayflower*, the *Fortune*, and the *Anne*, plus many related documents. Some of the original documents are scanned in as images; others have been transcribed as full text documents. If you suspect you have an ancestor on the *Mayflower*, this is the place to begin (see Figure 18-7).

♦ **Medal of Honor Citations (http://www.army.mil/cmh-pg/moh.html)**   This site contains the names and text of the citations for the more than 3,400 people who've been awarded the Congressional Medal of Honor since 1861.

♦ **Migrations (http://www.migrations.org)**   This site has two separate parts. First is a database of migration information submitted by volunteers (secondary source information, of course!), searchable by name and place. Second is a list of links to resources on migration. Migrations.org is an unincorporated noncommercial research project. The mission of the site is to provide genealogical and historical researchers and educators on the Internet with links to online migration and genealogical sources, as well as to offer a searchable public database that collects and analyzes migration data, providing migration patterns for genealogical, historical, and educational research. Migrations.org is maintained by Patrick Hays.

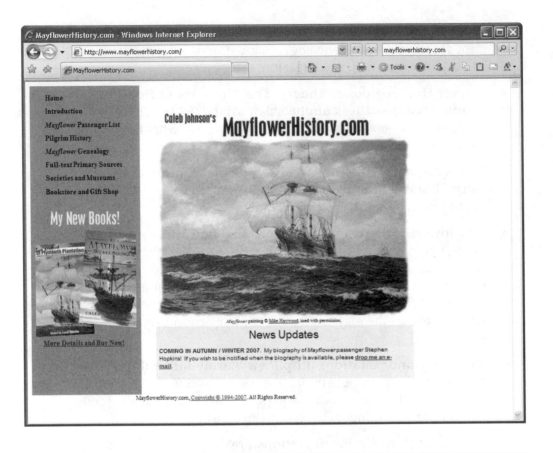

FIGURE 18-7. *The author of MayflowerHistory.com is Caleb Johnson, and he has been widely praised in the media for his work.*

- **Olden Times (http://theoldentimes.com/newsletterpage .html)** This site has historic newspapers online. You can subscribe to a newsletter for updates and additions.

- **Pitcairn Island Website (http://www.lareau.org/genweb .html)** This is the place to go for information on over 7,500 descendants of the crew of the *HMS Bounty*, of *Mutiny on the Bounty* fame.

- **Sons of the American Revolution (http://www.sar.org)**   This site has information on this organization's genealogical library, articles from its quarterly magazine, the history of the American Revolution, and more.

- **United States Civil War Center (http://www.cwc.lsu.edu)**   This site from Louisiana State University publishes book reviews, research tips, and articles about studying the War Between the States.

Libraries

Search the Web catalogs (Yahoo!, Lycos, Google, and so on) for "library" plus "state" or "national" or the region you need. Some state libraries also have special genealogical collections, which you might find with a search such as "Michigan State library genealogy." These are some of the best library sites for genealogy:

- **Abrams Collection, Library of Michigan (www.michigan.gov/familyhistory)**   The Abrams Collection Genealogy Highlights lists what researchers can find at this wonderful library. From assistance on specific genealogy topics, to an annual seminar, to an online newsletter, this page lists resources at the Library of Michigan and other libraries and research centers—the Abrams Foundation Historical Collection of genealogy materials covers more than just Michigan.

- **Connecticut State Library History and Genealogy Unit (www.cslib.org/handg.htm)**   This page explains the special collections and services the state library has for genealogists. The History and Genealogy Unit holds comprehensive collections of materials on the history of Connecticut and its people, as well as current and historical Connecticut newspapers. The history and genealogy staff responds to telephone, letter, e-mail, and fax inquiries regarding the unit's collections and services, as well as to brief, factual, nongenealogical questions on the history of Connecticut or its people. It offers a limited genealogical index search service for a fee in response to inquiries submitted on the Genealogical Index Search Request form found on the site.

♦ **Elmer's Genealogical Library (www.elmerslibrary.com)**   This nonprofit library is in Madison, Florida, and was founded as a place for folks to share documented family histories and records for present and future generations. As Florida has many retirees who moved to the state with their genealogy materials, the library often becomes the final resting place for individuals' family history. It also holds workshops and seminars (see Figure 18-8). The staff and volunteers will do research for a fee; membership in the library gets you reduced fees for research and copying.

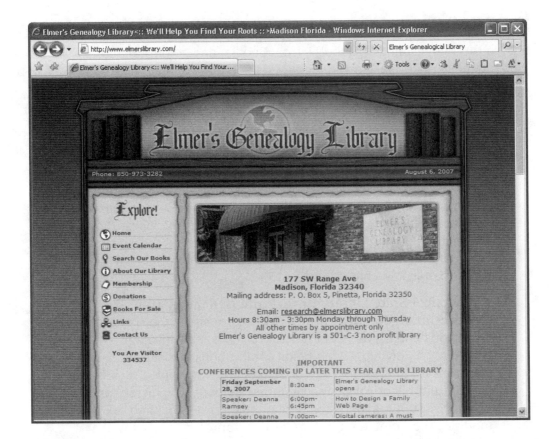

FIGURE 18-8.   *Elmer's Genealogical Library has over 16,000 genealogy books and research services for a fee.*

♦ **Gateway to Northwestern Ontario History (www.nextlibrary .com/tbpl/home.html)** This site has more than 1,000 photographs and drawings, as well as the full text of several books.

♦ **Genealogy and Local History Library (www.mcpl.lib.mo.us/ genlh)** This is a branch of the Mid-Continent Public Library, based in Independence, Missouri. The branch has its own page, building, and card catalog, and participates in interlibrary loans. The collection began in 1927 with early donations by the Independence Pioneers Chapter of the Daughters of the American Revolution (DAR). In 1971, the Mid-Continent Public Library (formerly known as Independence Library) acquired a collection of Missouri county histories, and the "Missouri Room" was opened at the Independence branch. The collection has over 10,000 circulating titles, 60,000 reference titles, and a vast number of periodicals and newspapers, as well as microforms, maps, and online databases. The current "Genealogy from the Heartland" circulating collection began in 1984 with a small collection of books donated to the Mid-Continent Public Library by the American Family Records Association (AFRA). Other collections have been added over the years: The Missouri State Genealogical Association (MoSGA), the Heart of America Genealogical Society (HAGS), and the Gann Family Association have added their libraries to the circulating collection and continue to add books that are donated to them.

♦ **Indiana State Library Genealogy Division (www.statelib.lib .in.us/WWW/whoweare/genealogy.html)** This site has searchable databases and an online card catalog. The Genealogy Division has developed over time to become one of the largest collections of family history information in the Midwest. The collection includes 40,000 printed items (family histories, indexes to records, how-to books, cemetery transcriptions, family history magazines, and more), as well as microfilmed federal census records, Indiana county records, passenger lists, and military pension information. The collection includes hundreds of CDs with family history information. The emphasis of the collection is on Indiana and bordering states, as well as on Eastern and Southern states.

- **Library of Virginia Digital Collections (www.lva.lib.va.us/ whatwehave)** A starting point, where you can search Virginia colonial records, as well as bible records, newspapers, court records, and state documents.

- **OPLIN Genealogy Gleanings (www.oplin.lib.oh.us)** Click "Genealogy" in the navigation bar to the left. This page archives all issues of Ohio Public Library Information Network's monthly online column on genealogy issues by Contributing Editor for Genealogy Donovan Ackley. You'll find tips on how to find reliable genealogical information on the Internet as well as in the library.

- **Repositories of Primary Sources (www.uidaho.edu/ special-collections/Other.Repositories.html)** This is a listing of over 2,500 websites describing holdings of manuscripts, archives, rare books, historical photographs, and other primary sources for every continent except Antarctica! This site is worth a look.

- **South Caroliniana Library (www.sc.edu/library/socar/books .html)** This is the online card catalog for the South Caroliniana Library, which houses an extensive collection of genealogy holdings, oral histories, manuscripts, and archives. You can also search all South Carolina university libraries from this site for books, photos, maps, paintings, and manuscripts.

- **Texas State Library and Archives (www.tsl.state.tx.us/arc/ genfirst.html)** This site lists available resources, including microfilm of the federal census schedules for all states through 1910, selected states from the 1920 and 1930 censuses, printed family and county histories, and a variety of Texas government records.

Maps, Geography, Etc.

"Where is that township?" is sometimes a hard question to answer. It can be even harder to find a community that no longer exists, or where county or state lines were moved. Searching for "historical maps" and the name of the county, state, province, or nation in question may turn up a hit in Google, Yahoo!, or other search sites. An excellent article on this topic can be found at www.rootsweb.com/ ~ srgp/articles/place.htm. It's titled "You Gotta Know the Territory—The Links Between Genealogy,

Geography and Logic." Some good sites to help with maps include the following:

- **The David Rumsey Historical Map Collection (www.davidrumsey .com)** This site has over 15,800 maps online. The collection focuses on rare 18th- and 19th-century North American and South American maps and other cartographic materials. Historic maps of the world, Europe, Asia, and Africa are also represented. Collection categories include Antique Atlas, Globe, School Geography, Maritime Chart, State, County, City, Pocket, Wall, Children's, and Manuscript maps. The collection can be used to study history, genealogy, and family history.

- **Deed Platter (http://www.genealogytools.net/deeds/)** If the deed with your ancestor has the metes and bounds, you can have this site draw a map. As mentioned in Chapter 5, learning to do this can sometimes help you see a connection you weren't aware of before.

- **The Hargrett Rare Book and Manuscript Library at the University of Georgia (www.libs.uga.edu/darchive/hargrett/maps/ maps.html)** This library has a collection of over 800 historic maps spanning five centuries. The collection can help you understand the minds and movements of early American explorers, revolutionary statesmen, cultural figures and politicians represented by the library's book and manuscript collections. The collection heavily emphasizes the state of Georgia and the surrounding region, but it has materials of other regions, too. To locate maps of geographic regions or time periods not represented on this page, use its list of links near the bottom.

- **Global Gazetteer (www.fallingrain.com/world)** This is a directory of over a quarter-million of the world's cities and towns, sorted by country and linked to a map for each town, with latitude and longitude.

- **GEONET Name Server (www.nima.mil/gns/html)** This site lets you search for foreign geographic feature names, and it responds with latitude and longitude coordinates.

- **U. S. Census Bureau Gazetteer (www.census.gov/cgi-bin/ gazetteer)** You can search by entering the name and state abbreviation (optional) or by the five-digit ZIP code.

- **Historical Maps of the United States from the University of Texas at Austin (www.lib.utexas.edu/maps/histus.html)** This site has dozens of maps under the headings Early Inhabitants, Exploration and Settlement, Territorial Growth, Military History, Later Historical Maps, and Other Historical Map Sites.

- **Old Maps, UK (www.old-maps.co.uk)** This site lets you search online for historical maps and order hard copies for a fee. You can search by county and then town, or look for popular sites, such as Buckingham Palace. Figure 18-9 shows Tenterden, Kent, UK, in 1876, one of seven available maps of that village.

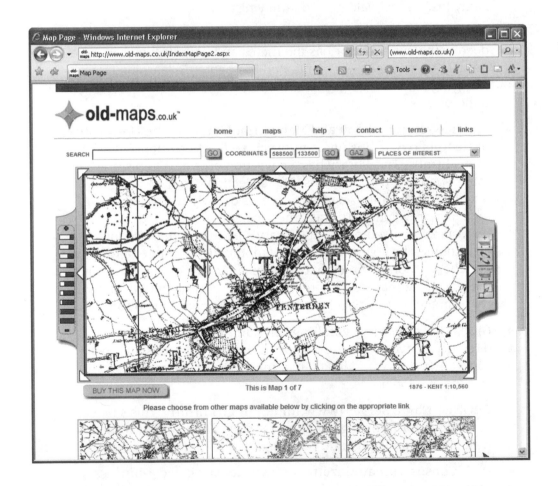

FIGURE 18-9. *Old Maps, UK sells copies of historical maps.*

Regional

If you need a regional resource, first go to Google, Yahoo!, Lycos, or another Web catalog and search for "archives." The following links are good examples of what you can expect to find:

♦ **Alabama Department of Archives and History Genealogy Page (http://www.archives.state.al.us/ge.html)**   This is a specific genealogy page with links to what records are available. The site accepts credit cards for reference requests (see Figure 18-10).

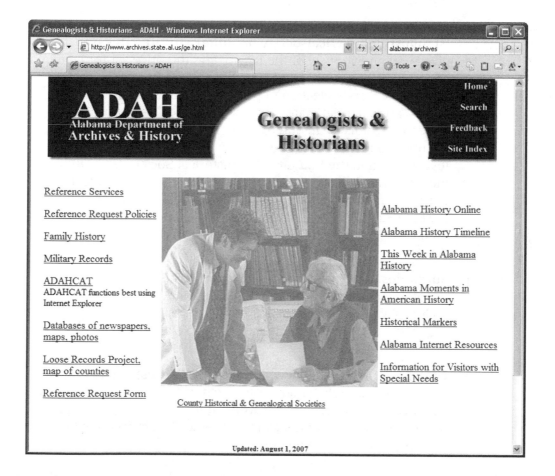

FIGURE 18-10.   *The ADAH Genealogy page is a good example of a state archive's website.*

♦ **Alabama Genealogy Sources (www.rootsweb.com/roots-l/ USA/al.html)**   This is just an example of the lists of links available at the RootsWeb. There is one for each state.

♦ **Canadian Heritage Information Network (http://www.chin.gc.ca/ English/index.html)**   This is a bilingual—French or English—guide to museums, galleries, and other heritage-oriented resources in Canada.

♦ **European Archival Network (www.european-archival.net/ archives)**   This page lists national archive sites by alphabet and region.

♦ **St. Augustine Historical Society Library (www .staugustinehistoricalsociety.org/library.html)**   This website gives you an overview of the facility and the price list for research services. The St. Augustine Historical Society Research Library has an excellent collection of printed, microfilmed, manuscript, digital, and pictorial materials relating to Florida history. The Research Library is an outgrowth of two of Florida's oldest cultural institutions: The Free Library Association of St. Augustine (est. 1872) and the St. Augustine Historical Society (est. 1883). It includes translations of the earliest (1594) church records in the nation, copies of official Spanish and British Colonial documents (1513–1821), the oldest municipal (1812) and county (1821) records in Florida, and genealogical data from the 16th century to the present, especially for people of Minorcan descent.

♦ **Surnames.com (www.surnames.com)**   This site discusses general genealogy, with some focus on the Arizona area. It includes a surname search and a map of genealogical organizations in the United States. The site also has a useful beginner's section.

♦ **Utah State Archives (www.archives.state.ut.us)**   Here you can access the research center for the archives' public services. This site includes research, places where questions can be answered, and places where records can be ordered. Not everything here is free, but it's very convenient!

Software

As noted in Chapter 2, software can help you gather, analyze, store, and compare information you find online and offline. Some good ones to investigate are:

◆ **Clooz (http://www.clooz.com)** This is a program that can help you organize your genealogy research by name, source, family line, and other categories.

◆ **Gene Macintosh (http://www.ics.uci.edu/ ~ eppstein/gene)** This page has information on David and Diana Eppstein's shareware program, Gene for the Macintosh.

◆ **GEDmark (http://www.progenygenealogy.com/gedmark .html)** GEDmark adds your name and contact information as a source citation on each record of your GEDCOM file. GEDmark costs $10 for a downloadable version (it's not available on CD-ROM).

◆ **GEDStrip (http://freepages.genealogy.rootsweb.com/ ~ hotrum/ gedstrip.htm)** This program takes the living people out of your GEDCOM file for privacy, if your current genealogy database program doesn't already do so.

◆ **RootsMagic (http://www.rootsmagic.com)** This is a new genealogy database program.

Starting Places

Here are some good places to begin your search for people, places, and pages:

◆ **Cyndi's List of Genealogy Sites on the Internet (http://www .cyndislist.com)** The best-organized and annotated list of genealogy websites on the Internet. A must-see!

◆ **Distant Cousin (http://distantcousin.com)** Distant Cousin is an online archive of genealogy records and scanned images of historical documents from a wide variety of sources, such as

newspaper obituaries, city directories, census records, ships'
passenger lists, school yearbooks, military records, and more. In
all, there are more than 6 million genealogy records from over
1,500 sources online. There are no fees or memberships required
to use the records at Distant Cousin.

♦ **Genealogy Home Page (http://www.genhomepage.com)**   This
page offers a wide-ranging index of genealogy resources on the
Internet. It includes links to maps, libraries, software, and
societies. It's plain text, so you can load and use it easily.

♦ **Genealogy Links.Net (http://www.genealogylinks.net)**   This site
includes over 9,000 links, most of them to online searchable
databases, such as ships' passenger lists, church records,
cemetery transcriptions, and censuses for England, Scotland,
Wales, Ireland, Europe, the United States, Canada, Australia, and
New Zealand.

♦ **Genealogy Pages (http://www.genealogypages.com)**   This site
provides a collection of links to free genealogical services, as well
as to over 29,000 online resources.

♦ **Genealogy Spot (http://www.genealogyspot.com)**   This is a free
portal with links to online genealogy resources for beginners and
experts alike. Sites featured here are hand-selected by an
editorial team for quality, content, and utility.

♦ **GeneaNet (http://www.geneanet.org)**   Based in France, this is a
genealogy database site you can search by name or geographic
location. It is not based on GEDCOM, but rather has its own
database format. Other resources are available, such as a list of
genealogy books, genealogy news briefs, and more. Much of the
emphasis is on French history, genealogy, and research, but there
are other resources, too.

Supplies, Books, Forms, Etc.

There are several good sources of free forms and supplies (see Chapter 1).
Check out DearMYRTLE's page (www.dearmyrtle.com/bookshelf/
supplies.htm) for some downloadable ones. The Ancestors series
Teacher's Guide has several PDF files of research forms for

downloading, too. You can buy supplies from Ancestry.com (see Chapter 17) as well. Here are a few other sites:

♦ **Heritage Quest (www.heritagequest.com/genealogy/microfilm/ html/order_info.html)** This site has books, microfilm, and other materials you can rent as well as purchase. It also has a database of information accessible from public libraries that subscribe to the service.

♦ **Global: Everything for the Family Historian (www .globalgenealogy.com)** This is the Global Genealogy Supply website. Shop online for genealogy supplies—maps, forms, software, and so forth—and subscribe to the *Global Gazette*, a free e-mail newsletter covering Canadian genealogy and heritage.

♦ **Family Chronicle (www.familychronicle.com)** This is the website for the *Family Chronicle* magazine, which is dedicated to families researching their roots. Check out their offerings and request a free sample of the magazine.

♦ **Genealogical.com (www.genealogical.com)** This site has genealogy supplies, articles about research, books, and CD-ROMs.

A Closer Look

Although one of the most exciting things about genealogy and Web browsing is the joy of discovery, some sites deserve a guided tour. The sites featured here are particularly interesting or useful to online genealogists, and each one has something special to offer. If you want to discover everything yourself, however, you have more than enough information to spend years researching online. Just skip past the rest of this section and be on your way.

AfriGeneas

AfriGeneas (www.afrigeneas.com) is a site for researching families of African ancestry (see Figure 18-11). The website has a mailing list that gathers and presents information about families of African ancestry. AfriGeneas is a guide to genealogical resources around the world. Members of the mailing list are invited to contribute information and

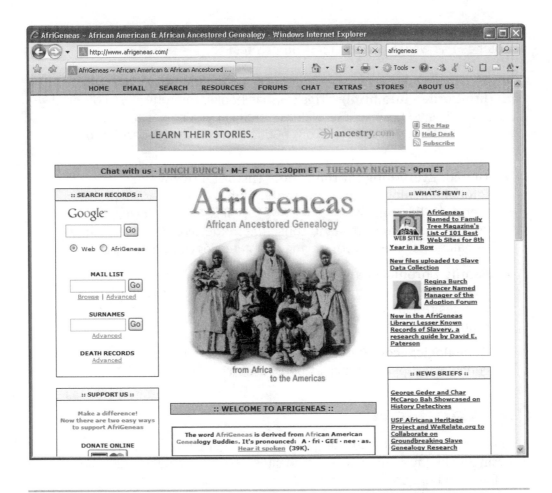

FIGURE 18-11. *African ancestry is the focus of the Web portal AfriGeneas.*

resources, sometimes going as far as taking responsibility for information for a certain area.

AfriGeneas has a searchable database of surnames (in addition to slave data) from descendants of slaveholding families, as well as from other sources, both public and private. Tips and topics help people in their search for family history through mailing lists, chats, newsletters, and the Internet. Volunteers do all of this; they extract, compile, and publish all related public records with any genealogical value. The site also maintains an impressive set of links to other Internet resources to help African Americans in their research:

- ◆ **Beginner's Guide**   This slideshow-like presentation steps you through online genealogy. It's a no-nonsense approach, showing what can and can't be done online. It also includes some success stories.

- ◆ **Mailing List**   This is the discussion list. You'll find the rules and the archives, plus information about how to subscribe and unsubscribe to the mailing list.

- ◆ **State Resources**   With a clickable map, this page links to sites for each U.S. state, with history, links to state resources, and queries.

- ◆ **World Resources**   This is along the same lines as the State Resources link, but only the United States and the Bahamas were up at press time. Volunteers are actively being sought for other countries.

- ◆ **Surnames**   This is a set of queries with names, dates, and places of known ancestors. You can search the ones there, as well as post your own.

- ◆ **Slave Data**   This area will help you find the last owned slave in your family. Records kept by the slave owner are frequently the only clue to African-American ancestors, particularly during the period 1619–1869. The site is also designed to help descendants of slaveholders and other researchers. Users share information they find containing any references to slaves, including wills, deeds, and other documents. This site also houses a search engine and a form for submitting any data you might have. To use the database, click the first letter of the surname you're interested in. This takes you to a list of text files with surnames beginning with that letter. Now click a particular file name. The text file may be transcribed from a deed book, a will, or some other document. The name and e-mail address of the submitter will be included, so you can write to that person for more information, if necessary.

- ◆ **Census Records**   These are transcribed census records. As a file is submitted, it's listed at the top of the What's New list on this page. Not all states have volunteers transcribing right now, so you can only click those states that show up as a live link.

- **Library**   This contains guides, articles, chat transcripts, and images for you to look at online or to download to your computer. Among the titles are "Researching in Southwest Louisiana" and "Cherokee Freedmen in Indian Territory."

- **Community**   This page shows how you can get involved, where and how to sign up as a volunteer, and testimonials about how much AfriGeneas has helped the people who use it.

- **Color profile**   Generic CMYK printer profile.

- **Newsletter**   The monthly newsletter looks at genealogy news from the African-American perspective.

- **Forum and Chat**   Chats on specific topics meet on a scheduled basis, and open discussions are usually available 24 hours a day. The forum is a Web-based list of messages sorted by date, with the most recent at the top.

- **AfriGeneas Links**   This page offers hundreds of fascinating links, sorted by topic, from good starting points, such as the WPA Slave Narratives and Canadian Black History.

AfriGeneas has come a long way from its beginnings as a mailing list, and it keeps getting better and better.

Cyndi's List

Cyndi Howell's list of genealogy links is on everyone's list of top-five genealogy places on the World Wide Web. With over 180,000 links, sorted into over 150 categories, it is the best place to start looking for genealogy sites. The links are categorized, alphabetized, and searchable, and the list has links to sites large and small, from national archives to personal genealogies.

The main index, accessible from the home page, lists each category in alphabetical order—from "Acadian, Cajun and Creole" to "Writing Your Family History." The topical index (www.cyndislist.com/ topical.htm) rearranges those topics into about a dozen different groupings. The "no frills" index (www.cyndislist.com/nofrills.htm) has every single category page, with no icons for the newest or latest update.

The Main Index page also has the FAQs about Cyndi's List, as in how she collects, verifies, and updates the links, and how to submit a link for her consideration. You will also find the newest links, sorted by month, and Cyndi's speaking schedule.

As you'll quickly see, Cyndi's List is indispensable for finding pages on genealogy.

DearMYRTLE

For the beginning to intermediate genealogist, there's no better spot than DearMYRTLE's place at www.dearmyrtle.com. DearMYRTLE has helped hundreds of genealogists with her daily columns, weekly chats, blogs, and online courses. Her site will help you learn and grow as a genealogist.

The first page of DearMYRTLE's site (see Figure 18-12) details her list of favorite things to do on the Internet for family history. The choices

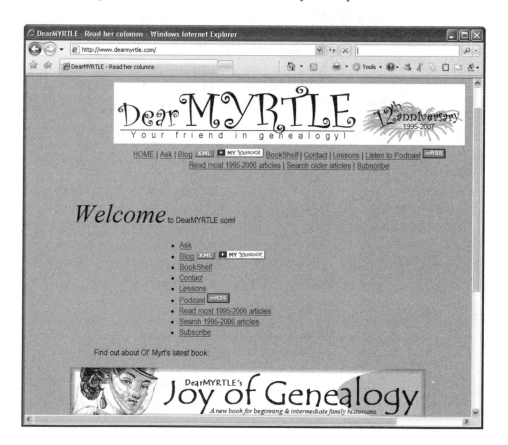

FIGURE 18-12.   *Genealogists at all levels can learn from DearMYRTLE's site.*

range from listening to her podcast talk show to her "step-by-step" guides.

Her "Best of the Internet for Genealogists" is a frequently updated list of helpful sites, especially for beginners. The Bookshelf is a collection of guided tours on genealogy. DearMYRTLE also has book reviews, and the Events page is her schedule of speeches, workshops. Her message board is hosted by RootsWeb and Ancestry, and you can subscribe to her daily genealogy column and have it delivered to your e-mail inbox.

Wrapping Up

- ◆ Thousands of websites exist to help with your genealogy search.

- ◆ Some of the most useful websites are collections of links to other sites, such as Cyndi's List and RootsWeb.

- ◆ A number of websites are more specific, with genealogies submitted by users (for example, GenServ).

- ◆ Several websites have data such as land records, family bible entries, and transcribed census data (for example, AfriGeneas, The Library of Virginia, and the Bureau of Land Management).

- ◆ Other pages have good information on how to proceed with your research (for example, DearMYRTLE and the Adoptee Search Resource page).

Part V

Appendixes

Appendix A

Genealogical Standards and
Guidelines Recommended
by the National
Genealogical Society

Standards for Sound Genealogical Research

Recommended by the National Genealogical Society

Remembering always that they are engaged in a quest for truth, family history researchers consistently:

◆ Record the source for each item of information they collect.

◆ Test every hypothesis or theory against credible evidence and reject those that are not supported by the evidence.

◆ Seek original records or reproduced images of them when there is reasonable assurance that they have not been altered as the basis for their research conclusions.

◆ Use compilations, communications, and published works, whether paper or electronic, primarily for their value as guides to locating the original records or as contributions to the critical analysis of the evidence discussed in them.

◆ State something as a fact only when it is supported by convincing evidence and identify the evidence when communicating the fact to others.

◆ Limit with words like "probable" or "possible" any statement that is based on less than convincing evidence and state the reasons for concluding that it is probable or possible.

◆ Avoid misleading other researchers by either intentionally or carelessly distributing or publishing inaccurate information.

◆ State carefully and honestly the results of their own research and acknowledge all use of other researchers' work.

♦ Recognize the collegial nature of genealogical research by making their work available to others through publication or by placing copies in appropriate libraries or repositories, as well as by welcoming critical comment.

♦ Consider with open minds new evidence or the comments of others on their work and the conclusions they have reached.

Standards for Use of Technology in Genealogical Research

Recommended by the National Genealogical Society

Mindful that computers are tools, genealogists take full responsibility for their work and, therefore, they:

♦ Learn the capabilities and limits of their equipment and software, and use them only when they are the most appropriate tools for a purpose.

♦ Do not accept uncritically the ability of software to format, number, import, modify, check, chart, or report their data and, therefore, carefully evaluate any resulting product.

♦ Treat compiled information from online sources or digital databases in the same way as other published sources—useful primarily as a guide to locating original records, but not as evidence for a conclusion or assertion.

♦ Accept digital images or enhancements of an original record as a satisfactory substitute for the original only when there is reasonable assurance that the image accurately reproduces the unaltered original.

♦ Cite sources for data obtained online or from digital media with the same care that is appropriate for sources on paper and other traditional media, and enter data into a digital database only when its source can remain associated with it.

♦ Always cite the sources for information or data posted online or sent to others, naming the author of a digital file as its immediate source, while crediting original sources cited within the file.

♦ Preserve the integrity of their own databases by evaluating the reliability of downloaded data before incorporating it into their own files.

♦ Provide, whenever they alter data received in digital form, a description of the change that will accompany the altered data whenever it is shared with others.

♦ Actively oppose the proliferation of error, rumor, and fraud by personally verifying or correcting information or noting it as unverified before passing it on to others.

♦ Treat people online as courteously and civilly as they would treat them face-to-face, not separated by networks and anonymity.

♦ Accept that technology has not changed the principles of genealogical research, only some of the procedures.

Standards for Sharing Information with Others

Recommended by the National Genealogical Society

Conscious of the fact that sharing information or data with others, whether through speech, documents, or electronic media, is essential to family history research and that it needs continuing support and encouragement, responsible family historians consistently:

♦ Respect the restrictions on sharing information that arise from the rights of another as an author, originator, or compiler; as a living private person; or as a party to a mutual agreement.

♦ Observe meticulously the legal rights of copyright owners, copying or distributing any part of their works only with their permission or to the limited extent specifically allowed under the law's "fair use" exceptions.

♦ Identify the sources for all ideas, information, and data from others, as well as the form in which they were received, recognizing that the unattributed use of another's intellectual work is plagiarism.

♦ Respect the authorship rights of senders of letters, electronic mail, and data files, forwarding or disseminating them further only with the sender's permission.

♦ Inform people who provide information about their families as to the ways it may be used, observing any conditions they impose and respecting any reservations they may express regarding the use of particular items.

♦ Require some evidence of consent before assuming that living people are agreeable to further sharing of information about themselves.

♦ Convey personally identifying information about living people— like age, home address, occupation, or activities—only in ways that those concerned have expressly agreed to.

♦ Recognize that legal rights of privacy may limit the extent to which information from publicly available sources may be further used, disseminated, or published.

♦ Communicate no information to others that is known to be false or without making reasonable efforts to determine its truth, particularly information that may be derogatory.

♦ Are sensitive to the hurt that revelations of criminal, immoral, bizarre, or irresponsible behavior may bring to family members.

Guidelines for Publishing Webpages on the Internet

Recommended by the National Genealogical Society

Appreciating that publishing information through websites and webpages shares many similarities with print publishing, considerate family historians:

♦ Apply a title identifying both the entire website and the particular group of related pages, similar to a book-and-chapter designation, placing it both at the top of each Web browser window using the < TITLE > Hypertext Markup Language (HTML) tag and in the body of the document, on the home or title page, and on any index pages.

♦ Explain the purposes and objectives of their websites, placing the explanation near the top of the title page or including a link from that page to a special page about the reason for the site.

♦ Display a footer at the bottom of each webpage that contains the website title, page title, author's name, author's contact information, date of last revision, and a copyright statement.

♦ Provide complete contact information, including, at a minimum, a name and e-mail address, and preferably some means for long-term contact, like a postal address.

♦ Assist visitors by providing on each page navigational links that lead to other important pages on the website or that return them to the home page.

♦ Adhere to the NGS "Standards for Sharing Information with Others" regarding copyright, attribution, privacy, and the sharing of sensitive information.

♦ Include unambiguous source citations for the research data provided on the site and, if not complete descriptions, offering full citations upon request.

♦ Label photographic and scanned images within the graphic itself, with fuller explanation if required in text adjacent to the graphic.

♦ Identify transcribed, extracted, or abstracted data as such and provide appropriate source citations.

♦ Include identifying dates and locations when providing information about specific surnames or individuals.

♦ Respect the rights of others who do not wish information about themselves to be published, referenced, or linked to on a website.

♦ Provide website access to all potential visitors by avoiding enhanced technical capabilities that may not be available to all users, remembering that not all computers are created equal.

♦ Avoid using features that distract from the productive use of the website, like ones that reduce legibility, strain the eyes, dazzle the vision, or otherwise detract from the visitor's ability to easily read, study, comprehend, or print the online publication.

♦ Maintain their online publications at frequent intervals, changing the content to keep the information current, the links valid, and the website in good working order.

♦ Preserve and archive for future researchers their online publications and communications that have lasting value, using both electronic and paper duplication.

Guidelines for Using Records Repositories and Libraries

Recommended by the National Genealogical Society

Recognizing that how they use unique original records and fragile publications will affect other users, both current and future, family history researchers habitually:

♦ Are courteous to research facility personnel and other researchers, and respect the staff's other daily tasks, not expecting the records custodian to listen to their family histories nor provide constant or immediate attention.

♦ Dress appropriately, converse with others in a low voice, and supervise children appropriately.

♦ Do their homework in advance, know what is available and what they need, and avoid ever asking for "everything" on their ancestors.

♦ Use only designated workspace areas and equipment, like readers and computers intended for patron use, respect off-limit areas, and ask for assistance if needed.

♦ Treat original records at all times with great respect, and work with only a few records at a time, recognizing that they are irreplaceable and that each user must help preserve them for future use.

♦ Treat books with care, never forcing their spines, and handle photographs properly, preferably wearing archival gloves.

♦ Never mark, mutilate, rearrange, relocate, or remove from the repository any original, printed, microform, or electronic document or artifact.

♦ Use only procedures prescribed by the repository for noting corrections to any errors or omissions found in published works, never marking the work itself.

♦ Keep note-taking paper or other objects from covering records or books, and avoid placing any pressure upon them, particularly with a pencil or pen.

♦ Use only the method specifically designated for identifying records for duplication, avoiding use of paper clips, adhesive notes, or other means not approved by the facility.

♦ Return volumes and files only to locations designated for that purpose.

♦ Before departure, thank the records custodians for their courtesy in making the materials available.

♦ Follow the rules of the records repository without protest, even if they have changed since a previous visit or differ from those of another facility.

Guidelines for Genealogical Self-Improvement and Growth

Recommended by the National Genealogical Society

Faced with ever-growing expectations for genealogical accuracy and reliability, family historians concerned with improving their abilities will, on a regular basis:

♦ Study comprehensive texts and narrower-focus articles and recordings covering genealogical methods in general and the historical background and sources available for areas of particular research interest or to which their research findings have led them.

♦ Interact with other genealogists and historians in person or electronically, mentoring or learning as appropriate to their relative experience levels, and through the shared experience contributing to the genealogical growth of all concerned.

♦ Subscribe to and read regularly at least two genealogical journals that list a number of contributing or consulting editors or editorial board or committee members and that require their authors to respond to a critical review of each article before it is published.

♦ Participate in workshops, discussion groups, institutes, conferences, and other structured learning opportunities whenever possible.

♦ Recognize their limitations, undertaking research in new areas or using new technology only after they master any additional knowledge and skills needed, and understand how to apply it to the new subject matter or technology.

♦ Analyze critically at least quarterly the reported research findings of another family historian for whatever lessons may be gleaned through the process.

♦ Join and participate actively in genealogical societies covering countries, localities, and topics where they have research interests, as well as the localities where they reside, increasing the resources available both to themselves and to future researchers.

♦ Review recently published basic texts to renew their understanding of genealogical fundamentals as currently expressed and applied.

♦ Examine and revise their own earlier research in light of what they have learned through self-improvement activities as a means for applying their newfound knowledge and for improving the quality of their work product.

Appendix B

How to Find a Professional Genealogist

Most of the fun of genealogy, online and offline, is the solving of puzzles and learning about your family's place in history, but sometimes you hit a brick wall.

You may need a consultant on a specific research problem or help finding a missing relative. Maybe you need a record translated from a foreign language or some handwriting deciphered. Maybe you need an experienced eye to look over what you have and help you develop a plan for what to do next. Maybe you want to surprise your mother with a genealogy for Christmas, or maybe there's just one whole branch of the tree you know you'll never find time for.

All of these are good reasons to use a professional genealogist. Professional genealogists can prove you are a descendant of someone for organizations such as the Daughters of the American Revolution. Professionals can help you with genealogy chores as simple as searching some records you cannot get to online or travel to physically, or they can take what information you have and trace the ancestry as far back as you are willing to pay for.

But hiring a professional genealogist is not as simple as a Google search. Genealogical research is a science requiring skillful analysis and intellectual concentration, as well as years of experience and education.

"I would not discount local history and genealogy experts in the areas where an ancestor once lived, but I find this is a touchy area," advised DearMYRTLE, the genealogy columnist and lecturer. "It is so difficult to evaluate the reliability of research when a person one might hire hasn't been certified or [is not an] accredited genealogist."

So, the solution, she said, is to look for someone certified as a researcher. First, there is the Certified Genealogist (CG) designation from the Board for Certification of Genealogists (www.bcgcertification .org). This organization tests and certifies researchers and teachers (the latter is a Certified Genealogical Lecturer, or CGL). A list of those certified is maintained on the website. The board has a Code of Ethics and Genealogical Proof Standard that the members must adhere to.

Another such certification body is The International Commission for the Accreditation of Professional Genealogists (ICAPGen), which certifies genealogists through comprehensive written and oral examinations. The ICAPGen website is www.icapgen.org, which offers the following:

♦ The agreement between the Accredited Genealogist (AG) professional and ICAPGen outlines the responsibilities of each AG researcher to ICAPGen, to the researcher's clients, and to the genealogical community. Should a dispute or client complaint occur, the agreement outlines the arbitration process.

♦ Out of a desire to protect the consumer, ICAPGen tests the competence of genealogists and provides assurance to those who want to hire a professional in the field.

Again, you can find a list of ICAPGen members on the website.

The Family History Library of the Church of Jesus Christ of Latter-day Saints (LDS) also has a staff of professional genealogists. The staff will test for AG status by the Genealogical Department of the LDS church. Examinations include specialized areas such as American Indian, Southern, United States, England, and Germany. These genealogists are not necessarily members of the LDS church, nor do they limit themselves to LDS clients. Accredited Genealogists sign an ethics agreement and agree to adhere to a code of conduct; they are required to renew their accreditation every five years. You can get a roster of these by sending a self-addressed stamped envelope (SASE) with the geographic or topical specialization needed to:

Family History Library
35 North West Temple Street
Salt Lake City, UT 84150-1003

Another organization to consult is the Association of Professional Genealogists (APG). Ethical conduct is extremely important to members of this association. Every member of APG signs a code of professional ethics, stating that the professional will:

♦ Promote a coherent, truthful approach to genealogy, family history, and local history.

♦ Clearly present research results and opinions in a clear, well-organized manner, with accurately-cited references.

♦ Advertise services and credentials honestly.

♦ Explain without concealment or misrepresentation all fees, charges, and payment structures.

♦   Abide by agreements regarding project scope, number of hours, and deadlines or reporting schedules.

♦   Refrain from knowingly violating or encouraging others to violate laws and regulations concerning copyright and right to privacy.

♦   Give proper credit to those who supply information and provide assistance.

Also, various certification boards in other countries may be of help, for example:

Australia

Australian Association of Genealogists and Record Agents
P. O. Box 268
Oakleigh, Victoria 3166, Australia
Send five International Reply Coupons for a roster. Tests and certifications in Australian and New Zealand records.

Canada

Genealogical Institute of the Maritimes
Universite de Moncton, Moncton
New Brunswick, E1A 3E9, Canada
Send SASE (with Canadian postage or two International Reply Coupons) for a roster. Tests and certifications for specialized research areas in Canada.

England

Association of Genealogists and Researchers in Archives
Hon. Secretary
31 Alexandra Grove
London N12 8HE, England
Send five International Reply Coupons for a roster. Peers recommend those listed as competent by long experience.

France

Chambre Syndicale des Genealogistes — Heraldistes de France
74, Rue des Saints-Peres
75005 Paris, France
Send five International Reply Coupons for a roster.

Ireland

Association of Professional Genealogists in Ireland
c/o The Genealogical Office
30 Harlech Crescent
Clonskeagh, Dublin 14
Send two International Reply Coupons for a roster. Membership is based on independent assessment and experience.

New Zealand

Genealogical Research Institute of New Zealand
P.O. Box 36-107 Moera
Lower Hutt 6330, New Zealand
Send large envelope and two International Reply Coupons for a roster. Members sign a code of ethics.

Scotland

Association of Scottish Genealogists and Record Agents
51/3 Mortonhall Road
Edinburgh EH9 2HN, Scotland
Send two International Reply Coupons for a roster. Members sign a code of practice.

Set Terms

Hiring a genealogist is a bit like hiring a contractor: You must have a clearly defined project and budget in mind before you sign a contract. You need to ask the genealogist for a letter of agreement that lists:

- The scope of work to be performed.

- How many hours to be worked for you, with some provision for time extensions under specified circumstances.

- A schedule of fees for various actions.

- Definition of what the retainer covers and how it will be applied toward final payment.

- How you will agree on more research activities after the original work is finished.

It is also a good idea to define who holds the copyright to the written research reports. Often, the professional genealogist wants to retain those rights, which means you cannot publish the report without the researcher's permission. If your researcher is a member of the Association of Professional Genealogists and you believe he or she has not worked within the code of ethics, you can file a grievance with the organization. APG will work with you and the professional to mediate the disagreement.

I know several people who ask at genealogy societies and clubs for the names of good professional genealogists before contacting one. Once you find one to talk to, it never hurts to ask for and check references. If the professional is reluctant to provide such a name, use your best judgment in deciding whether you want to hire this person. It's also a good idea to begin with a short, simple assignment, such as a research chore in a city you just cannot travel to. See how quickly and accurately the candidate can work and how important your business is. Then you can judge whether you have the confidence to agree on a larger project.

Most genealogists charge by the hour, but the fees can range from $10.00 to $95.00 per hour. An average is $30.00 to $50.00 per hour for the professional in the United States. However, you may find a researcher who prefers to charge a flat daily fee, such as $150.00 to $500.00 per day for their services. Indeed, several professionals prefer a minimum retainer, (usually $350.00 to $500.00) for a research project. This gives the researcher a good block of time and some working capital for transportation, copies, and so on. It also gives the genealogist some time to do a careful and thorough job on your project.

Once you have a specific list of research needs, a list of professional genealogists who meet your criteria in price and expertise, and you have checked their references, you can determine who to hire and sign an agreement. Then you give the researcher the information you have and the fees to begin.

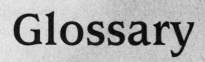

Glossary

A

a. (or c.)   about (or circa, in Latin), often used in front of uncertain dates.

AG   Accredited Genealogist, a designation conferred by the Church of Jesus Christ of Latter-day Saints (LDS).

ahnentafel   The word means "ancestor table" in German, and the format is more than a century old. The ahnentafel lists all known ancestors of an individual and includes the full name of each ancestor, as well as dates and places of birth, marriage, and death. It organizes this information along a numbering scheme. Any individual's father is twice that individual's number in the table; any individual's mother is twice plus one that individual's number in the table. Therefore, all males in the table are even numbers and all females are odd numbers. If you are #1 in the table, your father is #2 and your mother is #3. Your father's father is #4, your father's mother #5, and so on.

Ancestral File (AF)   A searchable collection of genealogical data submitted to the LDS archives in GEDCOM format to help genealogists coordinate their research.

anonymous FTP (File Transfer Protocol)   The process of connecting to a remote computer, either as an anonymous or guest user, to transfer public files back to your local computer. (See also: *FTP* and *protocol.*) Anonymous FTP is usually read-only access; you often cannot contribute files by anonymous FTP.

Atom   A syndication format written in eXtensible Markup Language (XML) language used for Web feeds and as a publishing protocol (APP is the acronym, but it is referred to as "AtomPub" for short) for creating and updating Web resources. It is a form of "push" technology that allows the user to retrieve information without the problems of e-mail and Web browsing.

B

backbone   A set of connections that make up the main channels of communication across a network.

BCG   Board for Certification of Genealogists.

browser   An Internet client for viewing the World Wide Web.

bulletin board   A way of referring to online message systems where you must log onto the site or Internet service provider (ISP) to read and post messages. Also called a message board, forum, or discussion board.

C

cadastre   A survey, map, or some other public record showing ownership and value of land for tax purposes.

catalog   A search page for the Web within an edited list, not the whole Internet.

chat   When people type messages to each other across a host or network, live and in real time. On some commercial online services, this is called a conference.

client   A program that provides an interface to remote Internet services, such as mail, Usenet, telnet, and so on. In general, the clients act on behalf of a human end-user (perhaps indirectly).

compression   A method of making a file, whether text or code, smaller by various methods. This is so the file will take up less disk space and/or less time to transmit. Sometimes, the compression is completed by the modem; sometimes, the file is stored that way. The various methods to do this go by names (followed by the system that used it), such as PKZIP (DOS), ARC (DOS), tar (UNIX), STUFFIT (Macintosh), and so forth.

CG   Certified Genealogist, by BCG.

CGI   Certified Genealogical Instructor, by BCG.

CGL   Certified Genealogical Lecturer, by BCG.

CGRS   Certified Genealogical Record Specialist, by BCG.

collateral line   A family that is not in your direct line of ancestry but of the same genealogical line.

conference   A usually large gathering with discussions, lectures, exhibits, and perhaps workshops. Genealogy conferences are held around the country every year.

D

database   A set of information organized for computer storage, search, retrieval, and insertion.

default   In computer terms, the "normal" or "basic" settings of a program.

directory   1. A level in a hierarchical filing system. Other directories branch down from the root directory. 2. A type of search site where editors choose the websites and services in the catalog, instead of a robot collecting them indiscriminately.

domain name   The Internet naming scheme. A computer on the Internet is identified by a series of words, from more specific to more general (left to right), separated by dots: www.microsoft.com is an example. (See also: *IP address*.)

domain name server (DNS)   A computer with software to translate a domain name into the corresponding numbers of the IP address. "No DNS entry" from your browser means a name such as www.first .last.org wasn't in the domain name server's list of valid IP addresses.

downloading   To get information from another computer to yours.

E

e-mail   An electronic message, text, or data sent from one computer or person to another computer or person.

F

Family Group Sheet   A one-page collection of facts about one family unit: husband, wife, and children, with birth and death dates and places.

FHC　Family History Center, a branch of the Family History Library in Salt Lake City, found in a local LDS parish.

firewall　Electronic protection against hackers and other unauthorized access to your files while you're connected to a network or the Internet.

flame　A message or series of messages containing an argument or insults. Not allowed on most systems. If you receive a flame, ignore that message and all other messages from that person in the future.

forum　A set of messages on a subject, usually with a corresponding set of files. Can be on an open network, such as ILINK, or restricted to a commercial system, such as CompuServe.

French Revolutionary Calendar　The French Revolutionary Calendar (or Republican Calendar) was introduced in France on November 24, 1793, and abolished on January 1, 1806. It was used again briefly during the Paris Commune in 1871.

FTP (File Transfer Protocol)　Enables an Internet user to transfer files electronically between remote computers and the user's computer.

G

gateway　Used in different senses (for example, mail gateway, IP gateway) but, most generally, a computer that forwards and routes data between two or more networks of any size or origin. A gateway is never, however, as straightforward as going through a gate. It's more like a labyrinth to get the proper addresses in the proper sequence.

GEDCOM　The standard for computerized genealogical information, which is a combination of tags for data and pointers to related data.

Gregorian calendar　Introduced by Pope Gregory XIII in 1582, adopted by England and the colonies in 1752, by which time it was 11 days behind the solar year, causing an adjustment in September 1752.

H

hacker   Originally, someone who messed about with computer systems to see how much could be accomplished. Most recently, a computer vandal.

host computer   In the context of networks, a computer that directly provides service to a user. In contrast to a network server, which provides services to a user through an intermediary host computer.

HTML (Hypertext Markup Language)   A coding system to format and link documents on the World Wide Web and intranets.

hub   A computer that collects e-mail regionally and distributes it up the next level. Collects the e-mail from that level to distribute it back down the chain.

I

IGI   The International Genealogical Index, a database of names submitted to the LDS church.

Internet   The backbone of a series of interconnected networks that includes local area, regional, and national backbone networks. Networks in the Internet use the same telecommunications protocol (TCP/IP) and provide electronic mail, remote login, and file transfer services.

Internet relay chat (IRC)   Real-time chat messages typed over an open, public server.

instant message (IM)   A type of chat program that requires users to register with a server. Users build "buddy lists" of others using the same program and are notified when people on their buddy list are available for chat and messages.

institute   A week-long set of courses on a specific area, usually held at the same site every year, with class size ranging from 15 to 30 students, allowing personalized instruction. Genealogical institutes are held yearly in many sites in the United States and other countries.

Internet service provider (ISP)   A company that has a continuous, fast, and reliable connection to the Internet and sells subscriptions to the public to use that connection. The connections may use TCP/IP, shell accounts, or other methods.

intranet   A local network set up to look like the World Wide Web, with clients such as browsers, but self-contained and not necessarily connected to the Internet.

IP (Internet protocol)   The Internet-standard protocol that provides a common layer over dissimilar networks, used to move packets among host computers and through gateways, if necessary.

IP address   The alpha or numeric address of a computer connected to the Internet. Also called "Internet address." Usually the format is user@someplace.domain, but it can also be seen as ###.##.##.##.

J

Julian calendar   The calendar replaced by the Gregorian calendar, which had also fallen behind the solar year.

L

LDS   Accepted abbreviation for the Church of Jesus Christ of Latter-day Saints, also known as the Mormons.

list (Internet)   Also called "mail list" or "mailing list." Listserv lists (or listservers) are electronically transmitted discussions of technical and nontechnical issues. They come to you by electronic mail over the Internet using LISTSERV commands. Participants subscribe via a central service, and lists often have a moderator who supervises the information flow and content.

lurk   To read a list without posting messages yourself. It's sort of like sitting in the corner at a party without introducing yourself, except it's not considered rude online. In fact, in some places, you're expected to lurk until you get the feel of the place.

M

mail list   Same as *list*.

MNP (Microcom Networking Protocol)   Data compression standard for modems.

modem   A device to modulate computer data into sound signals and to demodulate those signals to computer data.

moderator   The person who takes care of a message list, newsgroup, or forum. This person takes out messages that are off topic, chastises flamers, maintains a database of old messages, and handles the mechanics of distributing the messages.

Mozilla   A nickname for Netscape Navigator. In the early days, Netscape's mascot was a little dragon-like creature called Mozilla.

N

navigation bar   A set of words and/or images that appears on every page of a website, with links to other sections or pages of the same website.

NEHGS   New England Historic Genealogical Society, founded in 1845. Website: www.newenglandancestors.org. Published quarterly since 1847, *The New England Historical and Genealogical Register* is the oldest and most respected journal of American genealogy.

NGS   National Genealogical Society, United States.

NIC (Network Information Center)   An NIC provides administrative support, user support, and information services for a network.

O

offline   The state of not being connected to a remote host.

online   The state of being connected to a remote host.

OPAC (Online Public Access Catalog)   A term used to describe any type of computerized library catalog.

P

pedigree chart   The traditional way to display a genealogy, the familiar "family tree," where one person's ancestors are outlined. Other formats are the fan chart, decadency chart (starts with the ancestor and comes down to the present), and timeline.

Pedigree Resource File (PRF)   Genealogical information submitted by users of FamilySearch.com.

Personal Ancestral File (PAF)   A free genealogy program for use by members of the LDS church for submittal to the Temple in Salt Lake City.

podcast   A media file (sound, perhaps video) that is distributed to users though a "push" system such as syndication (Really Simple Syndication, or RSS) or downloaded from a site. Like "radio," this can mean either the content or the medium. A podcast is played with a program such as Window Media Player, iTunes, or RealAudio.

PDF (Portable Document Format)   An Adobe-copyrighted format that allows a document to be saved to look a certain way, no matter what computer is used to display it. The computer, however, must use Adobe's Acrobat reader (a free program) to display the file.

plat (v.)   To draw a map of a piece of land by the description of a deed. *(n.)* The map of a piece of land as defined by the deed.

PPP (Point-to-Point Protocol)   A type of Internet connection. An improvement on SLIP (see the following definition), it allows any computer to use the Internet protocols and become a full-fledged member of the Internet, using a high-speed modem. The advantage to SLIP and PPP accounts is you can usually achieve faster connections than with a shell account.

protocol   A mutually determined set of formats and procedures governing the exchange of information between systems.

push technology   A communication protocol where the request for a given transaction originates with the creator of content, and the user receives it with a special client (See: *Atom* and *RSS*). E-mail is a "pull" technology; RSS readers receive "push."

Q

query   A request for genealogical information. To be effective, it must have at least one name, one date, one geographical location, and your contact information.

R

register style   A format for a genealogy created for the NEHGS publication. It is a narrative style that assigns each ancestor a superscript number representing a generation. The first ancestor (the "primary") is 1, and each descendant of the primary individual is assigned a consecutive number; children are assigned lowercase roman numerals as well as arabic numbers. The result looks much like an outline, as we were taught to do when learning how to write a research paper.

remote access   The capability to access a computer from outside another location. Remote access requires communications hardware, software, and actual physical links, although this can be as simple as common carrier (telephone) lines or as complex as Telnet login to another computer across the Internet.

RSS   Really Simple Syndication is a family of Web feed formats used to publish frequently updated content, such as blog entries, news headlines, or podcasts. Atom is a similar format. They allow the user to retrieve content without the problems of spam and pop-up that often accompany e-mail and Web browsing.

S

search engine   A program on the World Wide Web that searches parts of the Internet for text strings. A search engine might search for programs, webpages, or other items. Many claim to cover "the whole Internet," but that's a physical impossibility. Getting more than 50 percent of the Internet is a good lick.

seminar An educational event highlighting the interaction and exchange of information, typically among a small number of participants. Genealogy seminars (sometimes called workshops) are often held by local organizations.

server A computer that allows other computers to log on and use its resources. A client (see the previous definition) program is often used for this.

shareware The try-before-you-buy concept in microcomputer software, where the program is distributed through public domain channels and the author expects to receive compensation after a trial period. Brother's Keeper, for example, is shareware.

signature A stored text file with your name and some information, such as names you're searching or your mailing address, to be appended to the end of your messages. Your signature should contain only ASCII (text-only) characters, no graphics.

SLIP (Serial Line Internet Protocol) A system allowing a computer to use the Internet protocols with a standard telephone line and a high-speed modem. Most ISPs now offer PPP or SLIP accounts for a monthly or yearly fee.

Social Security Death Index (SSDI) A searchable database of records of deaths of Americans with Social Security numbers, if that death was reported to the Social Security Administration. It runs from the 1960s to the present, although a few deaths prior to the 1960s are in it. The records give full name, place and date of death, where the card was issued, and birth date. Many websites have online searches of the SSDI, some with Soundex (see the following definition).

Soundex An indexing system based on sound, rather than on the spelling of a surname.

spider A program that gathers information on webpages for a database, usually for a search engine.

sysop The SYStem OPerator (manager) of an online community, or forum. The sysop sets the rules, maintains the peace and operability of the system, and sometimes moderates the messages.

T

tagline   A short, pithy statement tagged on to the end of a bulletin board system (BBS) e-mail message. Example: "It's only a hobby, only a hobby, only a . . ." Taglines are rarely seen on commercial networks, such as AOL, MSN, and CompuServe.

TCP/IP (Transmission Control Protocol/Internet Protocol)
A combined set of protocols that performs the transfer of data between two computers. TCP monitors and ensures correct transfer of data. IP receives the data from TCP, breaks it up into packets, and ships it off to a network within the Internet. TCP/IP is also used as a name for a protocol suite that incorporates these functions and others.

telnet   An Internet client that connects to other computers, making yours a virtual terminal of the remote computer. Among other functions, it enables a user to log in to a remote computer from the user's local computer. On many commercial systems, you use it as a command, for example, telnet ftp.cac.psu.edu. Once there, you are using programs and, therefore, commands from that remote computer.

terminal emulation   Most communications software packages will permit your personal computer or workstation to communicate with another computer or network as if it were a specific type of terminal directly connected to that computer or network. For example, your terminal emulation should be set to VT100 for most online card catalog programs.

terminal server   A computer that connects terminals to a network by providing host telnet service.

thread (message thread)   A discussion made up of a set of messages in answer to a certain message and to each other. Sometimes, worthwhile threads are saved in a text file, as on CompuServe's Roots Forum. Some mail readers will sort by thread, that is, according to subject line.

tiny tafel (TT)   A TT provides a standard way of describing a family database so the information can be scanned visually or by computer. All data fields are of fixed length, with the obvious exceptions of the surnames and optional places. Many TTs are extracted from GEDCOMs.

Trojan horse   A type of malicious code. This is usually a program that seems to be useful and harmless. In the background, however, it might be destroying data or breaking security on your system. It differs from a virus in that it rarely propagates itself as a virus does.

U

upload   To send a file or message from your computer to another. (See also: *download*.)

USB (universal serial bus)   A connection to a computer. Unlike a parallel port (where your printer probably plugs in) or a serial port (where your modem probably plugs in), a USB port enables you to "daisy chain" peripherals. If you have a USB printer, modem, and CD-ROM drive, you could plug only one into the USB port, and the rest connect by USB cables in a chain (in theory, say, computer to modem to printer to CD-ROM). In practice, however, sometimes it's a little tricky to get them in an order that makes all the peripherals happy.

V

virus   A program that installs itself secretly on a computer by attaching itself to another program or e-mail and then duplicates itself when that program is executed or e-mail is opened. Some viruses are harmless, but most of them intend to do damage, such as erasing important files on your system.

vital records   The official records of birth, death, marriage, and other events of a person's life.

W

World Wide Web (WWW or the Web)   A system to pull various Internet services together into one interface called a browser. Most sites on the Web are written as pages in HTML.

workshop   See *seminar*.

worm   A computer program that makes copies of itself and spreads through connected systems, using up resources in affected computers or causing other damage.

X

XML   eXtensible Markup Language, or XML, is a specification developed by the World Wide Web Consortium (W3C). It is designed especially for Web documents. It allows designers to create their own customized tags, enabling the definition, transmission, validation, and interpretation of data between applications and between organizations. Most "push" technology on the Internet is written in XML.

Smiley (Emoticon) Glossary

Because we can't hear voice inflection over e-mail, a code for imparting emotion sprung up. These punctuation marks used to take the place of facial expressions are called smileys or emoticons. Different systems have variations of these symbols. Two versions of this "Unofficial Smiley Dictionary" were sent to me by Cliff Manis (cmanis@csf.com), and I've edited and combined them. Several versions are floating around, but I think this one sums up the symbols you're most likely to see.

:-)   Your basic smiley. This smiley is used to show pleasure or indicate a sarcastic or joking statement.

;-)   Winky smiley. User just made a flirtatious and/or sarcastic remark. Somewhat of a "don't hit me for what I just said" smiley.

:-(Frowning smiley. User didn't like that last statement or is upset or depressed about something.

:-I   Indifferent smiley. Better than a frowning smiley, but not quite as good as a happy smiley.

:-/   Smiley showing puzzlement or consternation.

:-> >   User just made a biting sarcastic remark. Worse than a :-).

> >:-> >   User just made a devilish remark.

> >;-> >   Winky and devil combined.

Those are the basic symbols. Here are some less common ones.

> ## Note
>
> *A lot of these can be typed without noses to make midget smilies.*

- -:-)	Smiley is a punk rocker
- -:-(	Real punk rockers don't smile
;-)	Wink
,-}	Wry and winking
:,(	Crying
:-:	Mutant smiley
.-)	Smiley only has one eye
,-)	Ditto, but he's winking
:-?	Smiley smoking a pipe
:-/	Skepticism, consternation, or puzzlement
:-\	Ditto
:-'	Smiley spitting out its chewing tobacco
:-~)	Smiley has a cold
:-)~	Smiley drools
:-[	Un-smiley blockhead
:-[	Smiley is a vampire
:-]	Smiley blockhead
:-{	Mustache
:-}	Wry smile or beard
:-@	Smiley face screaming
:-$	Smiley face with its mouth wired shut
:-*	Smiley after eating something bitter or sour
:-&	Smiley is tongue-tied
:-#	Braces
:-#|	Smiley face with bushy mustache
:-%	Smiley banker
:-< <_	Mad or real sad smiley
:-=)	Older smiley with mustache

:-> >	Hey hey
:-|	"Have an ordinary day" smiley
:-0	Smiley orator
:-0	No yelling! (quiet lab)
:-1	Smiley bland face
:-6	Smiley after eating something sour
:-7	Smiley after a wry statement
:-8(	Condescending stare
:-9	Smiley is licking his/her lips
:-a	Lefty smiley touching tongue to nose
:-b	Left-pointing tongue smiley
:-c	Bummed-out Smiley
:-C	Smiley is really bummed
:-d	Lefty smiley razzing you
:-D	Smiley is laughing
:-e	Disappointed smiley
:-E	Bucktoothed vampire
:-F	Bucktoothed vampire with one tooth missing
:-I	Hmm
:-i	Semi-smiley
:-j	Left-smiling smiley
:-o	Smiley singing the national anthem
:-O	Uh-oh!
:-o	Uh-oh!
:-P	Disgusted or nyah-nyah
:-p	Smiley sticking its tongue out (at you!)
:-q	Smiley trying to touch its tongue to its nose
:-Q	Smoker
:-s	Smiley after a *bizarre* comment
:-S	Smiley just made an incoherent statement
:-t	Cross smiley
:-v	Talking-head smiley
:-x	"My lips are sealed" smiley
:-X	Bow tie or emphasized smiley's lips are sealed
::-)	Smiley wears normal glasses

:'-(	Smiley is crying
:'-)	Smiley is so happy, he is crying
:^)	Smiley with pointy nose (righty). Sometimes used to denote a lie, a myth, or a misconception, as in Pinocchio, or a broken nose. Also seen as :v)
:(	Sad midget smiley
:)	Midget smiley
:[	Real downer
:]	Midget smiley
:*	Kisses
:*)	Smiley is drunk
:<<N	Midget un-smiley
:<)<N	Smiley is from an Ivy League school
:=)	Smiley has two noses
:>>	Midget smiley
:D	Laughter
:I	Hmmm
:n)	Smiley with funny-looking right nose
:O	Yelling
:u)	Smiley with funny-looking left nose
:v)	Left-pointing nose smiley or smiley has a broken nose
':-)	Smiley shaved one of his eyebrows off this morning
,:-)	Same thing, other side
~ ~ :-(	Smiley is flaming, or has been flamed
(-:	Smiley is left-handed
(:-(	Un-smiley frowning
(:-)	Smiley big-face
(:I	Egghead
(8-o	It's Mr. Bill!
):-(	Un-smiley big-face
)8-)	Scuba smiley big-face
[:-)	Smiley is wearing a walkman
[:]	Smiley is a robot
[]	Hugs
{:-)	Smiley with its hair parted in the middle
{:-)	Smiley wears a toupee

}:-(	Toupee in an updraft
@@:-)	Smiley is wearing a turban
@@:I	Turban variation
@@ =	Smiley is pro-nuclear war
*:o)	Bozo the Clown!
%-)	Smiley has been staring at a computer monitor for 15 hours straight
%-6	Smiley is brain-dead
+-:-)	Smiley is the Pope or holds some other religious office
+:-)	Smiley priest
<:-<	Smiley is a dunce
=)	Teenage Smiley
> >:-I	Smiley is a trekkie
|-)	Hee hee
|-D	Ho ho
|-I	Smiley is asleep
|-O	Smiley is yawning/snoring
|-P	Yuk
|^o	Snoring
|I	Asleep
0-)	Smiley cyclops (scuba diver?)
3:[	Mean pet smiley
3:]	Pet smiley
3:o[	Smiley is a pet dog
8 :-)	Smiley is a wizard
8 :-I	Smiley is a propeller-head or Unix Wizard
8-)	Glasses
8-)	Smiley swimmer
8-)	Smiley is wearing sunglasses
8:-)	Glasses on forehead
8:-)	Smiley is a little girl
B-)	Horn-rims
B:-)	Sunglasses on head
C=:-)	Smiley is a chef
E-:-)	Smiley is a ham radio operator

E-:-I	Smiley is a member of net.ham-radio
g-)	Smiley with pince-nez glasses
K:P	Smiley is a little kid with a propeller beanie
O :-)	Smiley is an angel (at heart, at least)
O |-)	Smiley is an angel
O-)	Megaton Man On Patrol! (or else, user is a scuba diver)
X-(	Smiley just died

If you see	**The chatter means...**
AFK	Away from keyboard
Y	why
U	you
C	see
BRB	Be right back
< g >	grin
< bg >	big grin
< vbg >	very big grin
BTW	by the way
CUL	See You Later
CWYL	chat with you later
FUBAR	Fouled Up Beyond All Recognition
FWIW	for what it's worth
GIWIST	Gee, I wish I'd said that!
HHOK	Ha, ha! Only kidding!
HTH	Hope this helps
HTHBE	Hope this has been enlightening
IMHO	In my humble opinion
IMNSHO	In my not so humble opinion
IOW	In other words...
IRL	In real life
ITRW	In the real world
JK	Just kidding
LOL	Laughing out loud
OTP	On the phone

OTF	On the floor
OIC	Oh! I see!
OTOH	On the other hand
POV	Point of view
RL	Real Life
ROTFL	Rolling on the floor laughing
RTFM	Read the fine manual [or Help file]
TTFN	Ta ta for now
TTYL	Talk to you later
WRT	With regard to

Index